MAKING YOUR CHOICES COUNT

 **Michigan Faculty Series**

The Quest for World Order, by Robert Cooley Angell

Law, Intellect, and Education, by Francis A. Allen

Thinking About Morality, by William K. Frankena

Historical Americana, by Howard H. Peckham

Making Your Choices Count, by James N. Morgan and Greg J. Duncan

MAKING YOUR CHOICES COUNT

Economic Principles for Everyday Decisions

JAMES N. MORGAN □ GREG J. DUNCAN

Ann Arbor
The University of Michigan Press

Copyright © by The University of Michigan 1982
All rights reserved
Published in the United States of America by
The University of Michigan Press and simultaneously
in Rexdale, Canada, by John Wiley & Sons Canada, Limited
Manufactured in the United States of America

Library of Congress Cataloging in Publication Data

Morgan, James N.
  Making your choices count.

  (Michigan faculty series)
  Condensation and revision of: The economics of
personal choice, 1980.
  Includes index.
  1. Consumers. 2. Economics. 3. Finance,
Personal. I. Duncan, Greg J. II. Title. III. Series.
HB801.M6925   1982   330   81-22012
ISBN 0-472-06305-7   AACR2

Preface

Beware of the biases, special interests, and axes to grind of any person who is bent on helping you. Our own prejudices may become apparent as you read this book, but with some advance information you should be able to recognize them more readily.

One of our biases is toward the notion that everybody needs to understand some economics, since economics underlies many of the decisions individuals have to make in their lives. Detailed facts about the marketplace are not stressed here. Instead, a relatively few principles, applied in a variety of ways and situations, can serve to inform a great many important decisions and help to avoid later regret.

You may miss the pillorying of the bad guys and the passionate indignation about treatment of the average consumer. It is not that there are no problems, nor that we do not care; but easy indignation often tends to mask a failure in judgment or information gathering. The seller may or may not be the "guilty party," but the buyer need not be naive, and a clear head is better than a head of steam.

Our main work has been personal interview survey research at the Survey Research Center, Institute for Social Research, The University of Michigan, mostly on household behavior, attitudes, and conditions. That background has guided the focus of this book insofar as it leads to an understanding of how the majority of consumers behave; but we have tried to avoid burdening the reader with facts about consumer behavior in general. Indeed, human behavior is so varied that attempting to analyze it provides little guidance in terms of what the "average person" does. We have included enough about the processes of survey research to allow the reader to understand, and not be deceived by, the plethora of "facts" reported in the press.

We have attempted to retain the idea that economics is a set of "If . . . , then . . ." propositions, not a religion or a philosophy, and hence have tried to avoid telling the reader what to do. There are many noneconomic considerations that enter into any economic decision, and vast differences among people as to their goals, even in strictly economic terms. Most people at one time or another spend money or time on some luxury dear to their hearts. This book can help to determine what that luxury costs, but it cannot help to determine what it is worth to you.

Like any other investment, the time, energy, and thought invested in assembling information and making economic choices may or may not pay off. We have suggested some simplifications and shortcuts to minimize the time and energy and to make sure that the end result is worth it. Perhaps making a few large calculated decisions will allow you to relax and make the smaller choices more casually.

We hope you will come to think a little more like an economist and even to enjoy it. To add to your enjoyment, remember that careful consumers benefit others as well as themselves by making markets work better and by improving the correlation between price and quality.

It may appear from the examples given that the principles being illustrated are useful only to upper-middle-income, well-educated people. That is not true. The lower your income, the more constraints you face, and the more crucial it is that your economic decisions be the right ones for you. The same principles apply at all income levels. The very affluent may believe they can afford to ignore all this and simply enjoy their money. This is true for the small expenditures and minor decisions; but more money allows bigger mistakes, and exposes you to more alluring opportunities to make them. It is impossible to give examples that cover everyone's particular situation, so you should try continually to apply the principles to the choices or problems you are actually facing or likely to face soon. When the book talks about cars, for example, the same principles can apply to motorcycles or bicycles, as well as to snowmobiles, yachts, or even second homes. If you price ten-speed bicycles or washing machines at all of the retail outlets in your town, think of the implication of the price ranges for optimal shopping behavior, and of why the price differentials exist. If you talk with experts, many of whom have their own biases, perhaps the insights that you will have gleaned from this book can help you to ask the right questions, interpret what you learn from them, or avoid accepting incomplete or incorrect answers.

Finally, some things not stressed in this book, and why:

1. *Details of the federal income tax and its computation.* This is so complex, changing, and subject to interpretation that a brief treatment would be superficial, and a more complete treatment would soon be out of date. We have included tax considerations where they seem appropriate, pointing out that most strategies attempt to change the amount of one's *taxable* income. The benefits of this depend on one's tax bracket, more precisely the tax rate in that bracket, called the marginal tax rate.

2. *Details of the Social Security system.* This is another extremely complex system, subject to rapid changes in detail as taxes, benefit levels, and even special coverages are changed. We have given a general discussion of its logic and pointed out the ways its survivor provisions affect the choice of life insurance.

3. *Details of the operation of the stock market and other financial markets.* It is more important to understand general principles—such as the risk-yield mix, leverage, and the capitalization (calculation of present values) of expected future yields—than it is to know how a particular market functions or what a stockbroker does. Indeed, a basic knowledge of the theory of capital and interest will protect most people from the nonsense that is written and spoken about the stock market and other financial investments.

4. *The use of trusts and other devices to minimize income, estate, and inheritance taxes.* These details are of concern only to the affluent, involve rapidly changing laws and interpretations of laws, and require expert professional help. We have warned that they sometimes cost more to set up and to have administered than they save. Since most estates and smaller gifts are exempt from taxation, special devices are unnecessary to protect them.

5. *Detailed facts on consumer behavior, expenditures, and assets.* These are complex and require a great deal of interpretation to be of much value to anyone. As guidance for an individual, they are nearly useless: there is no average consumer.

6. *Technical details on nutrition, how appliances work, how to repair your car, etc.* These are again voluminous, changing, and of interest only when you have specific questions.

This emphasis on understanding and insight more than on factual details is the intentional result of our belief that the mass of detailed information available may leave us too little time to think about what we are trying to do and how best to do it. A Nobel prizewinner makes the point:

> In a world where information is relatively scarce, and where problems for decision are few and simple, information is almost always a positive good. In a world where attention is a major scarce resource, information may be an expensive luxury, for it may turn our attention from what is important to what is unimportant.[1]

With some effort and imprecision we have compressed the list of important economic insights to five items. These are explained briefly in the introductory chapter and are clarified as we apply them in one way or another in all subsequent chapters. Study them carefully, because once learned they will serve you well in almost every consumer decision you make.

Acknowledgments

The Economics of Personal Choice, the textbook from which this volume was condensed and revised, was written in response to the enthusiasms, questions, arguments, and confusions of hundreds of students spanning many years. We hope that new generations of students and the general public will find both the textbook and the present book clear, useful, and even enjoyable.

We are particularly grateful to Carolyn Shaw Bell of Wellesley College not only for repeated encouragement and advice, but for allowing us to appropriate the apt title of her course as the title for our textbook. We are also indebted for welcome suggestions and encouragement from Georgianne Baker of Arizona State University, Marjorie East of Pennsylvania State University, E. Scott Maynes of Cornell University, and Richard Porter of the University of Michigan. Some chapters benefited from reading by specialists including Alfred Conard in law (University of Michigan), Jeffrey O'Connell in law (University of Illinois), Sandra Newman in housing and urban planning (University of Michigan), and Jennifer Gerner in housing (Cornell University). Thomas Gies (University of Michigan) informed us on mortgages and banking. Two general readers, Alfred Hassler (former editor of *Fellowship*) and Renate Farmer, helped us make the books readable to noneconomists and nonstudents.

1. Herbert Simon, "Rationality as Process and as Product of Thought" (The Richard T. Ely Lecture), *American Economic Review* 68 (May, 1978): 13.

Many improvements in style and wording came from careful editorial reading by Joan Brinser and Richard Barfield. We also profited from comments by Charles Stallman, Sue Augustyniak, Ronnie Silverberg, Elwin Duncan, and a variety of readers of earlier versions. Our excellent typist, Barbara Browne, not only improved the appearance of the manuscript but also spotted inconsistencies and errors for us.

Contents

1. Introduction: Principles and Strategy *1*
2. Investment in Yourself *8*
3. Decisions about Work and Family *15*
4. Housing and Residential Location *30*
5. Long-term Financial Planning and Short-term Budgeting *57*
6. Borrowing and Consumer Debt *84*
7. The Investment of Savings *96*
8. Investments in Consumer Durables *126*
9. Risks, Insurance, and Estate Planning *144*
10. Meeting the Cost of Day-to-Day Life *180*
11. Consumer Information and Decision Making *210*

Appendix 1. Consumer Decisions Involving Costs and Benefits at Different Times *231*

Appendix 2. FTC Buyers Guide No. 7: Fair Credit Reporting Act *237*

Glossary *241*

Index *247*

of inflation, for reasons we will discuss in chapter 2. This means that we can use 3 percent as a "real" interest rate, and noninflated future dollars to convert future costs and benefits into present value amounts. This avoids the need to predict the future rates of inflation and interest. You do, of course, need to attempt to earn free market interest rates on your investments to make this device meaningful.

2. *Time is worth money*, and a decision that saves time or takes time has a benefit or cost. Sometimes it is helpful to value time at the amount you would make by working an extra hour on your job. (Sometimes you can earn double for overtime, or you may have no chance to earn more at all.)

3. *Costs or benefits that do not involve actual money payments can often be converted into dollar "imputations."* The cost of having your money tied up in owning a house is the interest you could otherwise be earning on it—the imputed interest. Cars and houses depreciate in value, and that depreciation is part of their cost—the imputed cost. Durable goods that you own also provide a stream of benefits as though you were renting them—the imputed rent.

4. *An uncertain dollar is not as good as a sure thing.* Where we can estimate probabilities, the dollar equivalent of an anticipated amount to the sure thing is the "expected value," that is, the dollar amount times the probability of realizing it. Thus, the expected value of an investment that has an even chance of paying $10,000 and an even chance of paying nothing at all is $5,000. If risk itself is something you want to avoid, then the expected value of this investment to you is less than $5,000.

5. *Costs and benefits count only after taxes.* Taxes are so pervasive and so large these days that, in making decisions which result in economic costs or benefits, it is worthwhile to consider the tax effects of each alternative. A decision to spend a sum of money may actually cost you less than the value of the entire sum, since it may reduce your tax bill; conversely, a decision which will add to your income may be worth less than its face value because it increases the tax you must pay. You may even gain more by saving money you have already earned than by earning more money; for example, saving $100 in fuel bills by turning down the heat while you are away from home results in a nontaxable benefit to you of $100, while adding an extra $100 to your income increases the amount of

income tax you must pay. Tax considerations make the motto "A penny saved is a penny earned" an understatement!

Implicit in these five rules for converting costs and benefits into comparable dollars is an important, counterintuitive principle: the past is irrelevant; past costs are "sunk costs" to be ignored. Money already overbet on a poor poker hand is irrelevant in a shrewd choice about dropping out of the game. Decisions about entering a new field of study are not to be based on the amount of time and money already invested in learning other fields, although that may affect the potential future benefits from more education. And even if I have just spent a lot fixing up my old car, an analysis of future benefits and costs may reveal that I should trade it in or junk it. The sunk cost principle is more than a matter of not "throwing good money after bad," however. If I pay an ex-friend $1,000 for a car that I discover is really only worth $200, then it still may be worthwhile to spend money fixing it up if the car's value could be raised above $200 by more than the cost of the repairs.

Now consider the decision to purchase and read this book. How far can we go in examining the costs and benefits of that decision, using our five principles?

In the first place, we must think in terms of today's dollars. Confusion is possible here because although the costs are incurred in the present, the benefits stretch into the future. However, the time of decision is now, so it makes sense to convert all the costs and benefits to present values. Suppose the knowledge you gain from studying the book might save you $100 each year for the next fifty years. What is the present value of that benefit? At an interest rate of 3 percent, it is now worth not $5,000, but $2,573. In fact, any fifty-year stream of costs or benefits has a present value of about half its total amount. (See appendix 1.) What about inflation? If prices rise, presumably you could expect to save more than $100 each year, but in that case the market interest rate will also tend to be higher by approximately the rate of inflation. A 10 percent inflation rate means a 13 percent interest rate, so the low 3 percent rate remains valid in today's dollar values. A lot of confusion and difficulty can be avoided by using the 3 percent "real" rate and not attempting to forecast the rate of inflation.

Our second principle converts the time you might spend reading this book into a money cost, using the pervasive principle that the value of anything is the cost of its alternative opportunity. What else could you do with this time? Could you be working and earning money? Would you insist on premium pay for overtime, because you value your leisure? In that case, perhaps the cost of reading this book should be evaluated at 150 percent of your hourly wage rate! On the other hand, if you have little else to do, you may feel the time invested costs you little or nothing. However, unless the value you place on your time is very low, *the major cost of reading this book is the value of the time spent reading it*. If you value your time at $3.00 per hour and spend 100 hours reading the book, then the time cost of reading it is $300.

Our third principle, converting noncash items to dollars by imputation, is used implicitly in estimating the value of the time you might invest in learning, although using a foregone alternative to value one selected is a somewhat different principle from imputing a money value to a nonmoney cost or benefit. The money cost of depreciation of a car, for example, is imputed from the decline in its market value.

The fourth principle is that uncertain benefits can be converted to an expected value by multiplying by the probability that they will be realized. Going back to our $100 per year for fifty years, you might feel that you have only a fifty-fifty chance of making these money-saving decisions, so you should cut that $2,573 estimate of the present value of benefits in half. The logic behind using probabilities is that if one chose that alternative many times, the average result would be the benefit times the probability. People object that they are making the choice only once, and they also sometimes distort the probabilities in biased ways, but the principle remains valid.

Fifth, and last, what part do taxes play in these calculations? If better consumer decisions save you money, there is no income tax on that saving, as there would be on an earned amount. Since most decisions have dollar effects that are small relative to your income, you can estimate federal income tax effects by using the marginal tax rate—the fraction of one additional dollar of income that would be taken or, in this case, saved in taxes. Table 1 gives some illustrative rates for joint (husband-wife) returns at different taxable incomes; the rate varies from about 12 percent to 50 percent. The marginal income tax rate you face is a crucial number. If it is 30 percent, then each dollar of tax-free income is worth a full dollar rather than

Table 1. 1982 Marginal Tax Rates for a Married Couple Filing Jointly

Taxable Income[a]	Marginal Tax Rate
$ 3,400	12%
5,500	14
7,600	16
11,900	19
16,000	22
20,200	25
24,600	29
29,900	33
35,200	39
45,800	44
60,000	49
85,600	50[b]

[a] Any income exceeding the amount listed is taxed at the corresponding rate.
[b] Maximum marginal rate for all taxpayers.

the seventy cents you would receive after taxes, or 43 percent (100/70) more than the taxable dollar. If your marginal tax rate is 50 percent, tax-free dollars are worth twice as much.

In summary, if you convert a future benefit to present value, reduce it because it is uncertain, increase it because it is a tax-free benefit, and subtract the cost of this book and the value of your time, you might have an estimate of the net benefits of learning some elementary economics. The final question is whether some other way of spending that time and money promises a higher net benefit.

Shortcuts

Even if you do not go through such calculations, some obvious rules of thumb derive from these general methods of comparing close alternatives and translating everything to present values. Anything with costs now and benefits in the distant future must provide a lot of benefits to cover the interest on the investment. Benefits that are not taxable, or (if you itemize deductions) costs that are deductible from taxable income, are better than taxable benefits or nondeductible costs.

There are a few other shortcuts. Decisions made by friends with similar tastes and incomes are clues as to what their information getting and decision making led to, and this is useful information, suggesting what you would find if you went through the same process. If a mechanically alert friend has just bought a particular brand of appliance and is satisfied with it, that may be all the information you need. On the other hand, people who spend other people's money—for instance, on expense accounts—may not make choices that you would want to make using your own money. You might also want to avoid situations where you might be competing with others who, because tax advantages benefit them more, are really paying less than you, or with people who are making careless decisions because of time or social pressure or because information is hard to get.

CHAPTER TWO **Investment in Yourself**

A character in Greek mythology named Procrustes chopped or stretched his visitors to make them fit his bed. In a similar if less dramatic pursuit of logic and order, the discussion of economic choices in this book will follow the sequence in which they are made in most people's lives. The first important economic decisions most people make are about how much time and money to invest in improving personal skills; similar decisions must be made throughout life regarding whether to seek advancement in a particular line of employment, whether to change jobs, or even whether to pursue a particular hobby or avocation. Of course, the early choices are the most crucial, since they provide beginnings and open up various opportunities for later learning. This chapter will discuss investing in the acquisition of skills and knowledge, either to increase earning power directly, or to improve the capacity to enjoy what is earned.

Capital Theory

Education, whether formal, like that accomplished in school, or self-education, as undertaken by reading this book, is partly an investment activity because it involves spending time and money now for some kind of future benefit we expect over a period of years. The theory of capital is involved because capital is the machinery (in this case, the skills) that results from investment and provides such future benefits as higher income in return. Houses and cars are "physical" capital, and they are easier to analyze than "human" capital such as that acquired by education. With human capital it is more difficult to quantify all benefits and costs, and there are more noneconomic considerations as well.

Investment in yourself means using time and spending money not for current consumption but to acquire skills and credentials that will provide future benefits. With learning, the benefits may be in future earning power, but they can also appear in enhanced aesthetic skills. Some human capital never seems to wear out or get obsolete the way physical capital does; it provides benefits over a lifetime.

The basic economic problem involved in decisions about investment in human capital is how to compare investment costs incurred now with benefits scattered into the distant future. It is compounded because the future (including the length of one's life) is always uncertain. Surely a distant uncertain benefit is not as good as a current and certain one. In addition, the availability of several alternative future possibilities may hinge upon a decision to invest made in the present. We shall want to take account of the options without double-counting.

Costs, Benefits, and Interest Rates

Since investment decisions must be made now, the sensible thing to do is to convert all costs and benefits into their equivalent present values. A dollar ten years from now is worth less than a dollar in hand now, for two reasons. First, by waiting ten years to receive it, I forego the interest I could otherwise earn for ten years if I obtained the dollar now and invested it. Second, if prices continue to rise as they always seem to, then a dollar will not buy as much in ten years as it will now. There is a way to simplify these calculations by taking account of both interest and inflation, relying on a historic tendency for market interest rates to average about 3 percent more than the rate of price inflation. The 3 percent rate represents the fact that complex, roundabout methods of production that require tying up funds (in capital or inventory) increase output sufficiently to pay 3 percent per year on the funds. Hence, anyone who lends resources to others can expect a 3 percent return in real terms (today's prices). If the market pays more, inflation tends to wipe it out. To see this, suppose that the market interest rate is 5 percent and the rate of inflation is 2 percent. This means that lenders are increasing their real (inflation-adjusted) wealth by 3 percent per year. If the inflation rate should rise unexpectedly to 6 percent, then the real rate of interest falls to 5 percent minus 6 percent, or -1 percent. Since borrowers can use "cheaper" inflated dollars to more than pay back their loans, the demand for loans will increase. Since lenders are better off keeping their money to themselves, the supply of loans will decrease. Both of these actions will drive up the nominal interest rate, and this will continue until the inflation-adjusted interest rate rises from −1 percent to 3 percent. With an inflation rate of 6 percent, this process will drive the nominal interest rates up to about 9 percent. (It is not always possible to obtain the free market rate of interest on savings in an inflationary economy, because the interest rates paid on savings accounts in banks or in savings and loan associations are artificially held down by law and lack of competition. You will also pay more than the "market rate" when you borrow because of risk and the costs to the lender of making and collecting small loans.)

All of this means that future benefits measured in future (inflated) dollars should be converted to present values at a market interest rate. However, dollars measured in real terms—or measured in today's prices, as payoffs in earnings usually are—should be discounted at 3 percent, which is all one could earn net of inflation if the funds were kept and put into financial investments instead of being used for investment in education. This also means, as we shall see later, that in working out programs of saving for retirement or future needs, we assume we can earn only 3 percent because any higher interest rates reflect, and are wiped out by, inflation. To do that, of course, requires trying to earn free competitive-market interest rates, even if the government allows banks to refuse to pay that much.

Present Values

Because of interest, costs and benefits that occur at different times are not comparable. And since decisions are made in the present, the simplest method of making them comparable is to convert them all to their equivalent values right now—"present values." The present value of a future cost is less than in the future, because if you have the money now you can earn interest on it until the cost occurs; the present value of a future benefit is similarly less, because you do not have it now to start earning interest for you.

Calculating present values becomes complicated in two ways. First, interest is earned on accumulated interest as well as principal invested. To account for this, we must use compound interest tables or calculators; a table employing an interest-per-time-period rate and listing a number of time periods will show the present value of a particular sum available at different points in the future. Second, an investment decision may involve "streams" of costs or benefits in the future; for example, a decision to obtain more education now may result in increased earnings per year for the next several years. When there is a stream of costs or benefits, each one must be reduced to its present value before it is added to the others, unless the series involves a constant amount for each period of time, in which case tables or calculators can estimate the present value of the whole series. Tables and calculators can also be set up to give the future values of present costs or benefits, or of streams of costs or benefits starting now.

Sometimes one is comparing alternatives of greatly different total size, so that finding their net present or future values alone does not reveal which option has more net benefits relative to the amount invested. A way around this problem is to estimate an interest rate for each alternative which causes its present value to equal zero. This is the "rate of return" on the investment, often called the "internal rate of return" to distinguish it from market interest rates. The alternative with the highest rate of return will thus be the most advantageous per dollar invested.

The reader who is interested in pursuing the actual mathematics of these calculations may do so by reading appendix 1, page 231, and studying the tables there.

We can use these principles to evaluate the profitability of obtaining further formal education. Whether one is trying to decide to go on from high school to college, to proceed from college to graduate school, or to go back to school after working for a time, the costs to an individual can be taken to include the direct costs of tuition and, more important, the indirect costs of the earnings foregone by attending classes rather than working full time. Scholarship money and part-time work will reduce these costs. The benefits of the education can be taken as the difference between the earnings of those who undertake the educational program in question and those who do not, during their working lives. This simple calculation, however, ignores any uncertainty about finishing the educational program, the value of the option of obtaining still more education made available by the first step, numerous nonmoney benefits of education, and the possibility that the increased earnings of those who obtain more formal schooling may be due to other factors such as motivation or ability.

Alternative Futures and Uncertainty Corrections

A decision to go to college, for example, should be based on the costs and benefits of college relative to the best alternative way of spending that time. The appropriate alternative for many people is to go to work right out of high school, so the base of comparison is the present value of an expected lifetime of earnings as a high school graduate. What can I expect from going to college? Clearly, it depends on whether I finish, and, if so, whether I go on to graduate work, and, if so, whether I finish an advanced degree.

In order to calculate some combined value for these uncertain alternative outcomes, we use our principle that the value of an uncertain gain is its amount times the probability that it will be realized. These products, which are called "expected values," can be calculated for each educational outcome and then added together. As long as the outcomes are mutually exclusive (I cannot both fail to finish college *and* go to graduate school), the products will sum to the proper expected value.

At any point in time, the decision whether to invest my time in one more year's education involves comparing the present value of my future earnings if I quit now and go to work, with an alternative present value of earnings that start later if I continue in school. But the second of these is more complex because each additional year makes it possible to choose to stay in school still another year. We call this an "option value," the value of the opportunity to do something. The dramatic case is deciding to finish high school, because I not only will earn more even if I graduate and go to work, but there is some probability that I will go on to college and earn still more in the future. To look only at the first benefit is to understate the value of one more year's education, but to evaluate the benefits fully requires estimating the probabilities of alternative completed amounts of education. If those chances are low, then earning the right to go still further is not worth much to me.

As I get more and more education each alternative future stream of earnings starts later, but will presumably be higher to repay the wait and any extra cost. Or I can calculate the internal rate of return on investment in education, and compare it with what I think I could earn by going to work and saving some money. Careful studies showed that the rate of return on a college education was in the 8 percent to 10 percent range in the early 1970's.

Popular discussions of the value of more education not only ignore the value of the right to get still more, but also add up the future extra earnings without discounting them to a present value. Since the earnings differences are usually in current prices, our usual 3 percent rate is enough, but even at that rate, extra earnings many years in the future are not worth much now. A dollar in twenty years at 3 percent is worth $.55, in forty years $.31. And a thousand dollars a year every year for forty years is not worth $40,000 but $23,115, even if there were no inflation!

The total value of another year of education is then the sum of the present values of various larger income streams (minus the present value if one dropped out), each multiplied by the probability that that will indeed be the option that is exercised. The basic rule is that the expected value of a series of *alternative* outcomes is the sum of their expected values times their probabilities, providing, of course, that the probabilities add up to unity.

In fact, most of us compare only one or two alternatives to keep the calculation simple, and most likely discount anyway for uncertainty or for the unconvincing nature of the evidence on added earnings.

On-the-Job Training

In addition to formal classroom education and informal self-education, on-the-job training is an important way of investing in human capital. Indeed, many economists suspect that the skill investments made on the job are more important in dollar terms than investments in formal education. The costs and benefits of on-the-job training are not so obvious as those of formal education, but the principles are the same. Jobs available to someone with a given level of education vary with respect to the wages paid and the opportunities for future promotion. Some jobs pay well initially but do not provide the possibilities for advancement that other jobs do. Frequently, the jobs with the greatest possibilities for advancement will pay less initially than those without, and the wage difference can be thought of as the cost of taking the job with the greater potential for promotion. The higher future wages, of course, are the benefits. The profitability of an investment in on-the-job training can be calculated with these costs and benefits just like the investment in formal education.

The implications of these investments in on-the-job training on occupational choice should be obvious. Careful consideration ought to be given to the choice between occupations which appear attractive at first but offer little chance of advancement and those which pay less now but promise more in the future. Those who do not expect to remain in a given occupation or who do not expect to be in the labor force continuously may find the on-the-job investments unprofitable.

Other Investments

There are ways of investing in the acquisition of skills and knowledge other than formal education or on-the-job training, such as adult education programs and learning by doing. Even changing jobs, or moving to a new area, is a kind of investment in changing the environment in which skills are marketed. In each case, the same analysis is feasible—a stream of future benefits and costs, or of net earnings, can be converted to a present value for each alternative, and then converted to a present expected value by discounting for uncertainty.[1] If there is a fifty-fifty chance of never using a particular skill, then we should take half the present value of the stream of benefits that would result from using it, and compare that with the cost in time and tuition of the lessons.

A great many decisions about investing in yourself, in learning skills, or securing the right to something, or changing jobs or job locations, involve only a single desired outcome; the main problem, then, is estimating the extent of the benefit and how many years it will last. Learning to play football might, with a low probability, provide a large stream of earnings as a professional, but for relatively few years. Learning how to use a library, or to whittle, might produce a smaller but surer and longer-lasting stream of benefits. Investing in skills is often combined with investment in related equipment—skis, a sewing machine, tools—so that in addition to the present cost there may be some future costs for maintenance and supplies.

---

1. Some people, including businessmen, suggest using a higher than normal interest rate to discount to the present. They sometimes do this implicitly by insisting that an investment "pay for itself" in five to ten years, which is the equivalent of a very high combination interest and risk-adjustment rate. This can lead to confusion by mixing up uncertainty adjustments and interest adjustments. A more straightforward method is to make the two adjustments separately or to calculate present values and then to multiply by a probability of the particular future events actually happening.

CHAPTER THREE **Decisions about Work and Family**

Having determined the state of my human capital stock of knowledge, credentials, skills, and seniority, I have a series of interrelated decisions to make about how much to work, at what kind of job, with whom to live and pool incomes and responsibilities, where to live, and how many children to have. If I want a traditional marriage, in which one partner stays home and takes care of children, then one of us must expect to earn enough to support a whole family. If I desire a more modern partnership, where housework and child care are shared, then both of us will need careers that allow something less than total devotion to work. If I expect to have no children, and a working partner, then we can work a lot less, or consume a lot more, or retire earlier with a comfortable income, or several of these. Each of the choices influences and is influenced by the others, regardless of the precise order in which they are made.

Most people will have selected an occupation, a partner, and at least a potentially permanent location and job, within ten years after leaving school. The statistics on occupational, geographic, and marital (marriage, divorce, and remarriage) mobility show a rapid dropoff after the age of thirty. Furthermore, the consequences of these choices are with us for a long time, and it becomes increasingly difficult and expensive to change them. For our purposes, we will start with the choice of a career as a logical next step after getting an education.

Selecting a Job

Finding the right job, like any other shopping and selection exercise, requires an expenditure of time and money for the purpose of securing information. Knowledge about some jobs may require actually working at them to find out what they are like. But simply finding out what jobs are available and what they require and pay takes effort, particularly since job openings are soon filled, nearly half of them by someone known personally to the employer or to other employees. Informal hiring methods are not necessarily unfair, dishonest, or even inefficient; the employer also has a problem of information about potential employees, and personal recommendation by a friend or trusted employee is an efficient and often successful shortcut. But since such informal methods have also allowed discrimination against women and minorities, we can look forward to more formal posting of and applying for jobs.

I must still invest some effort in learning about jobs and in figuring out whether a particular job provides options for advancement or transfer into other jobs. Some jobs are "dead end," while others open up new opportunities by providing on-the-job training. The latter may pay less at first for that reason.

The general interpretation of "investing in future promotion opportunities" is straightforward enough. Suppose that I must choose between two jobs, one with promotion opportunities and the other without. Suppose further that, relative to the job without promotions, the job with the future opportunities paid $1,000 more per year starting ten years from now but paid $1,000 less per year for the next ten years. The cost of taking $1,000 less for ten years at a 3 percent interest rate is the present value of that stream, or $8,530. The present value today of the extra earnings to start in ten years is 0.744 of its "present value" ten years from now. If that stream of extra earnings will last twenty years it would be worth $14,877 at its start. Converting that to present values today, I have $11,068 for the twenty-year stream. So because the future benefits are discounted more heavily than the more immediate costs, I must expect to work for nearly twenty years at the $1,000 higher salary to make it worth the ten years of the $1,000 lower salary while learning: at twenty years the net gain is $11,068 − $8,530, or $2,538.

Can one learn about the future earnings and advancement possibilities of occupations, if not specific jobs, from history, or from the forecasts of experts? The United States Department of Labor issues at intervals publications on the prospects for jobs within different occupational groups. But these have often had to be reversed within a few years. There have been rather dramatic shifts in the advantages of different occupations, with periods of oversupply and unemployment for construction workers, then engineers, then schoolteachers. What is worse, there are no longer the clear set of occupations and career lines we once thought there were. There seems to be a proliferation of specialties with no clear prerequisites of academic background and no unambiguous way of getting trained for them. Experts are fond of saying that the half-life of nearly any training (i.e., the time when it is half obsolete) is getting shorter.

One comforting consideration is that training in one area can often be used in another, and skills are rarely related to one specific job. Hence, mastery of almost any difficult subject is likely to be of some use somewhere, sometime. Developing the discipline and skills to master one subject can make it easier to master another, too.

How Much Work?

The job I select will limit my choices about how many hours to work. Most jobs require some minimum number of hours, often forty a week, and many do not allow, or do not pay for, time beyond forty hours. Some jobs I can forget about except when I'm actually working; others expect total devotion to thinking about the job. If I want more work than my job allows, I can change jobs, look for a second job, or find ways to do work around the house that I would otherwise have to pay for. Part-time second jobs are frequently poorly paid, and do-it-yourself direct production is difficult or unprofitable for many, so roughly one-fifth of the workforce say they want more work than they can find. This inability to find enough work is most common among those with the least education. The official government unemployment figures neglect this underemployment by defining as unemployed only those who did not work at all in a given week, were available and looking for work, were not between jobs, or not about to start work. This excludes those who wanted more work and also those so discouraged that they stopped looking.

Insofar as we have some freedom of choice about how hard to work, we have another important economic decision worthy of some systematic analysis. Working on a job involves time and some money costs as well—commuting costs, union dues, equipment and supplies (particularly for those who are self-employed), and perhaps outlays for child care for working parents. But the amounts of money are usually small compared with the value of the time spent. Income taxes also complicate our analysis somewhat, but we can handle the money costs and taxes by thinking of the money we earn net of the costs of earning it and of taxes. These net earnings are not equivalent to take-home pay, since take-home pay does not deduct some of the costs of earning the money, and does deduct some of the earnings which are "spent" for consumption costs (as when an insurance premium is automatically deducted) or "saved" (as with retirement deductions). It is inappropriate to subtract such consumption or investment (savings) from earnings, since if I paid the insurance premiums myself or managed my own retirement plan, my take-home pay would be that much higher. My income is also higher by the value of the other fringe benefits my employer provides. In calculating the "earnings" from unpaid production, like growing food or painting one's house, we can ask how much we saved by doing the work ourselves rather than hiring someone else to do it.

The main choice, then, is between work and its rewards, and leisure. The phrase "work and its rewards" is used because there is often some direct satisfaction from the work itself, apart from the money earned. Hours devoted to work produce money, valued output, or direct satisfaction, but hours left free for leisure also produce satisfaction more than covering the money costs of the recreation. Economists deduce that the amount of work that will maximize overall satisfaction is the point where the added satisfaction from the added earnings, minus the dissatisfaction (or plus the joy) of that added work, just equals the satisfaction given up if I am deprived of that last hour of leisure. If the hour of leisure given up by increasing work hours from forty hours per week to forty-one hours is less enjoyable than the money made from that forty-first work hour, then I would be better off working more. If I am not allowed to work as much as I would like, and can find no extra jobs or special part-time arrangements to get around the limits, then I may well feel my time is worth considerably less than my net hourly earnings. If I really would like to work less than the required forty hours a week, or am forced to work overtime, I may well feel the time is worth more than the pay. This will affect any calculations about other decisions which require that I value my time. One implication of these constraints is that for a person who really wants more work and does not value leisure much, then recreation that takes more time than money makes sense.

Even without overtime pay, many people are working more than full time (usually defined as fifty forty-hour weeks per year), many mothers are working, and many people say they want still more work. Apparently most of us do not value our leisure very highly. Philosophers may spend years trying to show that we all work too much, but the evidence from our actual choices of what to do with our time suggests the opposite.

Similar decisions "at the margin" must be made about working at unpaid jobs. Is the benefit of an additional hour of housework, child care, or gardening worth the cost of one less hour of leisure? Some of that work hardly seems discretionary, since most people do their own housework and take care of their own children. But there are choices even here, as indicated by the fact that some working mothers are reducing their double-job burden by paying to have some of the housework and extra child care done, and that we are all reducing housework hours by eating in restaurants more often. There is also some voluntary "home production" of food, repairs to car or house or clothes, and creation of new clothes. When we contribute to charity, we can choose to volunteer time or to give money in whatever proportions we choose. In fact, most people who give one also give some of the other.

The tax implications of choices are important in nonmarket unpaid production. I may have to earn $1,500 in order to have $1,000 after taxes to pay a house painter to paint my house, leaving him with $750 after his taxes. Even with this double tax on the division of labor and specialization, there is still relatively little do-it-yourself work done, indicating that the specialist must be far more efficient or able than the amateur. Indeed, this trend seems to be accelerating, with people earning more money at their main jobs and then paying others to do their cooking by eating out more and more.

The opportunities for reaching a better balance between work and leisure, and the constraints on free choices, depend not only on the kind of jobs one takes, but also on the partner one chooses to live with, if any. We now turn to the economic aspects of a decision once thought to be purely romantic.

Marriage and Other Partnerships

Although two cannot really live as cheaply as one, it doesn't √ cost twice as much either. Economists term such savings "economies of scale," and they are present when two choose to live together and share some overhead expenses. Overhead means not just the cost of a roof over one's head, but any living costs which can be shared, such as those associated with cars or other durable goods. It may sound absurd, if not dismal, to talk about selecting someone with whom to share income and expenses. Assortative mating has been the concern of the anthropologist and sociologist, and marriage the concern of the church and the novelist. But since it is true that alternatives to formal marriage are becoming more common and that more people are choosing to have no children at all, it makes sense to discuss the economic arrangements people make when they live together.

Sharing an apartment or house may mean merely sharing the rent, or may extend to sharing the costs and preparation of food, maintenance, and even the investment in owning the place. But it is sharing income and sharing responsibility for children that makes marriage or its equivalent a major and crucial economic choice. Particularly when it is assumed that both partners will have jobs working for money, the choice of partner is crucial. If two people are establishing careers, frequently by moving to different areas, or at least considering jobs in different locations, then sharing may involve some compromises in job choice by both partners.

The dominant pattern—women following their husbands, staying home with the children, and taking what jobs they can fit in with those prior commitments—is giving way to more balanced but more complicated joint career decisions. Some may even be postponing a final decision about a lifetime partner until both potential partners have some notion about their careers. Couples' decisions about how much work to do for money will vary depending on whether children are desired and expected, and on how much parental time each parent is expected to invest in those children.

It seems likely that new kinds of legal agreements, different from those in or implied by the standard marriage contract, will appear. It is important to make explicit and binding some otherwise vague agreements, which may be subject to mutual misperception or second interpretations or outdated law. When one partner compromises career decisions in the interest of the partnership, some longer-term commitment by the other partner to future cooperation and responsibility would seem proper. This is true for both sexes but, given past history, is probably more important for the woman. The commitment should involve life insurance on each partner, and a similar financial commitment if either partner decides to leave.

With views toward marriage changing, it has been suggested that some contractual arrangements be made and regularly remade between partners, spelling out what each is supposed to contribute to the partnership in tasks performed. Any economist will agree that this is inefficient and unduly rigid, and that it would be far better to agree on a pricing scheme that values both tasks and time contributions in dollar terms. Then negotiations could easily raise the "wage" for tasks that no one was willing to do at the old rate, and lower it for more pleasant tasks. Such an implicit price system and some rules for adjusting it allow flexibility, alternation of jobs, and adaptation to new situations. It might even be possible to combine time and money contributions in achieving a balance, at least in those cases where the woman holds a market job.

Having Children

Everyone does not first get educated, then find a job, then get married, then decide how many children to have, then decide about housing and residential location; but we can discuss the decisions in that order, coming next to the decisions about having children. Again, while this is not primarily an economic decision, it has crucial implications—costs and benefits—which need to be sorted out if only as a background for the noneconomic costs and benefits.

Over the years, the costs of children have been increasingly borne by society in a variety of ways: free elementary and secondary education, heavily subsidized higher education, public services focused on the family (parks, playgrounds, libraries), income tax allowances for dependents, and income maintenance systems like Social Security and Aid to Families with Dependent Children. But a child is still a very expensive "investment" for the parents, requiring large amounts of money and time during the very years when most parents need to concentrate on careers and to invest in cars, a house, and furnishings. Most published estimates of the costs of children seem to exaggerate the need for high-quality child care and the money costs of college, while ignoring the nonmoney costs of time demands. The cost of any added person in a family is the marginal cost of extra space, somewhat more wear and tear, and more food—overall a less-than-proportionate addition to costs. A first child might add one-sixth or one-fifth to the living costs of two parents (more when the child is adolescent and eating more). A second child might add a slightly smaller proportion. They may be cheaper by the dozen, but a dozen is still more expensive than eleven.

The present system of public education subsidizes large families, but overall, children are a poor investment, in crass economic terms, and the decline in the birth rate might indicate that the satisfactions from raising children do not appear sufficient to justify the investment. On the other hand, it may be the desires of women for careers, and the possibilities of luxurious living for a married couple without dependents now that good jobs for women are possible, that are influencing many couples to postpone or cancel plans to have children. One difficulty with postponing having children until careers are well along and household capital accumulated is the increasing probability of physical difficulties for mothers past thirty. It is worth noting, however, that an increase in the average age of parents at birth slows up the rate of population increase, even at the same net reproduction rate (total children born per woman), because each generational cycle takes longer.

Measuring Family Well-Being

Economic status is a complex result of decisions about education, job work hours, with whom to share, and how many children to have. It is useful to attempt to construct a composite measure of economic well-being that takes account of money, family composition, and leisure. Developing such a measure will help us to see how all of these decisions fit together.

The most common measure of family economic well-being is total annual family income, i.e., the total dollar income received by all family members from work, from dividends and interest, and from "transfers" (e.g., Social Security, unemployment compensation, welfare). But family income is clearly an inadequate measure of well-being because of vast differences in nonmoney income, family sizes (needs), and leisure time. Worse still, the money income used in most such discussions is neither what the family earns, nor what it has available for consumption, but something in between. It includes some transfer income such as Social Security benefits, welfare payments, and pensions, but leaves out nonmoney income from unpaid work and from living in one's own home (imputed free rent). It also leaves out nonmoney income from employer contributions to Social Security, private pensions, and insurance, and does not deduct taxes, costs of earning income, compulsory saving for old age, or alimony and child-care payments.

If money income is inadequate, even as a measure of current control over resources, ignoring wealth and other sources of security, a better measure is needed to help evaluate decisions about careers, marriage, and children. To determine how well off I am compared with ten years ago, or with before I got married, or with my friends and neighbors, first I need a measure of income. I may start with money income—wages, interest, rent, dividends, and regular transfer income like pensions—but adjust it:

1. Deduct income taxes, commuting costs, union dues, and compulsory payments like alimony and child support.
2. Add the amount of money saved in do-it-yourself projects and the value of the child care and housework done by the family.
3. Add other nonmoney income—employer contributions to retirement and insurance and imputed rental income from living in my own home. This rental income to homeowners amounts to roughly 6 percent of house equity per year and comes about because homeowners, in effect, rent to themselves and pay themselves a profit on their investment (more on this in chap. 4).
4. Add nonmoney transfer incomes such as subsidies for meals or rent.

Divide the result—call it net real income—by some standard of needs. The official federal poverty line, which shows the minimal income level needed to provide for families of different sizes (roughly $2,000 plus $1,000 per person per year in 1979), can be used for this. The ratio of net real income to needs shows what fraction or multiple of the poverty standard that income provides.

Before making further adjustments for leisure time, let us examine the implications of our measure of net real income relative to needs by comparing the economic status of two single-parent households—one with a female head and two children, the other a single male head living alone—before and after they marry. Suppose that the female head works full time and earns $8,000, while the male head works full time and earns $13,000. (That women earn about three-fifths of what men do is a well-documented fact.) If taxes reduce the man's income by $2,000 and the woman's by $1,000, and if the monetary value of housework adds $1,000 to the man's income and the value of housework and child care adds $2,000 to the woman's, then, barring other adjustments, the man's net income is $12,000 while the woman's is $9,000.

In 1979, the federal poverty needs standard was approximately $2,000 plus $1,000 per person in the household, so the needs standard of the man is $3,000 while the needs standard for the woman and her family is $5,000. The *ratio* of income to needs for these two families is $12,000/$3,000 = 4.00 for the man, and $9,000/$5,000 = 1.80 for the woman and her children. If they were to marry and continue to work as before, then their combined income would equal $21,000, their combined needs standard would be $6,000, and the income/needs ratio of the combined family would be 3.50—a vast improvement for the woman and her children and a moderate fall in the income/needs ratio for the man.

The above example shows that if family economic status is measured by net income relative to needs, then changes in status can come about from changes in family composition as well as changes in the sources and amounts of income. A recent study of such changes in status conducted by the Institute for Social Research at the University of Michigan found that they were not completely dominated by decisions about work hours and earnings. Rather, changing family composition accounted for substantial fractions of the overall change in family economic well-being. A dramatic illustration of this is the disastrous drop in well-being of women and children after a divorce. Changes in economic status were far more favorable for women who remained married as compared to those who divorced. That the children usually go with their mother after a divorce, that women, especially those who have raised children, are unable to earn and work as much as men, and that alimony and child-support payments are inadequate if paid at all, contribute to this situation. Large changes in economic status were also found to accompany births and deaths of family members and the timing of the departure of children from the parental home. Indeed, a major conclusion of the study was that "decisions about marriage, bearing children, and encouraging older children and other adults to stay in the household or leave it may be the main decisions that affect one's economic status."

A final adjustment to our measure of economic status is to make some allowance for the amount of work required to produce that income, and hence the amount of free time left to enjoy it. This requires combining a ratio of two dollar amounts (income and needs) with a ratio of leisure hours to a standard of leisure. We could do this by multiplying the two together, perhaps after weighting one more than the other. Making even the simplest adjustments for nonmoney income, different family composition, and different leisure left to enjoy the income will render a more realistic measure of well-being.

Taxes and Redistribution of Income

Modern societies frequently adopt programs which attempt to redistribute income, and thereby reduce differences in economic well-being, between the relatively well-to-do and the poor. The federal personal income tax is considered to be one of the major redistributive mechanisms in the United States. Since it has profound and differential effects on many consumer decisions, a summary of its main features is needed. It is a progressive tax, taking somewhat larger proportions of higher incomes first by totally exempting some income from taxation, and then by applying increasing tax rates to each successive block of income. The higher rate on each succeeding block of income does not apply to the earlier blocks, so you never end up with less after-tax income when you earn more. The fraction taken in taxes of an additional dollar you earn—your marginal income tax rate—is the crucial feature for many purposes. That rate varies from 14 percent to 50 percent.

A second crucial feature is the possibility of deducting certain items from income before it is taxed. Deductible if itemized are specified expenses like interest on debts (e.g., home mortgages), state and local taxes, uninsured casualty losses, charitable contributions, and (when they exceed some fraction of income) medical expenses. Itemizing deductions will lower your tax bill if the sum of what you can deduct that way is larger than the "standard deduction"; for most people this happens only when their income approaches $20,000 a year.

A third feature of the federal income tax is that it does

not tax some sources of income. Income from Social Security, unemployment compensation, and tax-exempt (mostly state, city, and school district) bonds is not taxed. Neither is the income that you "earn" from do-it-yourself work or from shopping around and paying a lower price for something as a result. The imputed rental income that you earn from owning your own home (and thus paying yourself a return on your investment) is not taxed either.

A fourth feature is that income from the sale of something you own that has appreciated in value (long-term capital gains) is taxed at only forty percent of the rate of other income. Capital losses, on the other hand, are fully deductible. These two facts produce a kind of subsidy to risk-taking.

Further discussion of some of the tax implications of deductibility of housing costs will be found in chapter 4, of casualty losses in chapter 9, and of special treatment of capital gains and tax-exempt bonds in chapter 7.

The importance of the income tax on consumer decisions warrants some illustrations. Suppose that you are in the 33 percent tax bracket—i.e., that the government would tax an additional dollar you earn at a 33 percent rate. The amount of charitable contributions you make can be deducted from taxable income, so each dollar contributed to charity lowers your taxable income by $1 and your tax bill by $.33. Thus, the government really "pays" one-third of that contribution because it can't collect as much in taxes, and the effective cost of that $1 contribution to you is really only $.67. By the same token, a savings account that pays a 6 percent interest rate before taxes is really giving you a return of 4 percent after taxes if your marginal tax rate is 33 percent. Since the interest payments on mortgages can be deducted from taxable income, a 10 percent nominal mortgage interest rate is really 6.67 percent. Income that you "earn" through do-it-yourself work is not taxed, so each dollar of it is equivalent to $1.50 of earned income that is subject to a 33 percent tax rate.

Your own marginal tax rate and whether you are itemizing affect the real (after-tax) cost of different things differently. But also, that other people with different tax rates are buying some of the same things you are means that you are competing with people who actually pay different prices than you do. For example, most tax-exempt bonds are bought by very high-income people whose 50 percent marginal tax rate makes the 6 percent bond yield as good as a 12 percent yield on something that is taxable.

The market interest rate on tax-exempt bonds is driven down because of this. So if you have a 20 percent marginal tax rate, a taxable investment that yielded 8 percent before taxes (and 6.4 percent after) would be better than a 6 percent tax-exempt bond.

A more important example is owning a home, where the untaxed free rent and the deductibility of interest and tax payments saves high-tax people more than low-tax people and thus lowers the cost of owning for them. The same principle applies to purchases in hotels and restaurants where people on expense accounts are spending someone else's money. That someone, the employer, faces a 46 percent corporate profit tax rate itself so that each $1 of business account expense reduces its before-tax profits by $1 and its profits tax by about $.46. The price of the hotel and restaurant expenses to the company, then, is cut in half.

Over the years a substantial number of special provisions, or "loopholes," have been written into the income tax law. They were usually justified for the case or cases that precipitated their acceptance, but for other people, particularly in combination with other special provisions, they lead to unfair, if legal, tax avoidance. There is a continuing process of closing these loopholes and a parallel process of opening new ones, so that it is difficult to see who is winning except the tax lawyers and the companies that have sprung up to help people with the complications of filling out their income tax forms. Indeed, recent revisions of the law dealing with charitable foundations were so complicated that even the lawyers claimed not to understand them, telling their clients not to start any more foundations nor to add to their present ones.

It is important for you as a taxpayer to know ways to reduce your taxes legally. Most ways involve changing income to a different recipient, a different year, or a different form. Although specifics are discussed throughout this book, a few general comments are in order here.

Almost all income now has to have a taxpayer number (usually the Social Security number of its recipient) attached, and this is transmitted to the Internal Revenue Service by the source (e.g., the employer, or the bank paying interest). But under the states' Uniform Gift to Minors Act, assets can be put in the names of minor children with an adult as trustee. Their yield is the child's income and hence not taxed while the child remains a legal dependent for the parents' tax return. When the assets are sold, say for the child's education, the capital gain is again the child's income and subject to little or no tax. Of course, as soon as the child becomes eighteen, the ownership is unrestricted and the child can legally spend the money.

One of the attractions of some United States government savings bonds is that, since no tax is payable on the interest until the bond is cashed (because no interest is actually paid until then), the owner can select a year of lower income and tax rates in which to cash the bonds. Similar freedom to choose the year exists with assets that appreciate in value. Such capital gains are taxed at less than half your regular rate anyway, and if you wait until you retire, your marginal tax rate may be still lower.

Assets that go up in value can also be given away at their market value, escaping income tax. Hence, converting income into capital gains has advantages beyond that of being able to choose the year to realize them. Investments in real estate and some other things that permit very large depreciation allowances essentially do this (see chap. 7). At most, you pay income tax on less than half the gain, and only if and when you sell the asset and "realize" the gain. If you bequeath an asset, your heirs pay no capital gains tax on gains before the date of your death, so your capital gain escapes tax altogether.

State income taxes vary from state to state, but are generally much less progressive than the federal income tax. In fact, since they are deductible from income for purposes of federal income taxes, they are even less progressive than they seem. Indeed, this is true of all state taxes. For instance, a straight state income tax of 10 percent of income regardless of its size is really 10 percent for the (low-income) person who does not itemize deductions for the federal return. Consider the person whose marginal tax rate is 20 percent and who itemizes, and thus can deduct his state income tax payment from his taxable income. His federal income taxes are reduced by 2 percent, so the effective rate of the state income tax for him is really 8 percent. A person with a 50 percent marginal federal tax rate (income around $40,000) really pays only a 5 percent state income tax. The federal income tax progressivity is eroded by the right to deduct other taxes—or perhaps all other taxes are made more regressive.

Tax laws are periodically revised, so a person has no choice but to keep up with them. The difficulty with the complexity and change, aside from the inequities, is the cost of compliance. Many people end up paying fees to "experts" to help them sort out the complications. The quality of these tax services is not always adequate, leaving the consumer with one more shopping problem and a decision about whether to invest instead in learning how to do it. The payoff to learning comes year after year in the saving of fees and also in increased sensitivity to ways of reducing taxes.

The two other main taxes most people face are property and sales taxes. Property taxes are the most maligned—accused of being erratically and inequitably assessed, of varying unconscionably from one area to another, and of being regressive. As explained in chapter 4, many of the accusations are simply wrong. Property taxes are a justifiable complement to other taxes, taxing the consumption of private and public services (free rent, police and fire protection, and schools) even by those who manage to hide part of their income from the income tax.

What about the sales tax? It depends on what is excluded from it. A sales tax that excludes food and medicine is roughly proportional over most income levels, at least before we consider it net of federal income tax offsets. But at high income levels, where people spend lower and lower fractions of their incomes on things subject to sales tax, the burden is lighter, even apart from the federal income tax advantages they have. Strangely enough, the lower middle income people—those hardest hit by the sales tax—often say they prefer it to an income tax.

The only other taxes with relatively clear redistributive effects of any importance are the federal estate tax and the state inheritance taxes, intended to reduce the inequality that results from inherited wealth. These taxes have never been very effective, because the wealthy have the resources, ingenuity, time, and legal help to devise ways to pass on most of their wealth to their children. Indeed, the affluent are much more concerned with avoiding estate taxes than income taxes, regarding the latter as somehow more justified because they come at a time when the money is being made. But once the money is part of the estate, the affluent feel it should be protected. The methods of protection are complex, involving trusts and special corporations and foundations, and we know very little about just how the intergenerational transmission of wealth really works. One of the purposes of the revised law on charitable foundations was to reduce their use as a method of avoiding estate taxes.

CHAPTER FOUR **Housing and Residential Location**

The decision about where to live includes not only location but whether to own or to rent. Decisions about jobs, living partner, and the number and timing of children all affect decisions about location and home ownership, and they affect each other—if you want to live in some areas, you have to own your home, whereas in others you may have to rent.

A residence is more than just something likely to account for a fourth of a family's expenses and a third of some people's cash outlays. It is a package deal which includes a neighborhood, commuting and other costs for all the workers in the family, a level of available public services and of property and income taxes, and probably some local styles and standards of living which may exert some pressure to conform. And because moving is expensive in money, time, and emotional turmoil, plans which include children may necessitate a house large enough to accommodate a kind of "peak load," even if it means some extra cost before and afterward.

Considering the difficulties and costs of moving, the decision concerning housing is worth careful thought before it is made. I have to decide how much housing I need and the true costs of that housing, whether I want to own or rent my housing, and where I want to live. Each of these depends on the others, but let's take them in order.

How Much Housing?

Rules of thumb for consumers are often misleading or just plain wrong, but in the case of home ownership, the following two rules about how much a family can afford to spend on housing without undue stress on the rest of the budget may help:

1. Your annual housing cost should not be more than one-fourth of your gross annual income.
2. Do not buy a house that costs more than two or three times your gross annual income.

Equating these two rules gives a relationship between the purchase price of a house and the rental cost of a similar place. If buying a house that costs twice your income is the same as renting a place that costs a fourth of your income, then the *annual* cost of owning a house is about an eighth of its price, and its monthly cost is about one-hundredth of its price (a $30,000 house would rent for $300 a month). The relationship between rent and house value comes about from competitive pressures in the housing market. If rents are much higher than they ought to be, based on house values, then some renters will become owners, and other investors will convert previously owner-occupied homes into rental property. If rents are not high enough to pay a reasonable return on the landlord's investment, then the reverse ought to occur. Both of these actions will tend to restore the relationship between rent and house value.

These rules are often misused, however, because of a misunderstanding about what constitutes the true "costs" of housing. Most homeowners, for example, consider that the mortgage payment is the principal cost of homeowning. But the mortgage payments are partly savings because they increase the equity in the house, and such saving is not a cost. On the other hand, the usual lists of housing costs exclude depreciation and the foregone interest on the money already invested in the house. Only by accident would the cash outlays of the homeowner reflect the real cost of a house.

It is crucial to know what housing alternatives really cost. The cost of rental is clear—rent payments plus utilities. But what is the comparable cost of a house for which only its price and the utility costs are known?

The True Costs of Owning

An economically sound estimate of the annual or monthly cost of owning a home can be made by estimating each of the components of cost. It turns out to be relatively easy, because almost all costs are roughly proportional to the price of the house. Let's look at those costs:

Depreciation is a major cost of any piece of capital equipment—the wearing out, using up, or gradual obsolescence that will ultimately require replacement. Depreciation can be offset by maintenance, but the sum of maintenance expenses and residual depreciation will amount to a roughly constant fraction of house value each year. In the case of houses, maintenance expenses include roofing and painting as well as periodic service to the plumbing, heating, and electrical systems. The sum of depreciation and maintenance costs of owning a home might be 1.5 percent of the current price per year. A 1.5 percent depreciation rate per year implies that an unrepaired house would self-destruct in $1/0.015 = 67$ years.

Repairs and maintenance to make certain the house lasts the sixty-seven years are implied in the 1.5 percent depreciation rate, but not the major alterations to make it last forever, which might be an additional 2 percent of house value per year. Experts claim that while repairs are less frequent on brick or stone houses, they are somewhat more expensive, and that the remaining difference is offset by the increased initial cost of the house. Total depreciation and maintenance costs, then, amount to roughly 3.5 percent of house value per year.

Inflation (appreciation) of house prices causes many people to say that one can ignore depreciation. This is a dangerous confusion. Capital gains—whether merely the result of inflation, or actually exceeding the general rise in prices—are important, but they differ from depreciation. One way to look at this is to think of alternative investments to a house. If inflation is driving up the prices of houses, it should also be driving up the prices of financial investments such as stocks and rental real estate, and some of these investments do not wear out or become obsolete: there is no depreciation to reduce the effect of inflation. You can point to houses in good locations that have had increases in value apart from general inflation, but there are also wise financial investments that have paid off. On the average, over the long run, most investments pay a real 3 percent plus the rate of inflation and plus enough to offset depreciation, if any. Hence, it is useful to take account separately of real depreciation and possible market appreciation of a house. Certainly if one moves to another or a larger house, that same inflation makes the new house more costly too. So holding capital gains aside as a possible benefit, rather than a deduction from cost, what other costs are there besides depreciation?

Interest costs must be considered. While most homeowners are painfully aware of the interest portion of their mortgage payments, few realize that a house with no mortgage has an interest cost which is almost as high. This is because the money tied up in a home could be earning interest if it were put in a savings account or in stocks, and this foregone interest is a very real cost of owning. Foregone and mortgage interest rates differ, since one must always pay more to borrow money than one could have earned by lending it (investing). But at a minimum, the foregone interest costs amount to at least what the money could earn elsewhere, which is 3 percent plus the rate of inflation. To this is added the extra cost of borrowing money, which will decrease to zero as the mortgage is paid off. Because inflation affects both the market value of a house and the interest costs (foregone or paid), it may seem that one offsets the other. But rather than count appreciation as a cost offset, and market interest rates as a cost, 3 percent of the house value can be taken as the annual interest cost in real terms, without having to predict future inflation rates. To this 3 percent are still added the extra real costs of borrowing money (above rates paid on savings).

So far I have a 3.5 percent depreciation cost, a 3 percent interest cost, and some differential interest cost if I must borrow. What else?

Property taxes will run between 1.5 and 2 percent per year of the current house value.

Utilities will cost 3 to 4 percent.

Insurance premiums will be 0.5 percent.

Summing these costs shows that living in a house costs somewhere between 9.5 and 14 percent of its value (i.e., current selling price) each year. Hence, the two rules about how much housing a family can afford really are equivalent. At a 12 percent cost rate, a $40,000 house costs $400 a month in equivalent rent-plus-utilities. If annual housing costs should be about one-fourth of income, and total purchase price should be about twice income, then the annual cost of housing should be about one-eighth of the total purchase price (12.5 percent).

That does not mean that the rules of thumb are right for everyone, however. Many people spend far more than 25 percent of their income on housing, and many spend far less, happily. It may make sense to own a larger house than needed right now because the extra space will be used later, or was needed earlier. It would not make sense to rent a place of the wrong size, since the costs of moving are so much less when renting and the risks so much smaller.

Tax laws make it advantageous to own and possibly to hold a house larger than present needs call for. Homeowners can deduct their property tax and mortgage interest from taxable income. They are also exempted from paying tax on the capital gains income brought about by increases in the market price of the house as long as they buy another house of equal or greater value within eighteen months after selling the old one, or are fifty-five years of age or older and elect a once-in-a-lifetime exemption from the capital gains on the house. In addition, the imputed rental income they receive by owning is untaxed. Imputed rental income is best thought of as the profit or return on his investment that a homeowner pays to himself rather than to a landlord if he were renting. To see this, suppose I sell my house, switch to renting, and invest the proceeds. Before I can use the investment yield to pay my rent, there is income tax on it. But as a homeowner, my investment "yield" was untaxed.

As a result of the various tax incentives for home ownership, benefiting those with higher marginal tax rates and higher interest costs (which are offset by inflating house prices anyway), the same house can have a real economic cost that varies depending on its buyer. With a 10 percent inflation rate and a reasonable set of other assumptions, a $50,000 house can have an after-tax cost of $5,800 a year for a low-income or older family with the mortgage paid off and a 20 percent marginal tax rate, but only $2,250 for a family with a 50 percent tax rate and a full mortgage. You may be bidding for a house against others for whom its real cost is quite different than it is for you!

Own or Rent?

The question of home ownership is filled with emotion, and there are strongly worded arguments on both sides. Some claim it is unsound, more expensive, and foolish to own. Others insist that it makes the owner a pillar of the community, establishes credit rating, forces saving for old age, promises larger capital gains, and has tax advantages. It has already been pointed out that the question of which is cheaper—if two roughly equal houses are available, one for rent and the other for sale—can be answered by making correct economic calculations of the current costs of each. The renter's cost is rent plus utilities; the owner's costs are the various percentages of house value listed earlier.

A common source of confusion in comparing the costs of owning and renting is that after paying off the mortgage, an owner ends up with a house worth tens of thousands of dollars while a renter ends up with nothing of comparable value. The key to this problem is that most of the owner's mortgage payment is really savings and has nothing to do with the economic costs of owning.

Compare the situation of someone who has just purchased a $50,000 house, and has a twenty-year mortgage at 3 percent, with a renter of an equivalent house. Assume initially that the rate of inflation is zero and the owner pays no excess interest costs on his mortgage. From the fourth column of table A in appendix 1 (p. 232) we see that for a twenty-year mortgage at 3 percent on a $50,000 house, the ratio (Amount of Mortgage)/(Yearly Payment) = 14.877, so the yearly mortgage payment is $3,361, and the monthly mortgage payment is $280. Most of the costs of owning involve payments unrelated to this mortgage payment: property tax payments of 2 percent of house value will cost an additional $83 per month, repairs and alterations at 3.5 percent will cost $146 per month, utilities at 3 percent will cost $125 per month, and insurance payments at 0.5 percent of the house price will cost $21 per month. These costs, which are unrelated to the mortgage payment (and will continue even when the mortgage is paid off), amount to $375 per month.

To see that most of the mortgage is savings, suppose that the renter pays his rent (which ought to amount to about $375 per month plus a normal return on the landlord's investment) and deposits $280 per month into a savings account that pays 3 percent. Both owner and renter consume identical housing services for twenty years. The sum of housing costs plus amounts being saved is higher for the renter than the owner by the amount of profit paid to the landlord. The owner ends up with a $50,000 house, but the renter ends up with a savings account balance of $90,283. (This is the value at the end of twenty years of the accumulated savings plus interest. From the fifth column of table A in appendix 1, $280 × 12 months × 26.870 = $90,283.) The renter accumulates more than the owner because he keeps the interest on his savings, while the owner pays the interest costs to the bank. Indeed, this is exactly the foregone interest cost that the owner incurs. To convert this cost to present value terms, it is useful to calculate the amount per month that the renter would have to put on a savings account to end up with a $50,000 balance after twenty years. Using the fifth column of table A, we see that $50,000/(Amount per Year) = 26.870, so that the monthly amount is $155. So if both owner and renter want to end up with something worth $50,000, the owner must pay $280 per month for it, while the renter pays only $155. The difference, $125 per month, is the foregone interest cost incurred by the owner. But if the landlord receives a 3 percent return on his investment, then the renter will pay the extra $125 per month as profit to the landlord. Consideration of tax effects will change these results somewhat in favor of the owner, while the excess interest costs of a mortgage will do the reverse. A potentially more important modification, however, is to allow for inflation. Inflation will drive up the house price, but it should also drive up the interest rate paid on the renter's savings. If the inflation rate is 3 percent per year, then the house price will inflate to $50,000 × 1.806 (table A, third column) = $90,300 in twenty years. But a 3 percent inflation rate will also drive up the interest rate on nondepreciating financial investments, if not always on savings accounts. If that interest rate is 6 percent, then the renter will accumulate $123,487 on his $280 monthly savings account deposits.

The other issues involved with the decision to own or rent are more difficult to quantify. Renting leaves one flexible, able to move with less cost—no broker's fees, no difficulty finding a buyer or seller. A renter can also adjust his or her housing to changing family needs, and thus economize. In addition, time need not be spent on activities that are the landlord's responsibility and that are less productive economically than sticking to one's own occupation.

Owning, however, provides a defense against inflation in the form of an asset whose value increases and a housing cost that—unlike rent—does not shoot up in tight housing markets.[1] Owning also allows more freedom in how to use the dwelling, and provides opportunities for tax-exempt do-it-yourself activities such as painting and repairing. Remember, there are those two income tax bites: on the money I earn to pay rent and on the money the landlord, or the painter he employs, earns. The income tax is a double tax on the division of labor. In my own house, I can be relatively inefficient at do-it-yourself activities and still find them economically worthwhile. The house also remains an asset, providing security even in

---

1. Also, a large house can be owned with a small investment—an example of "leverage" (see chap. 7).

bankruptcy. And there are tax advantages, property taxes and interest payments being deductible from income for federal income taxes, and the imputed rent and capital gains being untaxed.

Decisions about whether to own or rent, and about how much housing to buy, are also affected by liquidity considerations and a healthy respect for the interest charges associated with most mortgages. The amortized mortgage is a relatively recent invention and one of the first of many devices to help people manage their own finances. The villain in the old melodramas was always about to take over the farmstead because the mortgage had come due— not just a payment or the interest, but the whole thing. In those days, only the interest was payable regularly; the principal came due on the last day. An amortized mortgage, like ordinary installment credit, sets up a regular and constant monthly payment which returns both interest and principal, so that some fixed interest rate is paid on the remaining balance. Suppose that I have a $50,000 mortgage at a 10 percent interest rate and, to simplify the discussion, make annual rather than monthly payments for thirty years. During the first year, the bank has loaned the entire $50,000 amount to me and I owe $5,000 in interest charges for that period. With an amortized mortgage, my yearly payment will exceed $5,000 by just enough to reduce the remaining balance of the loan to zero by the end of the thirtieth year. In this example, the yearly payment turns out to be $5,304. The first $5,304 payment will cover the initial $5,000 interest charge and will pay off $304 of the principal, reducing the amount on loan to me during the second year to $50,000 − $304 = $49,696. Interest charges during the second year are 10 percent of $49,696, or about $4,970. So my second year payment of $5,304 pays off the smaller interest charge and a little more of the principal. In this example, the first payment is $5,000/$5,304 = 94.3 percent interest; the second payment is $4,970/$5,304 = 93.7 percent interest. In the last few years of the loan, the remaining principal and therefore the interest charges are small, and almost all of the $5,304 payments are principal.

Recent changes in regulations allow banks to vary the interest rate charged over the life of the mortgage and to allow smaller payments in the initial years of the mortgage and larger ones in the final years. In one type of arrangement, called variable-rate mortgages, interest charges are always calculated by applying the new interest rate to the remaining balance of the loan. With graduated-payment mortgages, the smaller initial payments may not be large enough to cover the interest charges. In that case, the amount of money on loan to me from the bank *increases* rather than decreases. Continuing with the example of a $50,000 initial loan and a 10 percent interest rate, a $4,000 initial graduated payment will fall $1,000 short of covering the $5,000 initial interest charge, so the remaining balance at the end of the first year will be $51,000, and the interest charges for the second year will be $5,100. Obviously, the total interest charges over the life of this loan will exceed those of a conventional mortgage with fixed payments because the bank is lending me more money. As in all other cases, the bank calculates interest charges by applying the interest rate to the current remaining loan balance.

Lenders do not allow indefinitely long mortgage payment periods, so my amount of housing may be limited by how much I can assemble for a down payment and the monthly payments. As we saw earlier, compound interest amounts to a great deal over long periods. A useful rule of thumb here is that if the interest rate times the number of years is close to 150, e.g., 10 percent for 15 years, or 5 percent for 30 years, then the total payments add up to about twice the price of the house. At 5 percent, a $30,000 house will cost $2,000 a year for 30 years in mortgage payments, or $60,000. Monthly payments can be cut only by paying for a longer period, and hence paying more total interest, or by making a larger down payment, which hides some interest cost in the form of the foregone interest that would otherwise have been earned on the down payment money. It is important, however, to examine the common notion that extending the period over which the mortgage is repaid makes a house easier to afford. In our $50,000, 10 percent mortgage example, the $5,304 annual payment could be reduced if the term of the mortgage ran for more than thirty years. But since the payments must cover the first year's interest charges plus enough extra to reduce the remaining principal to zero by the end of the loan, the annual payment can never go below $5,000. Payments are higher if the term is shortened to less than thirty years; a fifteen-year term increases the annual payments to $6,575. Extending the repayment period reduces the monthly or annual payments but substantially increases the aggregate interest paid over the whole period. Looked at the other way, by paying a little more each month one can drastically reduce the total interest cost. At $6,575 a year (24 percent more at each payment) the loan would be paid off in fifteen years and the total interest paid would be less than half as much ($48,605 instead of $109,120).

In addition to the sale price of the house, the buyer often must pay many additional costs such as title insurance, title search, mortgage insurance, and closing costs. Since most of them are associated with getting a mortgage, they can be thought of as extra interest cost. There is considerable variability in the costs, and it often pays to shop around among banks for the best "deal." Buyers must trade off differences in mortgage interest rates, and it is helpful to know how to convert one-time costs into implied additional interest charges.

To convert any or all such one-time charges, closing costs, or points into an addition to the interest rate requires a calculator that handles mortgage values, but table 2 will provide some examples. It tells you how much to add to the stated interest on a mortgage to allow for charges paid at the beginning. Charges are computed as a fraction of the amount of the mortgage. Thus, if the lump-sum costs on a $50,000, thirty-year, 10 percent mortgage amount to $2,500, then $2,500/$50,000, or 5 percent of the mortgage, will add $5 \times 0.12 = 0.60$ percent to the mortgage interest rate, where the 0.12 figure comes from the third row, fifth column of table 2. Since you are spreading the cost over the life of the mortgage, the added interest rate is higher if you pay off the mortgage sooner.

Table 2. Lump-Sum House Purchase Costs Converted to Additions to Interest Rate[a]

Stated Interest Rate	Amounts Added to Interest Rate on n-Year Mortgage			
	$n = 5$	$n = 10$	$n = 20$	$n = 30$
6%	.37%	.21%	.12%	.09%
8	.38	.22	.14	.11
10	.39	.23	.15	.12
12	.41[b]	.25	.16	.14[b]
14	.42	.26	.17	.15

[a] Assuming lump-sum costs equal 1 percent of the total mortgage. Thus, if lump-sum costs actually equal 10 percent of the total mortgage, multiply the figures listed by 10 to get the amount added to the effective interest rate. (This will underestimate a little.)

[b] For example, on a thirty-year, 12 percent mortgage, points, mortgage insurance, closing costs, title insurance, and other mandated charges amounting to 1 percent of the amount loaned to you add .14 percent to the interest rate. If you pay off the mortgage and these costs after five years, the interest rate cost has really been 12.41 percent for that period.

The federal Real Estate Settlement Procedures Act helps to protect the buyer even with the wide variety of customs as to how buyer and seller split closing costs. You can secure from the United States Department of Housing and Urban Development a guide to settlement costs that spells out your rights and obligations. For instance, you have a right to see an itemized list of services and fees the day before the closing. But even before that, you should have negotiated with the seller as to who pays what.

When a seller is asked to accept a purchase involving a Federal Housing Administration (FHA)- or Veterans Administration (VA)-insured mortgage, he should know that if the ceiling interest rate on such mortgages is below the going market interest rate for mortgages, he will be asked to pay "points." (Points represent added interest paid to the lender in one lump sum at the outset. They cannot by law be paid by the buyer, because that would openly raise the interest rate.) Any intelligent seller will, of course, raise the price of the house to cover this one-time charge, so just as with closing costs, the buyer ends up paying the equivalent of a higher interest rate anyway. How can one interpret points in terms of differential interest rates? One way is to take as a standard a 6 percent mortgage, and ask what the stream of payments such a mortgage promises is worth if the stream is discounted at higher interest rates of 8, 10, 12, or 14 percent. The difference in the value of these streams as a percent of the initial amount of the loan is called "points."

To bring the value of a mortgage up to 100 percent of the proper market interest rate, someone must pay the difference in cash. For example, a twenty-year, 6 percent mortgage for $100,000 would be worth $86,000 when the market interest rate is 8 percent and the seller would be asked for $14,000 in "points."

You can think of this as changing either the price of the house or the interest rate, but it is really the latter, since you wouldn't pay it if you had cash to buy the house, and would pay it as interest if you bought with a conventional mortgage at market interest rates. It is important to keep in mind, however, that added interest charges from points (or closing costs) are not tax deductible like conventional mortgage charges.

There are emotional considerations favoring home ownership. Many people feel it is a symbol of having arrived, of being a good stable family, of responsible citizenship. The desire to own real property probably varies from country to country and from subculture to subculture, but it exists almost everywhere. And the notion that home ownership is usually a sign of other things is true. Research suggests that homeowners *are* better off, *do* plan ahead, *are* more responsible. They had to be that way in order to acquire a home, and they continue to be because human behavior patterns persist. At equivalent incomes and ages, they tend to save more and to accumulate more liquid assets.

Because they are more stable and more responsible, and usually have lived longer in the same community, homeowners also engage in more community activities and do more volunteer work. Buying a house, then, becomes a symbol which may have a value of its own to some people. Indeed, the data show that, other things being equal, homeowners actually spend more for housing than other people. This may be partly the result of the difficulty in moving and adjusting one's housing to current needs, so that a home sometimes reflects future or past maximum family size and need. But in part it reflects people's willingness to put more into their own homes than they would put into rent, or greater interest in their housing on the part of those who own a home.

There is a long-term speculative aspect to the question whether renting or owning is cheaper. It has to do with rents and house prices in the future, relative to one another. In the past, at times when renting seemed cheaper than buying (just before World War II, for example, after years of depression), it proved unwise to rent; housing rapidly got tighter, and as rents rose, so did house prices, closing the escape of shifting to ownership. On the other hand, during boom times when building lags behind, rents may climb to the point where it seems cheaper to buy or build a new house, but this too may be temporary; as rents fall, the market value of houses may also fall. If the market values houses at only five times annual rent instead of the eight to ten times implied in our rules of thumb, there must be some temporary surplus of houses or shortage of rental places.

Most economists would argue that we are in for decades more of inflation and that owning a home is one of the few ways an ordinary consumer can hedge against it—one of the few places he can put his money where its value will increase at least as fast as the overall rate of inflation. Since a person can own more house than he has actually paid for yet, he has "leverage." The colloquial translation is that it will be easy to pay off the mortgage later with cheaper dollars, while the whole house is going up in price.

At times, when it may be otherwise advantageous to purchase a house because of rising prices, there may also be credit stringencies ("tight money") so banks tend to raise not only interest rates but "standards" as well; sometimes they refuse to make mortgage loans at all. They are more interested in keeping their business borrowers, who are repeat customers, than their one-time mortgage borrowers.

It is possible to own and rent at the same time by buying a condominium, or to own with limits in a cooperative. Cooperatives and condominiums offer some advantages of scale and some control over a neighborhood. The cooperation can vary from group acquistion of land to extensive and continuing cooperation and development of community facilities.[2] The more cooperation there is, the more management skills are required, of course, and there is a tendency to rely on the voluntary work of members to provide those skills. The old adage that everybody's business is nobody's business often applies. But a cooperative can develop a fine community efficiently, and provide the kind of services the members really want at a cost level they prefer.

In practice, it seems that the successful cooperatives (a) have had individuals of high ability willing to put a lot of managerial effort into the initial development, and (b) have restricted the demands for member participation to the minimum. After the first enthusiasm is gone, most members would rather pay for the community work than rake leaves or mow the community baseball field, which adds to cost. The number of cooperatives that have failed, with financial losses to members, is substantial; even some successful ones nearly failed in the process of developing. Yet there are obvious economies of scale and advantages in bargaining to get public services. So long as the member obligations are clear and the rules set early to meet most contingencies, there is a chance of success. It helps to have members or friends who know law, real estate, building, engineering, and organizational procedures. The community spirit and mutual help that may exist in a cooperative are also added benefits.

2. A cooperative may form a corporation to own the land or the buildings, or both. Or members may agree to sell back to the cooperative when they leave.

Condominiums, on the other hand, seem to have most of the disadvantages of cooperatives without the advantages. There are complexities about exactly what you own, difficulties in getting out, and the necessity of living with group decisions. In fact, a condominium usually involves a management company over which the "owners" have little or no control and which charges monthly fees for outside maintenance, club facilities, and management. The management company can raise charges and decide what facilities to add (and charge for). The company can develop many different properties, get most of its capital back by selling the condominium apartments or houses, and still be in a position to take most of the profits in monthly charges if the place develops well. If it doesn't, the owners are left with the losses when they try to sell.

Why do people buy condominiums? Some like the facilities and the freedom from responsibility for outside maintenance, the ease of leaving the place empty for periods of travel, and the possibility of renting it through the management company. Others like the income tax advantages, which are the same as for home ownership. And there are possible capital gains, tax-deferred if another place is purchased that costs at least as much. Many condominiums have been purchased as vacation or future retirement homes, with the understanding that the management company will attempt to rent them when they are not needed by the owner. There is always the chance that no tenant will be found, but the costs of holding idle property are mostly hidden (opportunity) costs, and the possible difficulties in getting their money out do not seem apparent to many buyers.

In the wake of some scandals, laws are being improved to deal with varieties of ownership and semi-ownership arrangements, but it is probably unwise to get into complicated arrangements that can be difficult to get out of.

Legal Traps and Tax Issues

Not only is a house a big investment for an individual, but there are some technical and legal pitfalls to be avoided when buying or building one. Clear title to the land can be a problem; legally, if you build a house on someone else's land, that person owns the house without any compensation to you. This fear is prevalent enough to support a profitable business in title insurance to cover the risk.

In building a house, one indirectly engages various artisans, who are protected by "mechanic's lien laws." These laws state that any "mechanic" not paid for his work on the property can place a lien on it. As the home buyer, you may have paid the contractor or the speculative builder, but if he fails to pay the workmen, you are responsible for paying them. Some people end up paying for their house twice. The "how-to" books urge you to secure a signed "waiver of lien" statement for each step in the building process before paying that installment on the house. Sometimes the banks will secure it for you, but it is a difficult process and still may not avoid trouble. The number of builders who go through bankruptcy should be enough to give one pause. When a builder gets behind, it is only too easy for him to use the money from one buyer to pay the workers for their work on a *previous* house.

Similarly, builders are sometimes careless about restrictions, such as minimum setbacks of buildings from lot lines. Buyers then find it necessary to go through complex and expensive negotiations to purchase a few feet of land from a neighbor in order to be legal. Some builders are also careless about drainage, and owners can find themselves with major engineering problems. But as we shall see later, the biggest risk comes from buying or building a house in a neighborhood not yet stabilized, i.e., one only partly built up. The value of a house depends heavily upon the neighborhood and can be diminished by persisting empty lots, or badly designed houses, or large apartment buildings, or various noxious commercial uses. Legal protection against such deterioration is weak.

Another legal detail about housing that everyone should know is the doctrine of easement. If someone wants to do something which infringes on another's property, such as using half of a joint driveway, the owner may be asked to agree to a formal easement. More important, if someone infringes on property for many years without objection, that person acquires the right to do so indefinitely; this is called a "prescriptive easement." To avoid this, people with private roads shut them off once a year with a "private property" sign, thereby retaining the right to close them in the future.

Legal details of leases or sales contracts are varied enough from state to state and complex enough that a lawyer is often needed. On the other hand, there are standard lease forms and local traditions about such matters as damage deposits which may help the unassisted buyer or tenant.

Spreading from the Midwest to other parts of the country is a different way of purchasing homes, where the title does not pass to the buyer until the last payment is made. These arrangements are called "land contracts." In ordinary times, land contracts are often used when the buyer has little or no down payment or even a poor credit rating, and hence carry an interest rate higher than on conventional mortgages. A major advantage of a land contract is that its terms are negotiated by the buyer and seller and not by a bank. The seller's risk is small, since he or she can reclaim the property without elaborate, costly, and time-consuming foreclosure proceedings. A land contract usually says that if any payment is missed, all previous payments are considered rent, and the owner can reclaim the property. But in fact, the courts have decided that a person cannot sign away such rights (accumulated equity in the house) that way, so the buyer does accumulate an investment in the property. Legally, the seller owes the property taxes until the deed is transferred, but the contract may call for the buyer to pay them.

An additional consideration in the decision whether to rent or own is the curious legal position of the tenant relative to the landlord. There are situations, more common in other countries, where the land is only rented to those who build on it. However long the lease, there are problems when it ends, and problems in the interim about adjusting for inflation or market changes. The "tenants" may do very well on fixed ground rents, as in Hawaii, until the lease runs out and the landowner escalates the rent.

Under the law of most states, the relation between landlord and tenant is not considered a contractual one, but a "leasehold estate," a kind of division of the ownership rights of the property. Because, under this arrangement, the landlord's right to collect rent from the tenant does not depend on his performing his duty to maintain the property in good condition, no matter how badly the landlord fails in his obligation to maintain, the tenant must continue to pay full rent at the proper time or face eviction. Some attempts at reform have been made, particularly in New York City, with systems for putting rents into escrow to be used for repairs.

A worse problem for the poor is that they often have no leases at all, but rent from month to month. This means that the landlord can evict them, or raise the rent suddenly, in retaliation for any complaints about unsatisfactory conditions. If the situation is bad enough, the tenant may move out, claiming "constructive eviction," and be free from any obligation to continue to pay rent, but it is often difficult to move and find another place.

Finally, where there is high turnover, landlords may demand a damage deposit, and sometimes keep it whether or not there has been damage. Various reforms have been suggested or instituted, including a public fund into which damage deposits can be placed, with independent determination of their disposition, and into which rents or parts of rent can be placed when needed repairs are not being done by the landlord. All this would increase the total cost of renting slightly, but would also treat tenants more equitably. It might eliminate a marginal supply of rental housing where the rents had been low because of bad maintenance or an implied obligation of the tenants to do any maintenance that becomes necessary. The damage deposit works a particular hardship on low-income renters, who are usually at a disadvantage in bargaining position and legal sophistication. The legal situation is changing, however, with many states providing new protections for tenants.

Buying and Selling

At any one time, only a limited number of places to live are available, and a buyer does not know what else may become available before a choice has to be made. Neither is there any very adequate or easy-to-secure information to help in the search. Realtors can be one source of information. They often keep records of past sales prices, know the reputation of areas and neighborhoods, and should offer good guesses as to the market values of the available houses. Direct inspection of a neighborhood late in the afternoon should reveal the age distribution (school children), traffic patterns, and general appearance. The assessor's office (city or county) can provide assessed values for specific properties, and the (county) registrar of deeds has data on the last few transfers of title. The city assessor can provide the average assessment ratio, for each area if it varies, which can then be used to estimate the market value for an individual house. Mortgage lenders also have notions about good places to live, often rather conservative, of course, and the office of the school system has information about school districts.

Besides the difficulty of getting information and the need to wait until something suitable comes on the market, there are other substantial costs of moving. Even from rented place to rented place there are the costs of moving furniture and possessions. In selling a house and buying another, each transaction costs both buyer and seller various amounts. The realtor takes 5 to 7 percent, title insurance 1 to 4 percent, and statutory fees up to 2 percent. The overall difference between what the buyer pays and what the seller gets ranges from a few percentage points to ten or fifteen. Technically, the seller pays the realtor, and pays any "mortgage points," though he probably raised the sale price of the house to cover the latter.

The buyer pays the closing costs (transfer tax and title insurance, totaling usually 2 to 3 percent) and sometimes prepaid property taxes, insurance, and special tax assessments, although these last three are not really transaction costs.

The realtor's fee will be divided between the realtor who arranged the sale and the one who got the house listed. This means that a realtor is rarely a disinterested source of advice, since the realtor gets the full commission on houses that he has put on the list, partial commission on those that other realtors have listed, and nothing on houses sold without listing at all. It is often difficult to sell or buy a house without a realtor, however, since the market is so unorganized and the "product" so heterogeneous. A realtor can provide a screening function for those who consider their time too costly to do much searching on their own.

There is frequently a kickback, from the title insurance company to both lawyers in the transaction, of part of what a buyer must pay for title insurance. Indeed, there are even lawyer-run title insurance arrangements, usually called "attorney's funds," with the profits going to the lawyers. This clearly deceives the consumer as to who is being paid for what—entirely apart from the conflict of interest on the part of the lawyers—in cases where there is a choice about title insurance companies, procedures, or need. In fact, there are communities where almost no one gets title insurance or lawyers' title guarantee, and other areas where almost everyone does. We do not know whether this reflects real differences in the risk and need for insurance, or merely the organized sale of a service in some areas. But the buyer has little choice if a mortgage is necessary and the mortgage lenders insist on title insurance.

Selling a house involves some additional decisions, the most important being how much to ask for it. The ideal way might be to set no price, but to try to get buyers to make offers and compete with one another, for instance by promising to take the best offer above some minimum by some deadline. This is a difficult tactic, but without it one of two mistakes is likely. The price can be set too low, and the first lucky person to discover it will buy the house at less than its market value. Or the price can be too high, wasting time and energy, and perhaps causing the house to be left empty for a while, in which case people may figure there is something wrong with it besides the price. It is difficult to believe that the houses that are sold before they ever get on the market could not have been sold for a higher price. However, it is often true that a particular house has only one person really interested in it and that a buyer often sees only one house that seems right. In such cases, there may be a wide range of prices within which both would be satisfied.

Where—The Question of Neighborhood

Conventional wisdom says that the value of a house depends on three things: location, location, and location. Selecting a residence is a package deal which includes a neighborhood and a community, commuting opportunities, different public services and taxes and other costs, and a different prospect for future development.

Selecting a location with an eye on the differential costs of living in different places may be misleading. A glance at any table showing comparative living costs will reveal that only the shelter costs really vary much from place to place. This is understandable; most other things are sold on a national market—you can even get your prescriptions filled by mail. The apparent differences in shelter costs may not reflect different costs of living, but rather different standards of living or different ways of paying for certain basic services. Some communities provide more services than others, and charge higher taxes. Some economists think that differential consumer preferences are best served when various neighboring communities provide alternative levels and combinations of services, each one attracting people who prefer that particular mix. This may be a slow process, however; people have to live somewhere near their work, and moving is difficult and expensive. That tax increases for specific services have to be voted on locally probably helps local communities better serve their residents' needs.

How does this affect the apparent cost of housing in a community? Suppose a community decided to increase recreational facilities and to tax houses in the area $200 a year more to pay for it. The value of owning a house or living in that area is presumably reduced by $200 a year, the extra cost. At 3 percent, $200 a year forever is worth $200/0.03 = $6,667 today. But if people value the recreational facilities at more than $200 a year—as most must since they voted for them—the net value of living in the area may go up a little. More important, if *most* people value the services more highly than they dislike the taxes, house values and rents will go *up*, not down. Note, however, that the cost of housing will look high in this community, simply because it includes more public services. Rents will be higher too, covering the landlords' higher taxes, and justified by the recreational facilities for which the taxes pay.

There might be differences in the efficiency with which different communities use their tax money, but that would be impossible to sort out. It is not even easy to find out what the community spends its money on, because there are both capital and operating costs, and federal revenue-sharing funds to help offset them. It makes more sense simply to select a community with the mix of services you want, if you can afford it.

So the community with more services may not have higher taxes relative to house prices, and the community with higher rents and house prices may even give more per dollar in the form of libraries, parks, fluoride in the water, community centers, recreational facilities, and police and fire protection. The real cost of living might be higher in a town where residents have to join a club to go swimming, buy all their own books, and generally cannot share many expenses with others.

Aside from costs and services, what makes a good neighborhood? No longer quite so important are issues of commuting costs and location with respect to schools, shops, and services. With the difficulty of forecasting the future location of jobs and schools, such considerations take second place to forecasts about the future of the neighborhood. Public transportation availability may take on new importance with high fuel prices.

Since the forecasts of experts have a self-justifying quality, coming true because people believe them, bankers and realtors are a good source of information about the future of neighborhoods. They tend to like homogeneous neighborhoods with uniform house and lot sizes, similar architectural styles, uniform land use, and similar types of people. In spite of democratic egalitarian opposition to the idea, most people prefer voluntary segregation by social class at least. No matter how much space one can afford around the house, there are still neighbors, and wide differences in living styles and standards of upkeep can be irritating all around.

There is vast literature on neighborhood and community design and beauty, most of it expressing the tastes of the writers and often ignoring the economic costs of what is proposed. What most people are concerned with, however, is not architecture or trees, but the simple neatness, cleanliness, and orderliness of an area. A study comparing the attitudes of architects and planners with those of ordinary residents found startling discrepancies in their ideas about what made a good neighborhood. The "experts" reflected the tastes of only the highly educated minority of residents. The rest of the people focused on cleanliness and neatness.

Homeowners' Protection

If the value of a house and the owners' satisfaction in living in it depend on what goes on around it, what defenses have they against changes that will ruin the neighborhood?

First, there are zoning laws restricting the uses of property and the kinds of dwellings allowed. Their efficacy has been reduced in the past because zoning boards have often capitulated to pressures to alter things, or have zoned too much land for more intensive uses in the first place. It is clearly safest to own a home in an area zoned entirely for single family houses. However, zoning almost never specifies the number of occupants per house or per square foot, and the definition of "single family" can be stretched. Furthermore, it is difficult to administer regulations against renting out rooms and particularly difficult to enforce regulations that have been ignored for years.

Property owners often form associations, either to press the zoning boards or the city administration for better safeguards, or to act in other ways. While they sometimes oppose things which would not really do much harm, such associations have in some cases managed to preserve a delightful neighborhood in the midst of decay and ugliness. The classic example is Beacon Hill in Boston, the Louisburg Square area in particular.

A third way of protecting a neighborhood is to introduce into the deed of sale a restrictive covenant requiring each buyer to abide by certain restrictions. Old racial restrictive covenants have been declared unconstitutional and therefore unenforceable. Others become obsolete, because they specify architectural styles, minimum dollar values per dwelling, or other standards of the moment. Still, they remain a possible way of specifying standard densities (minimum square feet per occupant, for instance) or other basic requirements.

Given the weaknesses of regulations or standards and the difficulties of enforcing them, the household choosing a neighborhood is really faced with a problem of predicting what may happen, assuming they will not have much power to affect the trend of events. There is some pattern to the way cities develop, and there are some rules of thumb used by realtors and city planners in making predictions. Old, small houses tend either to become the homes of lower-income or transitional families or to give way to apartments, even though a society with more and more well-financed older people might expect to develop such residential areas for them. New areas with much empty land can develop rapidly in good or bad ways depending on what the owners of the empty lots do. The sizes of lots often dictate the kind of uses, and it is very difficult to change that. Standards of lot size have risen as people's incomes have risen, and better transportation has allowed them the space, until single family homes on less than 10,000 square feet seem to be considered deficient and might have lower resale value. Developers often attempt to hide the smallness of lots just as they try to hide the lack of adequate space inside, partly by selling houses while there are still empty lots next door or behind.

Good standards for community services require both the willingness and the ability to pay for them. The former may be revealed by recent history. The latter is affected by the tax base relative to the potential needs. Some business or industry is often essential to help pay for things.

Design, Style, and Site

Choice of a residence also involves decisions about design and style, and about site or position of one house in relation to others. If you are buying, there are two sometimes competing criteria to be used—your own preferences and needs, and the resale value. One way to separate matters of taste from generally applicable principles is to ask what affects most people's satisfaction with their residences. The answer appears to be space, so the number of square feet of livable floor space in a house is crucial.

Builders commonly make houses seem larger than they are by using open planning with fewer halls but larger rooms. This results in the need to use rooms for halls—to walk through the middle of the living room in order to get from the front door to anywhere else in the house, for example. Occasionally, to get more rooms in a house, builders make all the rooms slightly undersized, which is hardly noticeable until the buyer tries to install furniture.

Basements and second floors allow the use of smaller lots, and apparently most people prefer the traditional two-story house with basement. Some people believe the one-floor house is far more efficient to live in, but in areas where people prefer more traditional design, resale of a one-floor house could be a problem.

The positioning of a house can affect the privacy it affords as well as its energy demands. The sun is a powerful oxidizing agent that can destroy a set of drapes in a few years. Rooms that face north and east can have good light without the heat of the midday sun. Because the prevailing wind direction is usually from the southwest, a southeast outside area can have the morning sun plus protection from the wind. Access to the house is important too, particularly from cars. It is also useful to be able to get into the house without letting in too much rain or snow or wind.

Property Taxes

Aside from construction and purchase costs and interest costs, the other major component of the cost of housing is the property taxes that must be paid on the house. They amount to between 1 and 3 percent of the value of the house each year, depending on the services provided and the cost of those services.

Property tax rates are commonly expressed as so many

"mills." A mill is a tenth of one percent of the assessed value of the house. Houses are commonly assessed at some fraction of their true current market value. A 40 mill tax on a $100,000 house assessed at $50,000 would mean 4 percent of $50,000 or $2,000 in taxes, or 2 percent of house value. In other words, the real tax rate, as a percent of house value, is the product of the official tax rate (mills divided by ten) times the assessment rate (ratio of assessed value to market value). Tax rates can only be raised by a direct popular vote in most places, but assessments can be raised as house values rise, or even to a higher fraction of market value, without a vote. When house values and assessments rise faster than other prices, or even faster than some people's incomes, the resulting increases in property taxes tend to be resented.

When comparing different areas, particularly cities with rural areas, it is unwise to look only at tax rates, or only at assessment ratios, since they may differ in opposite directions; rapidly growing areas tend to have higher tax rates but lower assessment ratios. When tax rates relative to market values of houses are high, it usually means that more services are being provided, and the houses are consequently worth more than they would otherwise be.

The property tax has several strikes against it in the popular mind. It is payable in lumps, during summer vacation season and right after Christmas in most places. It is seen as mostly financing the public school system (which it does), a public service that at any one time seems to benefit only those with children in the public schools, although almost everyone has had or will have some similar benefit. Indeed, what many people do not realize is that even if they will not personally benefit from or use some proposed new community facility or service, enough others will, so that everyone will "get his taxes back" in the form of increased value of his property.

The property tax is also claimed to be regressive, falling more heavily on low-income people, as personified by the retired couple on a fixed income who have trouble eating and also paying their rising property taxes. In fact, the statistics used to prove this point are misleading. They usually consist of property taxes paid (by homeowners only) as a fraction of the income of families in different income groups. But:

1. Income alone is not a good measure of ability to pay. The addition of nonmoney income, including the imputed rent on the owner's equity, reduces the amount of regres-

sivity. That homeowners can deduct property taxes and mortgage interest from their taxable income also reduces regressivity.[3] On the other hand, if we adjust income for family size, larger families have less income per equivalent adult and somewhat larger houses, so the impression of regressivity is increased.

2. Renters also pay property taxes, since (at least in the long run) the price of any product must include all its costs. But most renters have lower incomes and smaller quarters. If one estimates their indirect property taxes and combines them with the taxes of homeowners, most of the regressivity disappears.

3. The data often cut across tax districts, ignoring differences in services received.

We are left with some older people with currently low incomes living in houses too large for their real needs and paying heavy property taxes relative to their current income. Property tax relief is provided for them in many states, but usually not for older renters who may actually be in worse shape.

When house prices and, hence, assessed values and taxes rise faster than incomes or other prices, an already disliked tax becomes "intolerable," particularly since few state or local governments have the sense to reduce tax rates in such a situation. Solutions such as California's Proposition 13 which restrict property tax increases unless the property is sold produce inequity of a new sort.

As another example of the importance of understanding capital theory, let us interpret the recent trend to get rid of the property tax in favor of local income taxes. Since the level of services is presumably unaffected, what will this do to the market values of houses? They should go up, of course, by an amount equal to the present value of the stream of tax reductions. A property tax cut of $100 per year should add about $100/0.03 = $3,333 to the price of a house. This does not cut the cost of housing to anyone thinking of buying a house after the change—he will in fact have to pay more. It is doubtful that it will reduce rents in the short run, providing instead an immediate benefit to landlords. The change largely benefits homeowners who may want to leave the community and can now sell at a price that includes their capital gain. Those

---

3. The tax advantages become obvious if you rent your home to someone and spend a year in a rental house in another town. You have to pay income tax on the rental income you receive and so does your landlord. Exchanging houses rather than renting has clear tax advantages.

who stay can get theirs only as a dribble over the years. So what seemed like a nice liberal idea—to get rid of the noxious regressive property tax in favor of a fairer, even progressive, income tax—turns out to provide capital gains to homeowners who sell, some tax relief in proportion to house value (and income) for other owners, and a bonanza for landlords.

Other Costs of Housing

Another of the real costs of housing is the cost of the land and the services required. As the quality of sewer, water, and other services provided rises, the costs of installing and providing these services also rise. These costs can be reduced by more systematic development, using all the land in one area before extending services to new areas, and also by reducing lot sizes, although that reduces people's satisfaction too. Delay or restrictiveness in extending such services can produce a rise in the market values of those building lots that have basic services available, simply because of their scarcity; this rise in market value provides monopoly profits for the developers who "got in on the ground floor," and keeps the price of houses up. It is hard to escape the feeling that a kind of conspiracy exists in many areas among the bankers, realtors, and developers to keep the extension of services and the amount of building down to a level that will "preserve property values" (and profit levels, and speculative gains). That many people with interests in property serve on official bodies making such decisions is an unstudied example of conflict of interest.

Renters who are angered by rising rents traditionally go after landlords, who are often merely charging market prices, instead of seeking to increase the local supply of housing and reduce the local restrictions that create monopoly profits.

Various restrictive practices and regulations have proven very difficult to eliminate, and these work to keep the prices of houses high. The production of several key building materials is so concentrated as to allow market restriction. The craft unions, with their apprenticeship systems and licensing rules (administered by members of the craft), have managed to drive their wages higher than would be possible with "free entry." But perhaps the major obstacle to efficiency and competition in building has been the myriad of state and local building codes and regulations, and their varied enforcement (sometimes arbitrary and even corrupt). With no ability to standardize, to manufacture components efficiently that will be legally usable everywhere, it is difficult for mass production methods to be applied to the housing industry. In the face of this, it seems ludicrous for those interested in housing to focus continually on design innovations which are likely to introduce more complexities and still higher costs. To give an example of local codes: In many places the use of plastic pipe is still prohibited or restricted. Insulated sandwiches of plywood make stronger panels than the usual two-by-fours with plaster, yet are illegal where local codes specify minimum wall thicknesses.

The attempt to maintain the quality of housing by legal restrictions has focused on the inputs (materials and methods) of construction rather than the outputs (accessibility of the plumbing, safety of the structure), perhaps because it is easier. But this focus on acceptable materials and methods is much more rigid and resistant to innovation than standards of fire resistance, stress bearing, damp-proofness, and other aspects of construction would be.

CHAPTER FIVE

Long-term Financial Planning and Short-term Budgeting

*If your outgo exceeds your income,
your upkeep will be your downfall.*
    Ben Franklin

For most people, the term "budgeting" conjures up visions of hours spent recording and manipulating the receipt and expenditure of money. They agree that the goals of budgeting—keeping outgo in line with income, and accumulating sufficient savings for retirement or other future needs—are worthy enough; but they consider the procedure so tedious and time-consuming that few families budget effectively.

Budgeting is really an exercise in accounting, but we can keep it from being too difficult if we keep our language precise and use some convenient shortcuts. The basic trick to accounting is to bridge the gap between the flows of money (in and out) that are easy to see and record, and the more comprehensive *real* flows of consumption, income, and accumulation of wealth. Depreciation of a car, employer contributions to pension funds, and increases in the prices of common stocks are examples of expenses or income that do not show up as cash expenditures or receipts. Yet these are as important as the cash expended on groceries or the income from a paycheck. Further complications arise because some of the cash we receive (as from the sale of a house or common stock) is not income.

Note the ways in which such terms as *expenditures*, *expenses*, *receipts*, and *income* are used in the preceding paragraph. Expenditures and receipts are the visible flows of money that we spend or receive. Unfortunately, these cash flows often differ from the more important *real* flows of expenses (consumption) and income. Some expenses (such as depreciation of a car) do not show up as expenditures, while some income (such as an employer's contribution to a pension fund) is not received in the form of cash. Much of the exercise of accounting is getting from the easily visible receipts and expenditures to the crucial flow of income and expenses.

The comprehensive treatment of all income and expenses, and the details on how to monitor both precisely, will be saved for the last half of this chapter. Few people will find it worthwhile to keep detailed records of every income and expense item. Realistically, financial planning calls for two things: first, a simple way of keeping consumption in line with income; second, a way of setting savings goals that will allow one to meet such future needs as retirement, children's education, and bequests.

A Simple Budgeting Scheme

The simplest way to start watching financial affairs is to apply the bathtub theorem, which says that if it came in the faucet and isn't in the tub, then it went down the drain. If I choose a monthly accounting period, then I can measure the water in the tub at the beginning and end of each month by adding up cash, checking, and savings account balances, and measure the faucet flow by keeping track of the money received. Such receipts usually consist of some taxable income that must be recorded anyway. Monthly expenditures are the water down the drain, and instead of keeping track of every cent spent, I can calculate total monthly expenditures by subtracting the increase (or adding the decrease) in cash and bank accounts from monthly income. Monitoring these monthly expenditure totals is an easy way of ensuring that spending is consistent with income. (An even simpler, although ill-advised, method is to control expenditures by running out of money each month so that expenditures automatically equal receipts!)

Budgeting is not quite as simple as this, however. I soon discover that expenditures fluctuate from month to month and, more important, that these expenditures are an inadequate guide to consumption. Some of the variations in expenditures are due to the months with five Saturdays (if I shop on Saturday), or vacation months, or the months that the property tax bill or annual insurance premium comes due, but these variations tend to average out and can be handled by some "rubber budgeting" method of averaging expenditures over several months or watching a cumulative expenditure total. The biggest expenditure variations arise from "capital transactions": buying a car or an appliance, investing in common stocks, bonds, or real estate, or paying off debts. These expenditures are obviously quite different from the monthly expenditures for goods or services consumed during the month. A common stock purchase is not consumption at all, while the purchase of a car represents a little present consumption (i.e., the use of the car's services during that month), but is mostly consumption that will take place well into the future. It is crucial to distinguish current consumption from current expenditures because current consumption must be kept below income in order to avoid bankruptcy—or, more optimistically, in order to build up wealth.

I can take care of financial transactions like investing in common stock, bonds, or real estate by simply subtracting the value of any such new investments from the estimate of monthly expenditures. (Note that I do not have to add the money received from the sale of investments to monthly expenditures because that money also came through the faucet and, if not in any bank account or cash at the end of the month, must have been spent.) Can transactions involving physical capital like a house, car, or appliances be handled with a similar subtraction? Unfortunately, not completely. Although capital transactions do have an investment component which ought to be subtracted from expenditures, they also have a consumption component which ought to be counted as expenditures. Not only will a small piece of each item of physical capital bought in a particular month be consumed, but a small piece of *all* physical capital will be consumed—regardless of when it was purchased. This consumption consists of the depreciation and the foregone interest costs of money tied up in owning the household capital; this is an important consumption item which does not show up in monthly expenditure estimates. Fortunately, the consumption costs of household physical capital are relatively stable from month to month (or can be spread in a stable pattern),[1] so they don't have to be recalculated and added to expenditure totals every month. It is usually easier to set a monthly expenditure goal that takes account of the average depreciation costs being incurred. Alternatively, I could set a monthly goal for increases in cash and bank account balances to offset these depreciation costs. I could even keep these additional savings in a separate account and then use the money in that account to purchase new items of household capital when the old ones need to be replaced.

---

1. The simplest way to estimate the monthly depreciation costs of most durables is to estimate the expected life of the piece of capital and its resale value at the end of its life, and then divide the difference between initial cost and resale value by the number of months of life. See chapters 4 and 8 for ways of estimating depreciation costs for houses and cars.

Our "simple" scheme has become complicated, but only a little. In essence, it applies the bathtub theorem to estimate monthly expenditures and then converts expenditures to total consumption by adding to the expenditure estimate the depreciation costs of household physical capital and by subtracting any purchase of financial or physical assets.

A final adjustment is advisable because cash receipts are an imperfect measure of income. Employers frequently deduct from a paycheck some consumption costs (e.g., union dues, life or medical insurance, income tax) and some savings items (Social Security, pension accruals). Employers may also make contributions for current consumption (medical and life insurance) and for savings (Social Security, pension accruals).[2] The final adjustment needed to convert expenditures to consumption is to add (1) employer deductions for consumption items, and (2) employer contributions for consumption. To compare this comprehensive consumption measure with the total income received, I must add the value of all employer deductions and contributions to income.

We have used the bathtub theorem to manipulate receipts and cash-plus-bank balances to arrive at a comprehensive measure of monthly consumption (expenses). This consumption can then be monitored and compared with income to ensure that the consumption is less than income by an amount consistent with savings goals.[3]

Would it be easier to go from a monthly estimate of changes in cash-plus-bank-account-balances to an estimate of net savings (and then compare that actual savings with the savings goal)? Not really, because the changes in those account balances have to be adjusted by adding: (1) any net purchases of assets, physical or financial, since the cash expended for these purchases went down the drain but was really saved rather than being consumed; (2) employer deductions for savings programs (Social Security, pensions, or any other nonconsumption benefit); (3) employer contributions for such savings programs; and (4) interest earned on pensions or on the savings component

2. It may seem strange to classify insurance and income tax as consumption. Monthly insurance premiums buy "protection" for that month, and that protection is the service being consumed. Income taxes are consumption in the sense that they pay for the services provided by government.

3. For simply watching and controlling monthly consumption, I can use take-home pay as income and ignore the steady and semi-voluntary consumption handled by the employer.

of any life insurance policies, and by subtracting: (5) depreciation of household capital.

At this point you might wonder about the purpose of keeping all of these records without any idea about how much should be saved each month. One reason is that this simple scheme will indicate whether consumption and savings patterns are changing and drifting into trouble. Another is that the total expense estimate can be used to check up on the detailed expenditure records. But the ultimate reason for any such records is to keep savings (and thus consumption) within some target savings goals. Setting such goals requires a long-range plan. It is to the details of that plan that we now turn.

Long-Range Planning

There are two main aspects of long-range planning. One is the accumulation of savings for retirement and more immediate goals like children's education or the down payment on a house. The other is the pacing of the acquisition of a house, car, and appliances (and their replacements) so as to avoid the excessive interest charges associated with undue debt and to lessen the effects of the large depreciation and foregone interest costs of those investments. Indeed, the proper timing and monitoring of these lumpy and attractive expenditures may be the most crucial part of all household financial management and the potential source of most of the trouble.

Planning for an orderly acquisition of household durables is fairly simple if you maintain a separate savings or checking account for such expenditures. You may think that you could spend a considerable amount of money initially to build up a stock of housing, cars, and appliances, and then cut back drastically, spending only when replacements are necessary. In fact, most American families spend about 15 percent of their yearly income on such equipment. Perhaps it is the persuasion of advertising or planned product obsolescence, or perhaps it is real improvements in quality that encourage perpetual replacement and upgrading. Whatever the reason, some substantial fraction of income should probably be allocated each year to household capital. In terms of budgeting, a fixed proportion of income (15 percent) might be allocated to a savings account and the money in that account then used to repair the house or the other repairable items of household capital, or to buy new items.[4] In addition to that allocation, an amount to save toward longer-range goals should be determined.

Setting Savings Goals

All families constantly make decisions about saving, sometimes explicitly with savings goals, sometimes implicitly with expenditure decisions. How to decide how much to save and set aside for future use? For what purposes will these savings be used?

☐ A reserve fund for emergencies and to avoid using expensive short-run credit
☐ Providing for children's education (or the continuing education of adults)
☐ Accumulation of a down payment for a house
☐ Bequeathing an asset
☐ Providing for retirement

The first needs are relatively small and are usually accomplished within the first few years after completing an education. How much to invest in the children is a highly individual decision. It would not be difficult, using the tables in appendix 1, to figure the present value of four years of future college costs, and thus the amount to be paid into a savings account each year for, say, fifteen years that would accumulate to that goal at a 3 percent interest rate (e.g., $1,075 per year for fifteen years produces $20,000). Inflation will affect both college costs and the amount that must be saved each year to meet those inflated costs. If the rate of inflation is 3 percent and the market interest rate is 3 percent + 3 percent = 6 percent, then the $20,000 college costs will inflate to $31,160 in fifteen years. (This is calculated from table A, p. 232.) Even at a 6 percent interest rate, an annual savings of $1,075 will provide a sum of only $25,048, which falls short of the goal. However, if savings are increased each year by the inflation rate, then the savings goal will be met. Indeed, increasing an annual savings amount by the rate of inflation will always ensure that the inflated savings goal is met, provided those savings can earn market interest rates.

The need for a large down payment for one's first home

---

4. Note that this account is used for large maintenance and repair expenses of a house (e.g., new roof, paint). Building the equity in a house is part of the savings program and is not funded from this account. The capital account suggested here takes care of expenditures on cars and appliances, and lumpy intermittent repairs on them or the house.

depends on how tight mortgage money is and on house prices. In recent years, larger and larger amounts have been required on both counts.

The next purpose on our list, bequests, hardly ever becomes important until late in life, and then only for those who find that by luck or ability or oversaving they have more than they need for their children and their own old age. We return to bequests, gifts, and estate taxes when we discuss life insurance in chapter 9.

This leaves savings for retirement. Social Security and the rapid growth of company pension plans complicate the process of designing this savings goal. It is easier to work out a total retirement-savings goal, and then to estimate the fraction of the goal that Social Security and private pensions will provide for; the remaining fraction must come from private savings.

Savings Goals for Retirement

The process of saving for retirement and then living on the stream of payments provided by that savings fund involves the algebra of annuities. As detailed in appendix 1, the compound interest on savings accumulated over a long period of time produces a fund that is much larger than the sum of the savings payments. Even with a 3 percent interest rate, a forty-five-year accumulation period (e.g., from age twenty to age sixty-five) produces a fund that is more than *twice* as large as the payments into it. And remember that a retirement fund continues to yield interest after retirement.

Retirement planning may seem complicated by the uncertainty regarding the date of death. If I die sooner than expected, then I will not have used up all of my savings. A more serious risk is to outlive my savings by living longer than expected. Such complications are simplified by companies (usually insurance companies) that will sell me a lifetime annuity upon retirement, based on my life expectancy. The annuity is really just the stream of payments (which include interest) provided by the cash used to purchase the annuity. The companies eliminate the risk to them of my living too long by selling many such annuities. The funds from those who die sooner than expected provide for those who live longer than expected.[5]

5. Many kinds of annuities are available, including those that refund to the survivors of those who do not live long enough to "get their money back" the difference between the purchase price and the total payments made. Needless to say, these annuities are much more expensive than those without such refunds.

For a couple, the most sensible kind of annuity gives one-third of the total annuity payment to each partner and one-third to "joint or survivor." Thus, as long as both partners are living, the payments are one-third to each, plus one-third to "joint," so the couple receives the full payment. When one partner dies, the survivor receives his or her own one-third share plus the one-third "survivor" share. The smaller total needs of the surviving partner can probably be met with an annuity payment which is two-thirds as large as the payment when both were alive. The price of this annuity is obviously less than the price of one that gives the full payment until both partners die.

We will proceed with our analysis of retirement planning using the assumption that life expectancy at age sixty-five is fifteen years. This is too optimistic for the average man and about right for women. But it is also roughly correct for the "joint-or-survivor" annuity scheme just discussed.

We now have two rules of thumb to simplify our calculations—that the real interest rate will be 3 percent regardless of inflation, and that the average life expectancy is eighty. If I can fix three more things, then the fraction of my income I need to save for retirement can be calculated or looked up in the tables to follow. The three are: (1) my desires about my post-retirement standard of living relative to my pre-retirement standard, (2) the age I start accumulating, and (3) my expected retirement age.

Starting with the first of these, it is crucial to understand that I do not need a retirement income as great as my pre-retirement income. When I retire:

1. My income taxes go down, because neither Social Security payments nor the portion of my pension that was paid for with after-tax income are taxed, because I receive double income tax exemptions at age sixty-five, and because tax rates are lower on smaller incomes.
2. My Social Security tax stops.
3. Some expenses, like commuting and union dues, stop.
4. *I no longer have to save for my retirement.*[6]

That I no longer have to save for my retirement means that I should rephrase the issue of pre- and post-retirement

---

6. I could also list the fact that I start *receiving* Social Security income and a pension, but it may be simpler to ignore them, then count the contributions to those programs as part of the required saving. I could also take the changed taxes out of the picture by using income after income taxes and Social Security taxes as the base for calculations.

income, and ask instead what fraction of pre-retirement *consumption* (income minus saving) I need after I retire.

If I subtract the age I start contributing from my expected retirement age, I know how many years I shall be saving, and if I subtract my expected retirement age from a life expectancy (assume eighty), I know how much a lifetime annuity will cost, assuming 3 percent real interest on the remaining balance in the fund.

Tables 3–5 illustrate the various fractions of income

Table 3. Savings Goals if Post-Retirement Consumption Equals Pre-Retirement Consumption[a]

Years of Saving	Percent of Income to be Saved for n Years of Retirement					
	$n = 5$	$n = 10$	$n = 15$	$n = 20$	$n = 25$	$n = 30$
5	46%	62%	69%	74%	77%	79%
10	28	43	51	56	60	63
15	20	31	39	44	48	51
20	14	24	31	36	39	42
25	11	19	25	29	32	35
30	9	15	20	24	27	29
35	7	12	17	20	22	24
40	6	10	14	17	19	21
45	5	8	11	14	16	17

[a]This also can be interpreted as showing the fraction of an increase in income that must be saved if the extra yearly annuity is to equal the extra yearly income minus the extra savings.

Table 4. Savings Goals if Post-Retirement Consumption Equals Pre-Retirement Consumption[a]

Age When Saving Starts	Percent of Income to be Saved for Retirement Age x				
	$x = 50$	$x = 55$	$x = 60$	$x = 65$	$x = 70$
20	29%	22%	17%	11%	7%
25	35	27	20	14	8
30	42	32	24	17	10
35	51	39	29	20	12
40	63	48	36	25	15
45	79	60	44	31	19
50		77	56	39	24
55			74	51	31
60				69	43
65					62

[a]This is identical to table 3, with the categories rearranged to make it easier to see the consequences of retiring earlier, or starting payments later. An expected life of eighty years is assumed in these calculations.

that would have to be saved depending on years of saving, years of retirement, and the desired ratio of post-retirement income to pre-retirement consumption (income minus savings). Tables 3 and 4 assume no drop in consumption at retirement and show how the necessary saving varies with the accumulation period and the retirement period expected. By assuming a constant expected duration of life (eighty years) table 4 allows one to see more directly the dramatic effect of changing the age at which one retires.

Suppose I start working at age twenty-five and work until I am sixty-five. Then table 4, second row, fifth column, indicates that I must save 14 percent of my income to maintain my pre-retirement consumption after I retire. If I want to retire earlier, I have fewer years of savings, more years of retirement, and fewer years of interest accumulation on the savings. Moving to the left along the row in table 4 rapidly increases my required saving ratio to 20 percent, to 27 percent, and to 35 percent of my income. On the other hand, starting the savings later in life (and going down the same column of the table) only increases the required savings rate to 17 percent, or 20 percent, or 25 percent for five-year changes in starting age.

Table 5 shows the effect of allowing some drop in consumption standards after retirement, a reasonable assumption since the number of costs—commuting, lunches at work, interest on the mortgage, union dues, and "work clothes"—disappear or decrease.

A common problem that arises with these calculations is that they all assume a constant pre-retirement real income when, in fact, the real incomes of most workers rise over the years of earning. One way I can handle this problem is to estimate my most likely permanent or average real income level, find what fraction of it I should be saving, and then try to save that real dollar amount regardless of the year-to-year fluctuations in my actual income. That dollar amount will, of course, change by the inflation rate each year. Alternatively, I can treat each major change in real income separately. I cannot simply save the same fraction of any income increase as of the pre-increase income level. To see why this is true, consider an increase that comes just a few years before retirement. If I want post-retirement consumption to equal the new consumption standard that the additional income provides, it is obvious that I must save a much greater percentage of that increase than the percentage of income I was saving up to that point. Fortunately, however, the same tables can also be applied to any increases in pre-retirement income. *Any increase in pre-retirement real income can be thought of as a separate income stream.* If one substitutes "increase in income" and "increase in savings" for "income" and "savings" the tables will show the percentage of an income increase that needs to be saved. As an example, consider an income increase that occurs at age sixty, five years before retirement. Table 4, fifth column, shows that I must save 69 percent of such an increase.

The reason that I don't have to save all of any increase in income that occurs only a few years before retirement is that saving for retirement helps me in two ways: it provides funds for retirement, but it also reduces my current consumption level. It is that consumption level that determines my retirement income needs and goals.

The converse of this is that in a retirement plan that guarantees a pension that is some fraction of the income just before retirement, any salary increase late in life is very costly to the employer in terms of pension fund contributions. What seems like the same proportional salary increase to all employees really gives much more to the

Table 5. Savings Goals for Different Post-Retirement Consumption Standards

Retirement Age	Percent of Income to be Saved[a]			
	F^b = 1.00	F = .90	F = .80	F = .70
70	8%	8%	7%	6%
65	14	13	11	10
60	20	18	16	15
55	27	25	23	21
50	35	32	30	28

Starting Age	Percent of Income to be Saved[c]			
	F = 1.00	F = .90	F = .80	F = .70
30	17%	15%	14%	12%
35	20	18	17	15
40	25	23	21	19
45	31	29	26	24
50	39	37	34	31
55	51	48	45	42
60	69	65	62	59

[a]Assuming constant starting age (25) and expected life (80).
[b]F = desired ratio of post-retirement consumption to pre-retirement consumption.
[c]Assuming constant retirement age (65) and expected life (80).

older employees through added pension benefits. For personal planning it means that if I have a company pension that puts a constant fraction of my salary into a fund and I have salary increases late in life, then I should supplement these pension payments with private savings of my own. Or if I have an individual retirement account, I should contribute to it larger and larger fractions of increments of income, the later they begin. For women who start working late in life, or get most of their promotions then, this is particularly important. This inflexibility in pension plans in adjusting to income increases later in life is true of Social Security and largely true of private pensions under the federal Employee Retirement Income Security Act. In the latter, the only two allowable plans are "guaranteed contribution," which must be the same percent of salary for all employees, or "guaranteed benefit," where the last years' earnings cannot be weighted very much more heavily than earlier years.

Table 5 shows that the later the increase in income, the greater the percentage that needs to be saved, varying according to ratios of pension to pre-retirement consumption levels. Note, however, that the reasons for partial replacement—because some expenses drop on retirement—are less applicable to *increments* in income; required saving does not fall proportionately.

Social Security, Private Pensions, and Savings Goals

Now that we have the logic of determining the total saving required for a retirement program, we need to consider that some of the saving is already being done by Social Security taxes and perhaps a company pension. One way to handle the problem is to calculate the amounts going *into* these plans and deduct them from the savings goal, assuming that they will provide a 3 percent interest accumulation after taxes. With Social Security, this is relatively easy, although it is important to keep in mind that some of the Social Security tax pays for current benefits (the cost of what amounts to substantial disability insurance and life insurance), so only six-tenths of the Social Security tax ought to be treated as saving for retirement benefits. For most workers, Social Security saves roughly 5 to 8 percent of income for retirement benefits. Most companies have estimated the cost of their pension plans as a percentage of payroll. This has the advantage of making it unnecessary for the employee to predict either future income or future inflation.

The alternative way of accounting for these automatic savings is to estimate the actual amounts, presumably in current prices, that will be available upon retirement from Social Security and any company pension. You can count on Social Security, in spite of the alarmists. Such societal obligations are seldom defaulted. They were met in Germany even through defeat in two wars and a disastrous inflation or two. With the passage of recent laws, company pensions are reasonably safe, although they are always subject to change or cancellation of future accruals.

Estimating what your Social Security retirement check will look like can be done as follows: Ask your local Social Security office to give or mail you the latest version of their leaflet, *Estimating Your Social Security Check*, and a postcard you can mail in to the Social Security Administration in Washington requesting your "covered earnings" history. The process starts with averaging, for the best X years, the incomes on which Social Security taxes were paid. These incomes, or so-called "covered earnings," started with a yearly maximum of $3,600 in 1936 to 1951, are expected to hit $29,700 for 1981, and will continue to rise. For someone born in 1918, X is twenty-four years; each succeeding age group has to average covered earnings from a larger number of years. Earnings from early years are now increased to allow for inflation. The leaflet contains a table by which you can go from average yearly covered earnings to the amount of your monthly retirement benefits at sixty-five, or at earlier retirement ages. It also tells what other benefits there would be for dependents. The maximum possible benefits for a single person retiring at age sixty-five in 1978 were $489.70 per month; the table goes up to higher average covered earnings which will be impossible to reach until future years of higher limits are averaged in.

This method requires predicting earnings for the years until retirement, and averaging them in, up to the maximum for each year. Thus, retiring at sixty-five instead of sixty-two not only provides higher benefits at the same average earnings but also allows an increase in average earnings—substantially if early years of low earnings can be dropped and later years of high earnings added. Benefits are adjusted for inflation automatically by law now. Ten years of covered employment are required in order to receive any retirement benefits at all. In any case, it is unlikely that Social Security alone will be enough to take care of retirement.

Private pensions are now easier for the individual to evaluate because reforms dating from 1974 require clear information about the amounts you can expect, fairly rapid "vesting" so you do not lose the pension if you change jobs, and insurance in case the pension fund becomes insolvent.

It is possible to achieve some of the same deferral of income taxes by setting up an Individual Retirement Account (provided for by the same 1974 Employee Retirement Income Security Act). However, this seems to require finding an institution, such as a bank, mutual fund, or insurance company, to handle the account, paying them for managing your savings, and hoping that the account will be properly supervised and regulated. The history of mutual funds (chap. 7)—with excessive turnover of investments, relatively poor yield records, and large payments to brokers—might well be repeated with these retirement accounts. It may be advisable to treat the institution as your IRA agent and decide for yourself how the funds should be invested. Or you might see the Internal Revenue Service to help you set up and manage your own IRA.

One additional rule of thumb is to assume that Social Security takes care of replacement for income under about $8,000 a year and that company pensions and private savings plans should be organized to cover the rest. The simplest and best method, however, is to estimate current contributions to all kinds of retirement programs as a percent of current income, and to deduct this amount from the total saving goal. This requires the least forecasting of, or correction for, inflation.

For couples, the exercise can be done with pooled incomes, achieving savings enough to purchase three annuities, one-third on each life and one-third "joint or survivor," so that either survivor has two-thirds of the amount thought necessary for two. Such a long-term plan and commitment, in a world where the marriage law does not cover such issues, needs an explicit contract between partners, married or not, as to the ownership of the accumulations should their relationship change. With children, there is even greater need to assure that the accumulated assets will be available for their proper care until they are all grown. As we shall see (chap. 7), there may be other tax considerations influencing the choice of who should hold title to the assets, so the need for explicit contract cannot be avoided simply by having separate ownership of individual assets.

The Role of Social Security

Even though few of us have much choice about whether we contribute to the Social Security system, it is important to understand how to interpret it as part of a savings and retirement program. Any such program has a "rate of return" on the savings contributed to it that accounts for the benefits that come later. The first beneficiaries of the system had an enormously high rate of return because they contributed only a short time before they retired and were given benefits. Thus the system never accumulated a full trust fund that earned interest and paid the benefits. (It would have been disastrous to do so during the Depression when the system started—deepening the unemployment and raising issues about where all that money should be invested.) Succeeding generations contributed more and more relative to their benefits, and by law the number of years of covered earnings that must be averaged in determining benefits is still rising and will reach thirty-four years soon.

Estimating the rate of return on one's Social Security tax contribution is complicated because the Social Security system also provides disability, survivors, and Medicare benefits, and the retirement benefits are automatically adjusted for inflation. And the rate of return varies with one's level and period of earnings. But in general that rate has already been driven down close to zero in an attempt to keep the contributions of the working generations equal to the benefits to the retired generations—picturesquely called pay-as-you-go.

Why should we insist on pay-as-you-go, and how can it work when no interest is being accrued on people's contributions anyway? It happens that it will work if there is no inflation and the population grows steadily so that there are always more workers in each age group than retired persons in each of those age groups. But with population surges and substantial inflation, that simple rule is inappropriate, and an actuarially fair system—each generation contributing enough to justify, with interest added, its expected benefits—would have payouts exceeding contributions in some years and the reverse in other years. Ultimately, since people will insist that their contributions to the system, with appropriate interest added, be recognized in their benefits, it is likely that we shall give up the pay-as-you-go fiction and try to fix the rate of return so that each generation "pays its own way."

Summary of Budgeting Steps

This discussion of savings goals and budgeting can be summarized in the following set of guidelines:

1. Determine the fraction of your income (and of increases in your income) which must be saved each year to meet your post-retirement consumption goals.

2. Estimate whether your Social Security and private pension plans are forcing you to save enough to meet these goals. If they are not, develop a savings or investment program which saves enough to meet the goals. Thus, if you must save 15 percent of your income each year to meet your goals and find that Social Security "saves" 5 percent of your income for you and a company pension plan saves 5 percent, then set up a system that saves an additional 5 percent. Many banks will automatically deposit specified fractions of paychecks into savings accounts. A whole-life insurance policy also forces you to save, although it does not pay as high a return on your savings as most other investments you could make. Paying off a house mortgage is an additional method of forced saving, but you should count such savings for retirement only if you plan to "consume" the equity in the house upon retirement (e.g., by selling it or mortgaging it to purchase an annuity). Try to earn market interest rates on these retirement savings. As a general principle, a mix of investments in stocks, mutual funds, and money market funds (chap. 9) will provide a long-run market rate of return.

3. Define your other savings goals (e.g., children's education) and commit enough of your income each month to meet them.

4. Commit an additional fraction of your income (15 percent, on average) to a "household capital" savings account. Use this money to purchase or repair cars, appliances, and other items of household capital. Try to delay new purchases until this savings account balance is high enough to pay for them. If you deplete this account and must borrow from your other accounts (e.g., your retirement savings account, checking account, credit cards) or through a conventional bank loan, borrow as little as possible and delay further purchases or repairs until your "household capital" account is solvent.

5. Deposit the remainder of your income into a checking account or an interest-bearing combined savings and checking account. Fund all remaining expenditures from this account. If possible, restrict these expenditures so that this checking account remains solvent. If you must borrow from your other accounts, do so on a short-term basis only. If you consistently run out of funds in this account, keep detailed track of your expenditures and discover ways in which they can be cut back.

For many readers, these simple steps will be sufficient to meet and keep goals for savings, durables, and other budget items. If this applies to you, you can rejoin us at the end of this chapter on page 83. For the rest, a more detailed discussion may be necessary.

Detailed Financial Analysis

A proper financial analysis of the household rests on accounting principles which, in turn, rely on the careful use of such terms as *income*, *expenses*, *assets*, and *liabilities*. As stated earlier, the tricky part of financial accounting is to convert the visible flows of receipts and expenditures to the more basic real flows of income and expenses. *Income* is the accrual of rights over resources and includes such "invisible" items as an employer's contribution to a pension fund or the interest earned on such funds. Converting household physical capital to financial capital (e.g., selling a car for cash) produces cash but no income. *Expenses* are consumption, including losses of rights over resources. They too can be invisible (as with depreciation). Converting household financial capital to physical capital (e.g., using cash to invest in a car) is an expenditure but not an expense.

There are three basic accounting identities, all of which use *real* flows:

1. The income account: income minus expenses equals profit (change in net worth or equity).
2. The balance sheet: assets minus liabilities equals net worth (or equity).
3. The capital account: new investment minus depreciation equals increase in the value of the capital equipment.

Each of these is more complicated for a household than for a business firm, not just because the household has different goals, but because there are so many nonmoney flows to be counted, some without a market measure of their value. A full accounting could require inclusion of

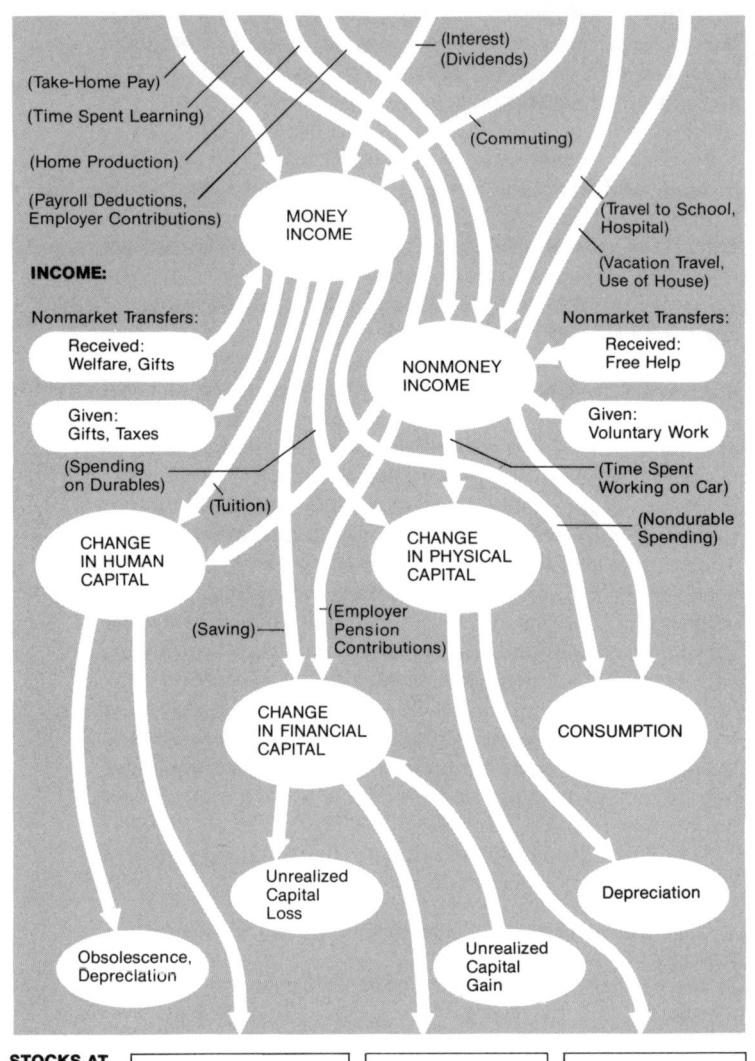

the value of human capital in assets and obligations to others (relatives mostly) in liabilities. The motives differ from those of a business firm, since the goal is not to maximize profit but rather to spread consumption evenly over a lifetime. The income account for a household is really "income minus consumption equals savings," and a major purpose of household financial management is to assure the proper rate of saving, not to maximize it.

The capital account is complex because it involves investment in three different kinds of capital: human, financial, and physical or household capital, the last being things to be used in the future, like a house or car.

Accounting procedures normally begin with a balance sheet, showing assets and liabilities at a point in time. Assets and activities produce income and expenses during a given period of time (typically a year). At the end of the time period, there is a new balance sheet. The three different kinds of capital on the household balance sheet complicate the process sufficiently to call for a chart (see p. 74). It starts at the beginning of the year with the following assets and liabilities:

1. Stocks of "human capital" and time (twenty-four hours per day per person) which can produce both money income from a job and household goods and services, including housework and child care
2. A stock of financial capital (e.g., savings accounts, common stocks, property) which produces money interest, dividends, rents, and capital gains or losses. The "unrealized" capital gains or losses will not be visible receipts or expenditures.
3. A stock of household physical capital, most of which produces a stream of services which the household consumes. Some capital also helps to make money on a job or produce household services (e.g., driving a car to work and using a washing machine to do the laundry).

By allocating time between working for money, producing at home without pay, and everything else—leisure, recreation, and maintenance (sleeping)—two kinds of income are produced (money and nonmoney) which are allocated four ways (consumption and changes in human, financial, and physical capital). It is worth the time to work through the chart systematically so we can understand this process.

Money income is produced by effort on a job (human capital) and by financial assets or investments. Nonmoney income is produced by effort around the home (housework) and by household capital in the form of imputed rental income (the return on my investment if I own my own home), transportation (if I own a car or bicycle), and so on. In the household production process, of course, household capital depreciates. This is shown in the lower right corner of the chart. Whether human capital depreciates is more difficult to say, although some of it may become obsolete. The acquired skill of knowing how to thread pipe, for example, is not worth much if everyone is now using copper tubing with sweated solder joints, or plastic with glued joints.

Two nonmarket mechanisms come into play to alter the amount of income (money and nonmoney) that is actually available for allocation to consumption and change in capital stocks. These have been picturesquely labeled (by Kenneth Boulding) the "economy of love" and the "economy of fear."

The "economy of love" refers to the giving and receiving of money or time without any reciprocal obligation: philanthropy by the giver, charity to the recipient. Some of it is to or from family members living elsewhere, although this is relatively small. There is a substantial amount of time and money spent helping religious or charitable organizations. Actually, if valued at what the time would be worth working for money, the value of volunteer work in the United States is about as large as the amount of money given to church and charity.

The "economy of fear" includes war and robbery, but mostly it refers to government taxes and "transfers." Income taxes and Social Security taxes are deductions from income, while unemployment compensation, welfare, and other such benefits are additions to disposable income. There are also nonmoney aspects of this (military conscription and free or subsidized public services), but we ignore them here.

What happens to the income, money or not, left to dispose of? Some may be invested in education and skills (human capital) in the form of tuition and time spent learning. Some is invested in financial capital, a process commonly called saving. Some is invested in the purchases of physical capital (car, house) or in repayment of debt on them, which is really purchasing them in pieces. The remainder is consumed. The term "remainder" is well chosen, because financial planning largely consists of decisions of how much to invest in the three forms of capital. The allocation of the remaining income to various forms of consumption is a relatively trivial problem by comparison.

Some of the disposition of income is automatic and constrained. Compulsory insurance (the survivor and disability insurance component of Social Security, worker's compensation, and unemployment compensation) probably belongs in the "economy of fear," but voluntary insurance premiums could be considered as part of consumption (since the insurance premiums purchase "protection" for a period of time). Insurance benefits can be considered as part of income. Time invested in learning is nonmoney income automatically invested in human capital. The housing and transportation services of a house and car are nonmoney income that are automatically consumed. Some employer's contributions and payroll deductions are automatically either a financial investment (as in a pension right) or consumption of nonmoney income (e.g., medical insurance or subsidized lunches).

The task, with what is left, is to allocate income (money and time) satisfactorily among consumption and the three investment categories: (1) investment in human capital (job skills and education); (2) investment in financial capital (stocks, bonds, bank accounts, real estate, etc.); and (3) investment in household (physical) capital for future consumption (house, car, appliances, skis). The allocation among investment categories is more difficult to do systematically and sensibly than the division of consumption expenditures, and it has more serious long-term implications. Consumption patterns can be rearranged with relative ease, but investing too much in household equipment may leave too little for saving and consumption, and with a need to borrow at high interest rates. Since there is a poor resale market for most consumer durables, and sometimes a sticky, slow one for houses, readjustment is difficult once the investments are made. The three capital accounts require more thought and planning than does consumption, which really should be considered a residual.

A major first purpose of financial analysis is to figure out how much to save and invest each year, so we know how much we can consume each year. We have already discussed the process of setting savings goals and controlling expenditures on household capital. What remains is a detailed discussion of monitoring the processes.

Sources of Income

If I want to account for all of my income from last year, I should examine thoroughly each of the following categories. Income that is automatically saved is marked with an asterisk.

1. Some income is in cash receipts: take-home pay, rent, interest, dividends, realized capital gains, and transfer incomes like pensions.
2. Some income is in cash, but not actually received: *employer contributions to Social Security, *employer contributions to a pension fund, employer-paid insurance and other fringe benefits. The first two of these are income that automatically becomes savings; the third is income that is involuntarily consumed.
3. Some income is in the form of payroll deductions, for: *Social Security, *pension plan, income taxes, insurance, and other things. Again, the first two of these are income *and* savings; the latter two are income that is automatically consumed.
4. Finally, there are some even less visible forms of income: *interest accruals in pension fund; *increased cash value of life insurance (chap. 9); *unrealized capital gains or losses in the value of human capital or financial capital; imputed income reflecting returns on my investment in house, car, and durables, which provide a stream of services that are consumed. (An estimate of this income might be 6 percent of the net equity in these investments.) I might even want to value my home production of food, repairs, etc., and add it to my income. The first three items are income that is saved, although the second is only an approximation of the interest earned on the life insurance saving reserve (see chap. 9). The third looms large if I have used the year getting educated, since increases in human capital are a capital gain. The fourth is income from the house or car that was consumed. If imputed rental income seems much too theoretical, consider the alternative of investing the same money in stocks and using the returns to pay rent. Each rental payment includes profit to the landlord, so it is only fair to give homeowners a profit on their investments also.

That completes an accounting of all income and some savings for last year.[7]

Estimating Savings

What about savings; how do I estimate that? I have already uncovered seven savings components. Two of these appear on my pay statement; I have to estimate the others. In addition, I must add the following five savings items:

1. Net reduction in debts (repayments on principal less new debt incurred). This can be negative if my debt increased.

---

7. I could also include expense account reimbursements and gift money in income and consumption, but they should probably be excluded from both, since they are not taxable, not wholly discretionary, and lumpy in amounts and timing.

2. Net purchases of financial investments like stocks, net of sales
3. Net purchases of physical assets (house, car, durables), net of trade-ins or sales
4. Contractual savings flows, if any, and accruals of interest in them (bond-a-month club, dividend reinvestment plans)
5. Increase in liquid assets (cash, bank accounts)

Not only is my income much more than my take-home pay plus some other receipts, but my savings is much more than the increase in my liquid assets that most people think of as savings. People who say they are "going broke" are often saving a great deal, but are periodically out of cash.

There is one final, crucial savings item: depreciation of my house, car, and other household assets. Depreciation is negative saving in the form of consumption with no matching income.

To recapitulate, I can estimate my savings for the year as follows:

1. increase in liquid assets,
2. net purchases of physical assets,
3. net investments (stock, etc.),
4. net reduction in debts,
5. Social Security contributions (employer and withheld) or some fraction of them,
6. increase in pension rights (employer contributions withheld, but not the interest accruals),
7. increase in cash value of life insurance, or any contractual saving balances,
8. *minus* depreciation.

My savings goals assumed a 3 percent return on the accumulation, so I should not include the interest on savings as part of the saving to meet those goals. It is just as well, because the interest accruals in pension plans and Social Security are impossible to estimate anyway. If my estimated saving last year was not adequate relative to my income, then I may want to try to increase it next year. At the same time, I can ask whether my net purchases of physical assets were on target, because my estimate includes both the savings for retirement and other purposes and the savings invested in physical assets. If I take 15 percent of income as an expected average investment in physical assets, first to build up a stock and then to replace and upgrade it, then in a year when I invest more than usual in physical assets, my total savings may look all right when my other, longer-term savings is really too small. I cannot merely monitor my total savings-plus-investment-in-durables, but must watch both against standards for each.

We now have some estimates of savings to compare with a savings goal or goals. It is instructive to ask what would happen both to savings and to the goals if I made certain large capital transactions.

Suppose I buy a car. This means that I shall have depreciation on it each year, and my other savings will have to be larger to offset the depreciation and to build up a fund which will enable me to buy a new car when the old one needs to be replaced. If I buy on credit, the repayment of principal will automatically reduce my debt and thus increase my savings. Indeed, some people seem to buy on credit as an automatic if expensive way of assuring that they will save enough of their income to offset the depreciation.

If I buy a house, I am likely to have a big, new contractual savings item—repayment of the principal of the mortgage—and, of course, a new depreciation item. They are unlikely to cancel out, because in the early years very little of the mortgage payment is applied to principal.

Before we proceed to discuss methods of watching monthly performance to make certain saving is adequate, it is useful to keep in mind that while real accounting for real flows is important, liquidity may also be important. There are periods in the family life-cycle where liquid assets are scarce and pressure to borrow is strong. Some extra saving, or slowing of the pace of acquisition of durables, may well avoid high interest costs and possible harassment.

There are also some tax considerations. These influence who "owns" the assets, and the kind of records that are kept about expenditures and about sources of funds for acquisition of assets. Where more than one person is involved, management and recordkeeping also require some collaboration. If some of the saving is for children's education, the funds can be put into their names with an adult as custodian so the interest or dividends are the children's income (escaping taxes) even though they can still be claimed as dependents.

Monitoring Current Expenditures to Achieve Savings Goals

Suppose that I have now set a goal for savings and a subgoal for investment in physical capital, partly by building up component needs for old age, children's education, and physical capital, and partly by asking how much I can expect to improve on last year's performance. There are always special situations that justify departures from norms.

First, I simplify things by deducting from my savings goal, and my recording, the unseen savings items and those that come out before I get my paycheck. They are reasonably stable and largely compulsory anyway.

This leaves four positive savings items that must take care of the rest of my savings goal and depreciation. So I have a new short-run savings goal: the total savings goal, minus Social Security and pension contributions, plus depreciation, equals a goal for the total of:

1. increase in liquid assets;
2. net investment in physical assets;
3. net investment (purchases) of financial assets; and
4. net reduction in debts.

I might even take out the repayments on principal of my mortgage both from the goal and from the "net reduction in debt" since it is contractual, varies continually, and is a nuisance to put in every month.

Each month, then, I want to see that the sum of those four items is sufficiently large to assure me that I am meeting my total savings goals. Actually, there are very few of the second and third (capital transaction) items in any one month, and if I took out the mortgage, there may be no other debt-change items. So I am really focusing on monthly changes in liquid assets, corrected for any debt change or other capital transactions. The only recordkeeping required for this is a monthly adding up of my cash and bank accounts, and a check to see whether they need "adjusting" for any capital transactions. I may also want to adjust for the receipt and expenditure of gift or expense account money. I don't want to think I undersaved the month I spend such money, or saved the month I received it and put it in the bank. So I adjust my monthly savings estimate by deducting such nonincome receipts, and adding back nonconsumption expenditures.

Monitoring Consumption to Achieve Savings Goals

I can eliminate the results of irregular income flows by monitoring monthly consumption rather than savings, since consumption is distorted only by erratic and unusual expenditures like vacations. To do this, I can rely once again on the "bathtub theorem" as it applies to the household: monthly receipts minus increases in liquid assets equals monthly expenditures. I need to add up my liquid assets every month anyway, and my monthly receipts are easily accessible, usually only a few items that are already recorded for income tax purposes.

My monthly savings goal implies a monthly consumption goal, from which I can derive a target for monthly consumption expenditures by deducting depreciation and expenses paid by my employer or deducted from my paycheck. I can estimate the relevant monthly consumption expenditures, first simply, then with corrections: expenditures equal receipts minus increase (plus decrease) in liquid assets minus the following corrections:

1. Purchases of physical assets (car, etc.)
2. Purchases of financial investments (stock)
3. Reduction in debts
4. Expenditures of gift or expense money

Note that a consumption estimate has to be corrected only for the use of gift or expense money. When such money is received, it affects both receipts and the increase in liquid assets, and one cancels the other. The same is true for *selling* an asset for cash.

There is also an advantage in a monitoring system that focuses on consumption maximums rather than saving minimums, in that it is easy to go on to a monitoring of some of the major *components* of consumption. I may want to see just where the major changes are occuring, or what it is that is drifting upward.

What has been proposed here is a very simple beginning that adds up liquid assets around the first of each month (a few days off will not matter), deducts the increase in assets from the previous month's receipts to estimate total expenditures for last month, and then makes whatever important corrections are needed to convert this to an estimate of consumption expenditures. If one is then motivated to know more, it is relatively easy to keep some track of major components of expenditures.

A summary way of thinking about keeping track of one's finances is to start with the simplest situation and note how one can handle the various complications that are likely to come along:

1. If I have no capital account or debts, my increase in cash is saving, and the rest is consumption.
2. The minute I own anything that depreciates, I must deduct

that depreciation from the estimate of my saving and add it to consumption.

3. My employer may pay for things, or deduct certain items from my pay; at least once a year I need to look at these as part of my income and of my consumption or savings.

4. If I incur or pay off any debts, these are, respectively, negative and positive savings.

5. If I have life insurance with a cash surrender value, it is probably also accruing an increased cash value, which is both interest income and savings (chap. 9).

6. If I buy (invest in) financial or household assets, that is savings and investment, not consumption; the subsequent depreciation of the household assets is consumption.

7. Realized capital gains increase my assets, so I have to count them as income too.

8. Loans to others and repayments of such loans can be treated like (risky) investments and disinvestments.

9. I can probably ignore unrealized capital gains—increases in the value of assets I own—since they are always potentially illusory until realized by a sale.

10. Finally, if I want to be precise in my analysis of finances, I should count as part of my income, *and of consumption*, the imputed income from my home and other depreciating assets, instead of counting only the depreciation as a correction to saving (see chaps. 4 and 8).

More Information on Financial Planning

Most of the "how to" publications on financial planning are written from the special points of view of those with something to sell—lawyers, trust experts, stockbrokers. They tend to sell complex solutions which require expert help, seldom providing frank details on the cost of that expert help. The budgeting guides tend to focus on trivia such as detailed record-keeping rather than the analysis and planning that tells what records are essential and how to interpret and act on them. The analysis requires a combination of economic analysis and accounting, but accounting books are written for business accounting, and economic analyses of life-cycle saving are not written for the layperson.

Indeed the best sources are the most recent pamphlets of the Social Security Administration, the Internal Revenue Service, and the Pension and Welfare Benefits Program of the Labor Department. Check the monthly catalog of United States government publications.

CHAPTER SIX **Borrowing and Consumer Debt**

In the usual sequence of things, even with the best financial planning, the need to borrow may well arise. A liquidity crisis is particularly likely if you have children, because pressures to accumulate household durables combine with family earnings which may be lower if only one parent works full time. Proper financial planning may allow you to avoid borrowing for the small durables and even for the car, but buying a house is sure to call for a loan.

Wherever you borrow and for whatever period, the loan will almost certainly call for repayment in regular amounts during the period. The old melodramatic villain demanding the full repayment on the due date is no more. Instead we have amortized loans.

Amortization Algebra

The characteristics of an amortized loan are simple enough. A regular monthly or weekly payment is calculated which over a stated period will return to the lender his principal plus interest at some fixed rate on the remaining balance owed. Calculating the monthly charge is a bit of work, so there are tables which can be used, similar to those in appendix 1 but for monthly or weekly payments. There are also inexpensive pocket calculators that will do this.

What confuses borrowers is that if they compare the two most available numbers, the amount borrowed and the total financing charges (extra amount paid back), they think the interest rate is just the charges divided by the initial amount borrowed. In fact, such a calculation gives an interest rate which is half as large as it should be. The reason is that the interest rate ought to be calculated as the ratio of finance charges to the average remaining balance rather than the initial balance. After the first month, since each payment is partly a repayment of principal, the amount on which interest should be calculated is smaller. On a twelve-month loan, the amount on loan varies from the full amount the first month to slightly more than one-twelfth of it for the last month.

The important point is that since on the average only a little over half of the initial amount of the loan is unpaid, the interest rate is really nearly twice what it seems. Another way to see this is to put yourself in the lending business with a portfolio of loans, a new one starting each month, and figure out how much capital you would have to have to stay in business. Slightly over $600 would support twelve $100 yearly loans!

Under the 1969 Truth in Lending law, the true annual interest rate on the remaining balance must be given on the loan contract, but it is still important to know how to estimate the rate of interest when you know the facts of a loan, or to estimate the monthly payments when you know the amount, period, and interest rate.

Interest is really rent paid for money, and the rent is so much per dollar per year. But the amount of money you are renting decreases each month because each payment contains both interest on the balance outstanding, and a repayment of some of the principal. Most of the first payment is interest, and since there is very little remaining principal at the time of the last payment, most of that payment is repayment of principal. What is the average amount of principal on which interest is being earned? It is roughly half the amount borrowed, just as the area of a triangle (the remaining debt) is the base times half the height. If, as many do, you divide the total interest (total repayments minus amount borrowed) by the amount borrowed, you underestimate the true interest rate by almost half (by overestimating the average amount on loan by nearly 100 percent).

Of course, you must also adjust to an *annual* rate by dividing by the number of years the loan runs, and you can make an adjustment for the fact that the payments come at the end of each month by multiplying the rate by $n/(n + 1)$ where n is the number of payments.

The resulting approximation is a slight exaggeration of the true interest rate, more so the longer the period and the higher the interest rate, but it is still a useful approximation:

$$\frac{\text{Interest charges}}{\text{Half the amount borrowed}} \times \frac{1}{\text{Number of years}} \times \frac{\text{Number of payments}}{\text{Number of payments} + 1}$$

In this formula, "interest charges" are the difference between the total amount paid back and the initial amount borrowed. Inexpensive pocket calculators are now available to provide a precise interest rate or payment. Indeed, any loan involves a time period, an amount borrowed, a payment, and an interest rate, and if you enter any three into the calculator it will provide the fourth. Hence there is no excuse for various approximations like the "sum of the digits" method, which is increasingly unfair to the borrower who repays early, the longer the term and the higher the interest rate.

A few lenders claim to deduct the total interest charges at the beginning of the loan; this is commonly called "discounting." But that should not confuse you if you remember that the amount you really are borrowing is the amount you get. And don't divide the interest charges by the amount borrowed plus the interest charges; that is a meaningless number.

That the early payments are largely interest and the last few largely repayment of principal leads to some additional confusion when a loan is repaid early. Halfway through a loan period, I still owe more than half the loan. In addition, some added prepayment penalties may be justified, because there is a fixed cost of making a loan (credit check, forms, etc.) that has to be covered out of what seem to be interest charges. The bank or lender counted on spreading those fixed costs over the whole loan period.

Even lenders get confused by the fact that interest is really earned and paid on the remaining balance. They occasionally worry that the market value of a car bought on credit can drop below the total installment payments still due on it. The vision of people defaulting, thinking that they could get a better car with the same money, is clearly only a nightmare, since it ignores the unearned interest included in the total "payments still due." The lender is safe so long as the market value of the car exceeds the remaining principal. Actually, even if the value falls below the principal of the debt, there is little cause for concern since borrowers would ruin their credit ratings by defaulting, and in fact the car is not the total security for the debt—the borrower's wages can be garnisheed too.

Varieties of Lenders

Loans vary in size, duration, and risk. Risk, in turn, depends partly on the property, if any, which is used as security for the loan. Home mortgages, with a house for security and FHA or VA insurance against default to boot, ordinarily carry interest rates only a little above the rates paid on savings accounts. Installment credit and credit card interest rates can be twice as high, finance company loans can be double the installment rate, and illegal backstreet lenders could double the rate again.

There are costs in making a loan, and they are generally included in what we think of as interest charges. For rather small, short-term loans, what seems like a high interest rate may actually be mostly the costs of checking on credit rating and the work of making the loan. There are also different risks of default, which are largely handled by charging more for unsecured loans or by restricting credit to customers with certain characteristics. Not everyone can get even a credit card. The use of centralized organizations to keep track of people's credit ratings has led to concerns about the dossiers of unchecked information on individuals that can harm them unjustly. There are also problems concerning whether methods of classifying credit applicants into risk groups are proper and fair. We return to these issues later in the chapter.

An individual needing to borrow should shop for a "best buy," which means the highest class of loan for which he or she is eligible, and the best terms available in that class. Studies done in the past have indicated a wide range of different interest rates even within the same city.

We have already discussed mortgages, but not their rates. There is not much competition among mortgage lenders, but the total finance charges are so large that shopping for slightly lower interest rates may well pay off. If rates are similar, there may at least be better provisions for speeding up repayment with less penalty, and fewer restrictions against refinancing should interest rates drop.

The Truth in Lending Act has made it easier to discover and compare interest rates, but the act and the printing of the rates tends to give them an air of authority and official sanction which allows one particularly confusing practice known as "packing" to continue. It is called packing since it packs part of the price of the purchase into what the buyer thinks are interest charges.

Packing involves writing the installment contract at a very high interest rate, which low-income borrowers or poor credit risks may think is what they have to pay, but then selling the actual installment contract to someone else for a sum larger than the remaining principal. The extra is really the result of rediscounting the obligated stream of repayments at a more realistic interest rate, and the difference goes to the seller. The seller thus gets more for the product than the buyer thinks he paid, and the interest is really less than the buyer thinks. The same result can be achieved if the seller sends you to a particular lender who has agreed to set up a "bad debt reserve" and refund the unused amounts in it to the seller. It is easy to set aside far more than is needed, a delayed extra payment for the buyer with higher "interest" charges. There is nothing illegal about this, but it is obviously a deceptive practice. One way to find out whether it is going on is to bargain with a car salesperson about the price of a car on the assumption that you are going to buy on credit, and then offer to pay the best price in cash. If the salesperson suddenly checks with the manager and finds they cannot offer that price after all, or adds the figures again and they total $100 more, it seems likely that they were counting on "pack"—a little something extra paid by the bank or finance company out of your "interest" charges.

A similar kickback from an insurance company to a lender of part of the premium you paid for "credit life insurance" on a loan may deceive you as to what cost what (chapter 9).

Sources of Loans

Loans for purchase of things which themselves serve as security for the loan are available from banks, installment finance companies, and credit unions. Loans based not on specific objects but on your general credit rating are available from banks, credit unions, stores, and with credit cards.

Credit unions are technically cooperatives, some established under the Federal Credit Union Act and others under state laws. They are presumably organized and run by their members, although some members primarily keep their savings there and others primarily borrow. They claim to have more of a consumer orientation and avoid some of the worst practices of other lenders. For instance, they generally place no penalties on prepayments. On the other hand, their managers sometimes start sounding like bankers wanting to increase business and profits, for example, by suggesting you buy a new car every two years, and only pay off enough to be able to refinance the new one, thus maximizing the amount of borrowing and interest charges you pay.

Lenders reduce their risks by insisting the borrower carry insurance that will pay off the debt in case of trouble. With homes this is usually limited to fire and casualty insurance, although life insurance may also be part of the deal. With cars it includes collision insurance and sometimes life insurance on the borrower. With other loans it tends to be life insurance. These insurance coverages are costly, and should be avoided if possible. Credit life insurance in particular violates the principles of how much insurance to carry (chap. 9) and is expensive in these small pieces. "How-to" books suggest avoiding these "package deals" and at least getting credit and insurance separately. As with any compulsory package deal, there may well be confusion as to just how much you are paying for what.

Charge accounts used to be the free credit of the affluent, but most have given way to store credit cards, available to more people and charging substantial interest unless each monthly bill is paid within a short period after it is received. Competing with store credit cards are bank, gasoline company, and general credit cards. From the consumer's point of view, they all have similar characteristics: a limit on the amount you can buy with them, a billing date, and an interest charge each month if you do not pay within a stated number of days after that date. Most bank credit cards (Visa, MasterCard) are either free or require a modest annual charge. This means that you can still get the low-cost credit of the charge account by paying bills within the deadlines, although some are set up to deduct charges immediately from a checking or savings account. Most general credit cards (American Express, Carte Blanche) charge a larger annual fee.

It is easy enough to see why a store or gasoline company would issue a credit card, but what about the bank credit cards or the general credit cards which are honored wherever their signs are displayed? In addition to the interest charges on delayed repayments, these companies thrive by giving the vendors less than the amount of the sale, by about 4 to 6 percent. If I pay a hotel bill of $100 with my MasterCard, the hotel gets $95 or so. Why should a business stand for this? Because they think it brings more business, saves them handling their own credit, and reduces cash and theft problems. On the other hand, someone willing to pay cash could justifiably ask for a discount, and Consumers Union won a court case declaring that the vendors could not be prohibited by their credit card contracts from giving such discounts. For those who find it unpleasant to negotiate discounts, it is possible to use the credit card to save some interest even though the interest you save until you have to pay the bill is far less than what the store pays by having you pay with the card rather than with cash.

Think of paying for a $100 item:

1. If you pay cash, you pay $100 right away, and the store gets it right away. If you pay by check, there is only a slight delay.
2. If you use the store's credit card and pay before the interest charges start, you may have as much as forty-five days to pay. You save the 50¢ or so in interest if you keep your money in a savings account, and the store loses interest on its money for the same period.
3. If you use the store's credit card and take six months to pay, you pay slightly over $105 including interest, and the store nets about $102 because their interest costs are lower.
4. If you use a bank credit card (and the store may not allow this, particularly if they have their own credit cards) and pay before interest is charged, you pay $100 and save a little interest. The store gets about $95 with a little delay.
5. If you use a bank credit card and pay over six months, you pay some $105 including interest, and the store gets $95.

What all this means is that the store is subsidizing the user of bank credit cards at the expense of the cash customer. And the credit card user who delays and pays interest is helping to pay for the free credit of the credit card user who pays before interest is charged. Where a store credit card is involved, those who use the card and pay on time are subsidized by those who end up paying interest—and perhaps also by the cash customers, although most stores try to make their credit operation self-financing, i.e., no burden to the cash customers.

The customer can, of course, do a little better by keeping track of billing dates, using whichever card gives the longest time to pay on that purchase date, and paying at the last day possible. He or she may save half a percent in interest compared with paying cash.

The store does best if customers use store credit cards and pay over months with interest. They do next-best with cash, somewhat worse if their customer uses the store credit card and pays on time, and worst of all if the customer uses an outside credit card (6 percent discount to store) regardless of when the customer pays the credit card company. Some hotels now ask for a check instead of a credit card, for this reason.

Obviously, except for the confusion and possible nuisance if they are stolen, a variety of credit cards allows the consumer to get a lot of free credit, avoid carrying cash, and still have a record of expenditures without writing many checks. Unfortunately, some of the credit companies have so abbreviated their billings that it is difficult to sort them out, and proving you paid a particular bill is more difficult than if you have a canceled check.

The new combined checking and savings accounts that keep most of your funds in a savings account until they are needed to cover your checks clearly make this careful timing easier. Pay-by-phone also facilitates it. But there are costs—the opportunity cost of your time to schedule everything, and the (negative) expected value of the cost of being late with a payment and incurring financing charges (the charges times the probability of incurring them). And the savings account interest in combined checking and savings accounts is usually lower than you could get elsewhere. (See chapter 7 on money market funds.)

As explained in chapter 5, most households can expect to spend almost one-sixth of their incomes on consumer durables. There are two common ways of budgeting these expenses, with very different implications for the interest charges a household will pay. The first method is to fund purchases of durables from a (positive) savings account balance. An initial period of sacrifice with minimal expenditures can build the account balance to the point where durables can be purchased outright, rather than on credit. The advantage of this method, of course, is that this savings account earns interest. A second method is to finance the purchases by borrowing, gradually repaying the debt and then incurring new debt when the original one is mostly paid off.

For some, the choice may seem to be between buying on credit or not buying at all. It is easy to get into such a situation and stay there all your life. But a small, one-time delay of a few purchases can make a permanent shift from persistent borrowing and paying interest to regular saving and earning interest.

Credit Ratings

Getting credit cards, like getting a loan, requires establishing your credit rating. People used to say that a person should borrow some money and pay it back, if only to establish a credit rating. Credit rating bureaus rely on more than that, but there is an argument for taking out one of the bank credit cards and using it like a low-cost credit charge account, partly to establish your credit rating.

What is in your record at the credit rating organizations is important, because it may affect your ability to get low-cost loans or even to get a job. The concern for privacy and the possible misuse of various public records, plus some extreme cases of unwarranted damage, led to the Fair Credit Reporting Act of 1971, provisions of which are summarized in appendix 2. The main concern is that unchecked erroneous information can get into such files and do a great deal of damage to an unsuspecting individual. It may have been a different Pat Jones, or Pat may have had a legitimate complaint, or the whole thing may have been amicably settled, or the charges may have been dismissed, or Pat declared not guilty; but the record may not contain the final outcome, only the report of trouble. Now, at least you have the right, if you are denied credit on the basis of a credit bureau report, to see it and have it corrected, or at least have your own version added to it. You can also find out who has been given the incorrect information and have the bureau send them corrections.

Credit ratings are also based on general characteristics of individuals as well as their personal credit ratings. This can be unfair to individuals who find themselves in a geographic area or population class that is rated as a high risk by lenders. Increasing demands are heard that these ratings be justified by actual experience or that they be made less stereotyping (prejudicial). There is justification for charging more where risks are high, but broad risk groups, such as everyone in a low-income area, are bound to be unfair to some of the people in those areas or groups.

We have said little about the small-loan companies and the illegal lenders. The latter lend to those whose credit is so bad that even the high legal maximum interest rates, varying around 36 percent, of the small-loan companies are too low to cover the risk. The obvious advice is to avoid them and to borrow only what you can borrow from lower-interest lenders.

Some people try to avoid the problem by borrowing from friends, often at no interest at all. This is very economical but sometimes loses friends. If a national sample of individuals is asked how much money they owe to other individuals, and how much money other individuals owe to them, the aggregate amounts recalled should be about equal; but in fact the average amount people remember they owe is substantially smaller than the average amount people remember as owed to them! It is clearly wise to secure a signed receipt promising some specific interest per year and repayment of the principal by some fixed date if you lend to anyone, however lovable. With the receipt, you might have a chance to recover the debt in small claims court, or be able to deduct the loss on your income tax. It is easier to wait for a long-delayed repayment if interest is accumulating. In drawing up such a loan agreement, however, make certain that the stated interest rate does not exceed the maximum legal rate dictated by state usury laws.

Trouble: Repossession, Garnishment, and Bankruptcy

If you do find difficulty keeping up with the payments on a loan, a whole new world of complications opens up, even apart from what happens to your credit rating and your chances of borrowing in the future. There may be friendly dunning letters, from a collection agency if the creditor is a small store or a doctor who doesn't want to bother personally. If a purchase was the reason for the loan and the loan involved an item as security (chattel mortgage), the item may be repossessed. Actually, repossession rates have been quite small, generally less than 1 percent on cars, for instance, indicating that people have been handling their credit rather well or that lenders have been carefully selecting those to whom they would lend.

For small debts, there are small claims courts, set up to help individuals secure justice but largely used by sellers to collect from customers. There are limits to the amounts that can be collected this way. When substantial amounts are involved, the process goes from warnings to repossession to garnishment to bankruptcy.

Garnishment is technically a legal action requiring an employer to turn over part of an employee debtor's salary to a creditor. The rules vary from state to state as to how sure one must be that the debtor was notified and given a chance to object that this was not a proper obligation, and as to the amount of earnings exempt from garnishment. Some states even set exemptions in dollars, unadjusted for family size or inflation. Texas does not even provide for garnishment at all.

The threat of garnishment is often enough to make people pay up, even if they have to borrow elsewhere to do so. Employers dislike the nuisance and feel that an employee cannot be working well when most of the wage is being diverted. Consequently, many companies fire anyone whose wages are garnisheed a second time. People selling shoddy merchandise or services on credit may use the threat of garnishment and loss of job to collect what might otherwise be regarded as illegitimate claims. A Federal Trade Commission study of the Washington, D.C. area indicated that most of the garnishments were secured by eleven sellers selling mostly to low-income people. The real question is whether the use of garnishment against dishonest or disorganized consumers justifies its availability to dishonest sellers. Technically the claim must be a valid one, but uninformed victims with no legal help can do little. Sometimes they are not even notified until their paycheck is cut.

Faced with the threat of garnishment, or unable to pay anyway, the debtor may find the only way out is to go bankrupt. Many people think of bankruptcy as something businessmen do, but the vast bulk of bankruptcies are personal. To go bankrupt you must file a form giving your assets and debts and last year's income.

Some critics have felt that bankruptcy was too easy a way for a debtor to evade obligations, and have urged an alternative—court-enforced scheduled repayments. The federal bankruptcy law contains a provision, Title 13, under which the federal judge assigns a lawyer to negotiate with creditors, take over the debtor's paycheck, and make scheduled repayments to the creditors and an allowance to the debtor. It is quite clear from the official statistics that the use of Title 13 depends on the judge. The ratio of Title 13 cases to regular nonbusiness bankruptcy varies dramatically from one federal judicial district to another, being very high in Alabama, southern Georgia, and western Tennessee.

Once a debtor goes bankrupt, he is not allowed to do so again for six years, not even in another state, since the law is federal. In fact, some high-pressure credit sellers or lenders seek out recent bankrupts as better than average credit risks among the poor, since they can no longer escape into bankruptcy and can thus be put under the full duress of garnishment. A new Bankruptcy Act signed into law late in 1978, while failing to follow some of the recommendations of a National Commission on Bankruptcy Laws such as counselling on alternatives, did provide a few additional consumer protections. It allows the debtor to opt for the uniform federal exemptions that protect some property from distribution to creditors. The federal exemptions are generally more favorable to the bankrupt than those allowed by many states. If a creditor tries to protect his claim from discharge by claiming that the debtor made a false financial statement, he may be subjected to liability (sued for damages) if he loses, and would have to pay the court costs and attorney's fees. On the other hand, in response to some abuses, educational loans cannot be discharged by bankruptcy until five years after the loan is due, by which time most people would have enough assets so that bankruptcy might not appear so cheap.

The Title 13 scheduled repayments, unlike bankruptcy, can be repeated whenever necessary. In both cases legal fees are about the same—several hundred dollars. One ingenious researcher decided to investigate the notion that Title 13 taught people how to handle their money and preserved their credit ratings. He investigated in Alabama and found that many of the victims were going through the scheduled repayment process for the third or fourth or fifth time! Clearly, paying lawyers to schedule their repayments was not teaching them to stay out of trouble. In fact, we really do not know whether the availability of bankruptcy aids more people to get out from under impossible or unjust obligations than it aids dishonest people to avoid repayments they could perfectly well make.

A specialized group of "credit counselors" or "debt adjusters" has arisen to help those in trouble. They range from genuinely professional counselors, sometimes in nonprofit organizations, to frauds on a par with the small-loan company offer to consolidate your debts by lending you money (at 36 percent) to pay off a lot of small debts (most of them with lower interest charges or none at all). Some of the more progressive labor unions and employers have encouraged credit unions and provided credit counseling, as do the Armed Services. In the final analysis, following the budgeting procedures described in the previous chapter constitutes an individual's best defense against falling into such financial trouble in the first place.

CHAPTER SEVEN **The Investment of Savings**

Most families at some time accumulate some savings which can be invested until they are needed. The financial analysis in chapter 5 indicated that most saving is contractual—payments into the Social Security system or into private pensions, paying off the mortgage or other debts, and increasing the cash surrender value of life insurance (chap. 9). Someone else decides how much those savings amount to each year and where they are invested. But when we do manage to accumulate some money that we control, we need to know where to stash it until it is needed.

Theory of Investment

Before talking about the characteristics of different kinds of financial investments, it is useful to understand the theory. Any investment is expected to produce a flow of future benefits. If the investment is in physical capital, such as a house, car, or washing machine, the benefits are streams of services: housing, transportation, clean laundry. This chapter will consider financial investments, whose benefits take the form of interest, dividends, rents, or gains in resale value (capital gains). The present (discounted) value of those future benefits, less the present value of any future costs, is what the asset is worth, i.e., its price. Physical investments have limited life and depreciation costs, but financial investments usually involve little or no future costs, and the benefits may extend into the indefinite future.

Some investments, like land which pays a net rent, or shares in a corporation which has no necessary lifetime and pays dividends, provide a regular return or yield practically forever. The present value of a stream of money payments that goes on indefinitely is easy to estimate. If the proper interest rate is 3 percent, the value of $100 per year is 100/.03 or $3,333.33. You can check that out by noticing that if you had the $3,333.33 now and put it in a bank account that paid 3 percent it would give you $100 a year. The present value of something that produces that

$100 a year forever is only $3,333.33 because far enough into the future the present discounted value of that annual $100 approaches zero. In fact, the value of $100 available 50 years in the future is only $22, in 100 years only $5, and if you have to wait 200 years for it only $.27. At higher interest rates, of course, the future is even less important.

This means that a competitively traded bond which promises a fixed dollar amount each year for a number of years and a lump sum at the end of that period will have a different price depending on the going market interest rate. Prices will also be discounted for risk—the more the risk, the lower the price that will be established for the bond.

Suppose there is no inflation and a bond promises to pay $30 a year for twenty years and then $1,000 in cash (a 3 percent bond). If the market rate of return on equally risky investments is 3 percent, what would the price of that bond be now?

Present value of $30 a year for twenty years at 3 percent	$ 446.32
Present value of $1,000 in twenty years at 3 percent	553.68
Total price	$1,000.00

The price of this bond will remain at $1,000 over its twenty-year life as long as the market rate of interest is 3 percent. But what if you expect 6 percent inflation each year and the market rate of return is driven up to 9 percent? Consider the same bond:

Present value of $30 a year for twenty years at 9 percent	$274, not $446
Present value of $1,000 in twenty years	$178, not $554
Price	$452

How does paying $452 for that bond earn you 9 percent? The first year's $30 is only 6.64 percent of your $452 investment, but the market price of the bond will rise by the other $10.68 to give you a total yield of $40.68, which is 9 percent of $452. Why will the bond be worth $10.68 more in one year? There is one less $30 payment due, but all the remaining payments are a year closer, so the present value of the interest payments only drops by $5.35. (You can think of dropping the payment twenty years away, and $5.35 is the value of $30 in twenty years at 9 percent). At the same time the present value of the $1,000 redemption value goes up because it is one year closer—present value of $194, or about $16 more. The difference between these two amounts is the increase in the price of the bond—$10.68.

One way to think of it is that the closer to redemption, the less you must discount the price of a bond for its deficient interest yield, because there are fewer years to wait and earn that low interest before you can take your cash and invest it better.

The yield on a bond bought at a discount is also subject to lower income taxes because the part that is not paid as interest, but appears as an increase in the price of the bond (the fact that you bought it for $452 but will get $1,000 when it comes due in twenty years), is treated as a capital gain and taxed at only 40 percent of your marginal tax rate, and then only at the end of the twenty years. This means that such bonds are a better bargain for people with higher tax rates, because the after-tax yield is higher than on their other investments, by a larger differential. The annual increase in the price or market value of such a discounted low-yield bond goes up more rapidly as you approach its maturity, and the investor is referred to as "riding the yield curve."

The other side of the coin is a bond which pays a higher interest rate than the market demands; such a bond will sell for more than its redemption value, and its market value will fall to $1,000 as it approaches maturity. The yield is a high cash (taxable interest) income plus a capital loss.

The same principles apply to the stock market, although there is no fixed dollar dividend comparable with bond interest, and no fixed redemption value at some maturity date. One could treat a stock as an infinite stream of dividends, but most of us intend to sell the stock and use the money at some time in the future, and find it difficult enough to think about an infinite future. Besides, a major part of the short-run return on stocks is the increase in their market value, which is why one year's dividends relative to market price of the stock is usually less than the market interest rate.

Suppose I pay $100 for a share of stock that gives me $5 in dividends and has a market value of $105 by the end of the year. My return is then 10 percent, half of it in capital gain. Ordinarily, this return should be higher than the going rate of return on safer investments. Historically, stock rates of return have averaged 8 to 9 percent higher than the rates of return of corporate bonds. The fortunes of the company and its future earnings, dividends, and increase in stock prices are uncertain to some degree. There is a large competitive market for stocks, and their prices presumably reflect the prevailing assessments of many investors about risks, future profits, and dividends. The individual buying stock can either assume that the market is reasonably efficient in reflecting possibilities—that apparently high rates of return reflect higher risks—or can try to outguess the experts. However, the individual might also want to take a longer view of the future than many investors, and look for companies with good long-range prospects.

In the case of common stock, the investor owns a fraction of a company, and that same fraction of its annual earnings (profit) after taxes and interest costs. Part of those earnings is paid as dividends, and part (retained earnings) is reinvested—theoretically to increase earnings and dividends in the future. So the annual yield on a share of stock is the dividends plus the increase (or minus the decrease) in its market price, and the rate of return is this sum divided by the initial price.

What is important to remember is that earnings should affect stock prices either because they produce dividends or because they result in increases in the price of the stock. Remember also that it is *future* earnings that matter most.

The market value of a stock also depends on the interest rate used to evaluate the stream of yields. When comparing stocks with alternative investments adjusted for differences in risk, the stock price has to fall or rise to make the expected rate of return better than that of alternative investments. If market interest rates go up, and safe, liquid, short-term alternatives are available at 12 percent interest, stock prices have to fall until they are expected to yield something comparable. It used to be assumed that stocks were a good investment to protect against inflation, but when the inflation leads to a monetary policy of very high interest rates, large investors sell their stocks and take the high interest rates available on other investments. For the individual counting on the dividends (which usually keep rising with inflation) and not intending to sell the stock for some time, this fall in stock prices is less of a problem—except perhaps emotionally.

If a company paid out all its earnings in dividends, one might expect that it would not grow, and the value of the stock per share would also not grow, other things being equal. But most companies reinvest at least half their earnings. If every dollar reinvested increased the value of the stock by a dollar, the yield would be the company's earnings divided by the initial market value of the stock, which would be the inverse of the price-earnings ratio printed every day in the newspaper.

What determines how much retained earnings will increase the stock price? Presumably, the more those reinvested funds increase future earnings and future dividends, the more they will increase the market value of the stock. So one would like to find a stock which either reinvests most of the earnings, provided reinvestment is profitable, or otherwise pays most of them out. And of course one would like to find a stock with a high ratio of earnings per share against market price per share, that is, a low price-earnings ratio.

How then could price-earnings ratios get to thirty and higher in 1968? Did people assume some extremely promising reinvestments or earnings? Or did they simply assume that a past record of increased stock prices would continue, and then proceed to drive prices up by buying more, fulfilling their own prophecy? Investors may have been entranced with capital gains (stock price increases) because those were only taxed when realized, and then at only 40 percent of the rate of other income. (Remember, however, that the tax benefits from getting capital gains rather than fully taxable income are greater for those with high tax rates, who can afford to pay more than most people.) Conversely, a low ratio of stock price to per-share earnings might mean that a company is reinvesting unwisely, or that it has made bad past decisions or had troubles and that earnings (and stock price) are about to fall.

The whole stock market can respond to generalized uncertainty about the future, or generalized expectations about the future profitability of business, or the yields available in alternative investments. The ordinary individual is often unable to consider some of those alternative investments if they involve sending funds abroad, or require very large minimum purchases.

Desirable Characteristics of Investments

The general principle of valuing any financial investment by estimating the present value of an expected set of future yields, including capital gains, applies to any investment. But there are other things besides rate of return that concern us about investments. You may weigh them differently, but each has some importance. The characteristics by which to judge alternative investments, in addition to rate of return, are:

Liquidity. I may want some assurance that I can get my money back rapidly when I want it, without having to wait until the market is in better shape. Illiquidity involves both the simple time delay in finding a buyer and completing a sale, and fluctuating prices so that any particular time may be a bad time to sell. Some investments (such as some bonds) have a fixed price at which they will be redeemed—usually at some date in the future—some have fixed annual yields in dollars, some have neither or both.

Safety. I want to be reasonably sure that I can get the principal of my investment back, even if not immediately. What we earlier called "risk" is a combination of low safety, low liquidity, and variability of yield.

There is a tendency for high-yield investments to be high-risk as well. What I want is the best combination of high yield and low risk.

Risk can be reduced through diversification, which means reducing the variability of my total yield by reducing the correlation between the individual yields or even by selecting investments with negatively correlated changes. For instance, some stocks suffer in inflationary periods and some benefit, so a mixture of the two reduces my risk.

Inflation Protection. A third desirable characteristic of investments is inflation protection. It is provided when yield and price go up with the rising price level. I want to "hedge" against inflation, which means I want to make a commitment that offsets the risk of some other commitment already made or inevitable. For example, a baker who makes a contract to provide bread over the next year at a given price may also "hedge" by promising to buy wheat for future delivery at a specified price. This will prevent his being caught between rising prices for wheat and a fixed price for his bread. Of course, if the market price of wheat were to *fall* below the specified future delivery price, he loses some profits he would otherwise have made.

Most people think the best inflation hedge is an asset whose yield is mostly capital gain, but an investment can be good or bad protection against inflation regardless of whether its yield is mostly in cash or in increased sale value. For instance, if I buy a bond at a discount because its interest rate is lower than market, then part of my return is the increased market value of the bond at maturity (capital gain) and part is the cash interest paid; but both of these are fixed and cannot respond to an acceleration in prices or in real national income. In fact, more inflation means a higher market interest rate, which will reduce the market price of the bond. On the other hand, a share of common stock could be in a company that paid out all its earnings in dividends, but the earnings (and thus the dividends) would rise with rising prices. In this case there is good protection against inflation but very little capital gain. So the tax advantages of capital gains, and the hedging advantages of investments whose yields rise with inflation, do not always go together. However, both do seem to be associated with somewhat more risk.

Tax Considerations

In addition to the advantage of taking my yield as capital gains rather than as currently taxable dividends or interest or rent, there are other tax advantages of those investments that allow me to postpone the legal receipt of income, or to change the timing to a year when my tax rate is lower. There are also special tax provisions that make it advantageous to invest in oil wells, or cattle raising, or reforesting land. Wherever my own management or effort increases the value of my investment, a kind of labor income is converted into a capital gain taxable at less than half the rate, and then only when the capital gain is "realized" (i.e., when the asset is sold). On the other hand, if I want to put assets in the names of minor children (for their later education, for example) so that the dividends will be *their* income and hence not taxed, even though they remain dependents on my tax return, I might want assets that require little or no management, such as a mutual fund with automatic dividend reinvestment. Stockbrokers usually know the rules for reducing taxes by putting assets in the name of minors with someone as trustee. The rules vary from state to state and can be affected by Internal Revenue Service rulings. A recent IRS ruling makes it difficult for a parent to be the trustee, and having someone else do it may raise the cost. A more complex way of tax avoidance is the setting up of a trust or even a private foundation, and some investments are more appropriate or acceptable for that purpose.

Estate taxes also engendered another legal trick: putting assets in the names of more than one person, generally by "joint tenancy with rights of survivorship and not as tenants in common." In common tenancy, both parties have to sign for everything, whereas in joint tenancy either one can. And either can run off with it all. The "survivorship" phrase makes the survivor automatically owner of the whole, escaping probate and estate taxes in at least some states. But it can later be construed as a gift of half the total value unless it can be proved that both parties contributed to the estate. Joint ownership used to allow playing games as to whose income the yield was, but now it is necessary to specify who is reporting the income for tax purposes.

Women have a legitimate complaint that officials, in deciding who paid for an asset that is jointly owned, ignore the contribution of unpaid work done mostly by the wife, and assume that the contributions were in proportion to dollar earnings.

It is possible to postpone taxes on retirement savings by setting up an Individual Retirement Account under the Employee Retirement Income Security Act of 1975. For the tax postponement you give up liquidity and control over how the funds are invested, and you also must pay management fees to the institution handling the account. If you manage your own Individual Retirement Account, or similar Keogh plan if you are self-employed, you need investments that satisfy the regulations. Or you can postpone taxes on the yield of savings already taxed as income by buying a deferred annuity. You can even cash the part that is your own investment first, paying taxes on the accumulated interest or dividends as you take the last dollars out. The possibilities of trouble are great in an area so new, with so little regulation, and with customers blinded by their eagerness to postpone taxes. If you need the money before retirement, you have to pay all the taxes on it immediately.

It seems that most of the devices used to avoid or postpone income taxes require giving up some liquidity by tying up funds in various ways. If you need cash, you may even have to borrow and pay interest, even though you own assets.

Information and Management Costs

The less fixed the yield, and the more uncertainty about the quality of an investment, the more I must invest in getting information to select it and in continually acquiring information as to whether to keep it. There are also transaction costs—brokers' fees, federal transfer taxes, legal fees. In some investments, such as rental real estate, the management costs are extensive, and it may even be difficult to find individuals or firms to handle the task. On the other hand, for those who have the time and skill and desire to do the management and even maintenance work themselves, such investments are a source of income that is legally property income and does not disqualify them from receiving Social Security or other retirement benefits. Managing your own assets, whether real property or financial investments, may be an excellent post-retirement occupation.

Characteristics of Available Investments

Each of us must weigh the various characteristics of investments, or ask ourselves how much yield is to be traded for other advantages. With the various characteristics in mind, it is useful to go through a list of the main places where savings can be invested. We will consider financial investments roughly in the order of the prevalence of their use.

Savings Banks or Savings and Loan Associations

Savings accounts in either savings banks or savings and loan associations (many people do not distinguish between the two, even though the savings and loan associations generally pay higher interest) are perfectly safe, provided that the particular institution is insured by the Federal Deposit Insurance Corporation or the Federal Savings and Loan Insurance Corporation. Although there can be a long delay in getting one's money in the case of default, this is rare. In practice, a savings account is nearly as "liquid" as cash or a checking account. The banks will even write an occasional check for you. You may be able to have the bank automatically transfer funds from your savings account to your checking account so you can maximize the amount on which you earn interest without any danger of overdrawing your checking account. Many people are using savings accounts not so much for long-term savings as for accumulating funds for large expenditures. When interest rates rise, large differences in rates may develop between areas, between institutions, and particularly between a savings bank (subject to restrictions if it is a member of the Federal Reserve System) and a savings and loan association. Since banking can easily be done by mail, it is surprising that the movement of funds does not wipe out these differences, but many people prefer to keep their funds locally or perhaps do not trust distant institutions.

Of course, in return for their safety, simplicity, and liquidity, one accepts lower yields in savings accounts and no increase in value with inflation. But keep in mind that one of the "returns" from liquidity is avoiding the necessity of borrowing at very high rates; another is being able to take advantage of bargains.

Government Bonds

A bond must specify its interest rate in advance and cannot raise it as market rates change, the way a savings bank can. Hence, there is a risk with a bond that rising market interest rates may leave you stuck with the old lower yield and unable to sell the bond before maturity without a loss. After World War I, people who had patriotically bought government bonds suffered substantial losses when they cashed them, because market interest rates had risen. To avoid this problem, the United States government, beginning during World War II, has issued some savings bonds with a schedule of guaranteed redemption values at least as high as the purchase price. But still there is a loss in the opportunity cost sense. If you buy a fifteen-year bond at 4 percent and discover the market interest rate has risen to 6 percent, you cannot earn the 6 percent. Had you kept the money in a savings account, you could switch. The scheduled bond redemption values do not earn even the full 4 percent if you cash the bond before the end of the fifteen years.

The reverse of this picture is also true. Falling market interest rates will raise fixed-rate bond prices. That increase is technically a capital gain, taxed at less than half one's usual marginal rate; and the gain can be taken whenever it is most advantageous by timing the sale of the bond.

State and local government bonds, including school bonds, have another feature—income from their interest is exempt from federal income taxes. Of course, they have lower yields because of this, which may more than offset the tax advantage except for very high-income people. There are pressures to eliminate this exemption on the argument that the implicit subsidy to states and localities from lower interest costs could be given in other ways that do not provide a tax loophole for the wealthy.

If your marginal federal income tax rate is 30 percent, then you keep 70 percent of ordinary income including interest, 88 percent of capital gains, including increases in the value of discounted bonds, and 100 percent of interest from tax-exempt bonds. If your marginal tax rate is 50 percent, you keep 50 percent of ordinary income including interest, 80 percent of capital gains including increases in the value of discounted bonds, and 100 percent of interest from tax-exempt bonds. (Forty percent of any realized capital gain is taxable income.)

When considering tax-exempt bonds, it is useful to convert their yields into equivalent rates of return on taxable income for comparison. For example, at a 50 percent marginal tax rate, a tax-exempt bond that pays 5 percent is equivalent to a taxable bond that pays 10 percent. At a 30 percent tax rate, a 5 percent tax-exempt bond is as good as a taxable bond paying 7.14 percent (5/0.70). Similar calculations are possible for bonds bought at a discount so that part of the yield is capital gain taxed at half the rate. Remember, again, that you may be competing against others for whom the same bond provides a greater tax saving.

The safety of government bonds is rated by two different organizations—necessarily, because many institutional investors like insurance companies are restricted to the safer ratings. The two ratings can be interpreted as follows:

Moody's	Standard and Poor's	
Aaa	AAA	Highest quality
Aa	AA	Just off top grade
A	A	Fair to good
Baa	BBB	Medium to fair
Ba	BB	Poor to medium

Some experts feel that the result of rating is the forcing of higher yields for those bonds with the lower ratings, out of proportion to the increase in risk. Risk of default exists even with the top-rated bonds, although it is generally assumed that safety is higher for bonds issued by the counties than those by the cities, the states than the counties, and so on. There is also the risk of loss through changing market interest rates if you have bonds with a distant maturity date, even if you do not need to cash them, because you miss the opportunity to earn more.

Real Estate
Probably nothing has been so romanticized or exaggerated as the potential profits from speculating in land, particularly empty land.

If we think of the "Rule of 72"—that the years it takes for an investment to double in value at a compound interest rate of r is $72/r$—then how do we interpret a story about a man who bought land for $10,000 and sold it ten years later for $20,000? Even if he had no other costs, he got only 7 percent per year on his investment—and the advantage that the return was a capital gain. But if we take account of his property taxes and any maintenance costs, he might well have done better in the stock market. Houses and rental real estate also provide a rental income, and have risen dramatically in price in some periods.

But real estate, particularly rental real estate, has certain advantages as an investment. Its value goes up with inflation. Current tax laws allow deductions for accelerated depreciation on investment in rental real estate, so that for tax purposes one understates the current income and converts the rest into a capital gain. The technical aspects of "double declining balance" depreciation need not concern us, except to note that depreciation is allowed more heavily at first, as a fraction of the remaining value (net of depreciation already taken), *and* at double a reasonable rate. This means, for instance, that on an apartment house purchased for $100,000, some $4,500 can be taken in depreciation the first year. If the net income (net of interest on the mortgage, taxes, and other operating costs) is $4,500, then there is *no* taxable income and yet a $4,500 "tax-free cash flow." When the apartment house is sold, the capital gain must of course be figured on the depreciated value—$100,000 minus all the annual depreciation deductions—but that gain is taxable at only 40 percent of the usual income tax rates and can be carefully timed to take place in a year when other income is low. The boom in rental real estate, particularly small apartment buildings, is in part a result of these tax laws, which were designed originally to stimulate business investment in plant and equipment.

There are even ways in which such real estate investments can be combined with a personal corporation. Rules about the proportion of corporation income that must be paid out in order to avoid penalty taxes depend on whether the income is from active or passive investments, and rental income is considered "active." The rules are subject to change, administratively and through tax reform, so there is little point in describing the present loopholes and special provisions. It may be of interest to note that the present rules about personal corporations were designed to prevent such prior abuses as incorporating one's yacht along with some stocks or bonds and then using the yields from the latter to maintain the former, reporting no net income.

The success of investment in real estate can depend heavily on whether you have knowledge of special opportunities (from, say, having been in a community for many years, or in an occupation where you accumulate such information), and on whether you have the skills and time to put into maintaining and managing properties yourself. If you do your own investment analysis, management, etc., you save two income taxes—your own and the one that would have to be paid by the specialist you hired.

As we saw in chapter 4, there is no evidence that buying and renting out single-family houses is profitable. It may be the high and rising cost of labor for maintenance and repairs, or the way rental occupants usually treat a house, or the willingness of people to pay a great deal more for their own house than they would pay to rent one of similar quality. In any case, no one would recommend the rental of single-family homes as a good investment except in situations such as an expected escalation of house values.

A final disadvantage to renting real estate is due to common misconceptions about fair price and the belief that during inflationary periods rents should not rise. The assumption is that since the owner bought the place at an earlier time, he need not raise the rent when prices go up. That the owners would be making more if their money were elsewhere, or that they are being asked to take less than a market price to provide a benefit for their tenants, escapes the critics. Even the old notions that rent on land, that gift of God, is unjustified, and that capital gains are ill-gotten returns, contribute to making "landlord" an odious term. When people say, "Rents are too high," it might mean that there are undue restrictions on the supply of new dwellings or some conspiracy among owners of rental property. But it is more likely to mean that no one has asked, "Compared to what?"

Common Stock

It is difficult to talk about common stock briefly, since it covers such a wide range of combinations of yield, safety, and capital gains. The proportion of American families owning some common stock has risen in the years since World War II, from 10 percent to nearly 25 percent, although a large proportion of these own rather little and seldom buy or sell. The vast bulk of the trading that dominates the stock markets is done by institutional investors, mutual funds, and a small number of wealthy people. This very fact affects the nature of stock as an investment, since no individual can keep himself so well informed about short-run prospects of individual companies as the highly paid experts responsible for the investment of huge sums of money.

Technically, owning a share of stock is owning a piece of a corporation equal to the fraction one owns of the total number of shares. But the stockholders' claims come after those of other creditors, so what they really own is the "net worth" of the corporation, the value of its assets net of all other obligations. Corporate accounting is conservative, based largely on original investment costs minus depreciation, so the "book value" of a share of stock may bear little relation to its market value. After all, it is the earnings a company can be expected to make in the future that really matter. In rare cases, the book value of a stock may be more than the discounted value of the expected future earnings of the company, in which case it may be ripe for liquidation (or may have failed to depreciate its plant and equipment adequately and be ready for bankruptcy).

One clue to past accounting is the relation of the depreciated value of plant and equipment to its original cost value in the corporate balance sheet. If there has been a regular pacing of investments, and reasonable depreciation, one would expect the accumulated depreciation allowance to be about half the value of the plant and equipment, unless the company is very new or has not had to keep expanding much in recent years.

But it is the level and stability of the earnings history and expectations that matter. One technical aspect which affects the level and stability of earnings available to the stockholders is "leverage." Leverage refers to *any technique of controlling more assets than one owns*. To illustrate, let us compare two very simple companies.

Company A has $100,000 worth of assets and no debts, so the common stockholders owning the 1,000 shares of stock benefit directly from the company's earnings. If the company makes $10,000 in a year, the stockholders may get half of their $10 per share earnings in dividends and the other half in increased stock values through reinvestment. If the company earns $5,000, the stockholders get a benefit amounting to $5 per share. If it earns only $2,500, the stockholders get $2.50 per share in cash or capital gains.

Company B also has $100,000 in assets from selling 1,000 shares of stock, but borrowed another $100,000 by issuing corporate bonds at 5 percent. Thus, they have $200,000 in assets with which to earn money, but must set aside $5,000 each year to pay the interest on the bonds. If they make 10 percent on their assets, or $20,000, there is $15,000 left for the stockholders, or $15 per share. If they make only 5 percent, or $10,000, then there is only $5,000 left for the stockholders after the bond interest is paid. And if they make 2.5 percent on the $200,000, there is barely enough to pay the bond interest and nothing for the stockholders, in either dividends or reinvestment. Hence, in the two cases the stockholders have the following:

Rate of Return on Assets	Rate of Return on Stock	
	No Leverage (A)	Leverage of 2:1 (B)
10%	10%	15%
5%	5%	5%
2.5%	2.5%	0

Whenever the corporation can earn more on the borrowed assets than the interest on the loan, the additional earnings benefit the stockholders. But because the interest is a fixed obligation, it can also reduce the stockholders' return. Leverage applies to individual investors as well. Capital gains in the housing market imply larger rates of return to those with low-interest mortgages on their homes than to those who have completely paid off their mortgages. An individual investor can increase his leverage in the stock market by buying stocks with borrowed money or by using puts and calls (explained on p. 117), as well as by buying stocks in leveraged companies.

Leverage is used more by companies whose earnings tend to be stable, such as public utilities, so it is simpler to compare past fluctuations in earnings per share, which combine the effects of leverage with the actual market fluctuations.

Over a period of years, a company may issue new stock or declare stock dividends or splits. This makes long-term comparisons difficult. If the new stock is sold at market prices and not at special prices to executives, it can be disregarded, although it may reduce the total leverage. Each share represents ownership of a smaller fraction of a larger company. But if each stockholder is issued another share of stock for each share he has (i.e., a stock split), then the assets per share and the dividends per share are cut in half, and so is the market price of the stock. The folklore about stock splits is that they raise the value of the stock, but in fact the stock price tends in most cases to reflect the split exactly, falling just to the point at which the value per share times the number of shares outstanding is the same as before the split. The market value of the expected future earnings of the company is not affected by the legal details of ownership. Often the purpose of stock splits is to cut the price per share, in order to make trading easier and less expensive (since broker fees are considerably lower if stocks are purchased in blocks of 100 shares). The stock is split *because* it is going up!

The ordinary investor is not helped by the conventional ways of expressing stock prices and earnings. We noticed earlier that the price-earnings ratio is the *reciprocal* of a kind of "rate of return" on money invested in the stock. A price-earnings ratio of 20 means the company is earning at a rate equal to 5 percent of the market value of all the stock out, so the stock may yield about 5 percent—not all of it in dividends, however. Dividends per share are not meaningful by themselves, either. The two figures that *are* relevant are earnings per share divided by price per share, and dividends per share divided by price per share, each calculation giving a cash yield in percentage terms for comparison with other stocks. Neither of these figures is available without some extra calculation. The fluctuation of these figures over a few years reveals something about the stability of a single stock. The relationship between them also reveals something, since the common practice is to pay out about half a company's earnings in dividends. A company paying out much less than that may be reinvesting a great deal in expectation of future profits, or it may be having a difficult time and need the cash. A company paying out more than half of its earnings may be doing insufficient reinvesting, may be unwilling to cut its dividend payments in the face of falling earnings, or may lack profitable uses for the funds.

The ordinary person who is thinking of investing in stock is faced with a bewildering number of choices, difficulty in getting good information about the earning prospects of companies, stockbrokers who know little and are themselves often victims of folklore, and an active rumor mill which is sometimes right in the very short run just because so many people listen to it. There are three choices: stick with large companies which already spread the risk over many products, purchase a variety of stocks, or go to mutual funds or investment trusts which invest in an assortment of stocks.[1] Before we can discuss the merits of these choices, we must discuss mutual funds.

Mutual Funds or Investment Trusts

One way to pay someone else to select stocks for you is to purchase shares in a mutual fund or an investment trust, which then reinvests the money. These have different stated objectives. Some put most of the money in bonds, or real estate, or preferred stock. Some invest in foreign corporations. Some specialize in new ventures, risky but potentially profitable. Hence, the investor still has a problem of selecting among investment trusts. Of course there is a fee for this service, partly a fraction of the yield, ranging up to 1 percent per year of the investment but averaging closer to 0.75 percent, and partly (at least in the case of most funds) a "load," or percentage cost paid when the shares are purchased, often around 8 percent of the price. This is the commission the agent or salesperson gets.

The 0.75 to 1 percent of the investment that pays for the management fees and operating costs of the mutual fund leads to another piece of folklore, namely that a fund is a bargain because the market price of its shares is less than the market price of the shares of common stock it owns. People who say this forget that this differential has existed from the beginning and will probably continue, so when you sell the mutual fund, you will sell below the market value of the shares of common stock it owns per share of its own stock. The difference reflects the capitalized value of the management fee charged by the fund—unless that fee is offset by higher than average yields on the stocks. Indeed, the bigger this difference, the bigger the fund's charges, and perhaps the less of a bargain the fund! A reverse difference can reflect the belief that the fund managers are able to buy undervalued stocks.

In order to induce brokers to sell their funds, some have an 8 percent commission, or "load" (difference between buying and selling price), which goes to the seller. For these funds, of course, the net yield is quite low until that

---

1. A highly readable analysis and counsel is Burton A. Malkiel, *A Random Walk Down Wall Street,* rev. ed. (New York: W. W. Norton, 1975).

transaction cost has been amortized over a number of years. There are, however, some "no load" funds. You save the load, but have to deal with the company that operates the fund directly. And there are funds whose stock is sold like any other stock. Wiesenberger Investment Services annually publishes a book entitled *Investment Companies, Mutual Funds, and Other Types* which is available in libraries and lists all the funds with their experience.

Funds are organized as open-end or closed-end funds, which means only that some continue to issue new shares and invest the proceeds in the market, while others maintain a fixed size, managing the fund already invested and the capital gains that are reinvested and not paid out. There is no particular reason to prefer one over the other. The total size and record is more important. Some of the funds are sold on the stock market like any other stock, making them easy to keep track of and easy to purchase through a stockbroker, who charges only the usual fees. For 100 share lots of moderate price, the fee falls about 2 percent of the sale price.

Assessing the records of funds is difficult, because one must decide how fast to write off the 8 percent loading, and how to compare a new, rapidly growing fund with an older, more static one. The promotional literature of the funds themselves is often difficult to understand or even deceptive in selection of base years. It is easier for a new, rapidly growing fund to produce a good record, because it can invest in good prospects without the extra costs of getting out of some previous investment first. For this reason, many a "great" new fund becomes average after only a few years. The extrapolation of past success into the future is dangerous anyway. Supposing that there is a large random element in individual fund experience, then the very fund which has recently shown the most capital appreciation may be the one most likely to suffer reverses in the future as it regresses toward the average.

Various studies have tried to determine whether one does better buying a mutual fund or a random assortment of stocks. Does the fund's better selection pay for its management fees and for the 8 percent loading? The answer, of course, will depend on the period studied, the number of years allowed to amortize the 8 percent, and the exact random selection of stocks; but in a substantial number of studies the mutual funds appear to be no bargain. Only if the investor is as judicious in selecting a mutual fund as in selecting stocks does it seem to pay. Indeed, the risk spreading implicit in large, diversified corporations may well be as great as that in a mutual fund, particularly one that focuses on an industry such an electronics, or computers, or chemicals.

Selecting Stocks or Mutual Funds: Information and Advice

Unfortunately for the average person interested in investing rather than speculating, most of the standard sources of information on common stocks seem to be geared to short-run fluctuations and speculation. The stock market report in the newspaper gives such recent information as the high and low price for the day and perhaps for the year to date (rather than for the last twelve months), the dividends (often for the year to date rather than per year), and the number of shares traded yesterday. The information sheets distributed by stockbrokers are better, but frequently go back only a few years and provide very little information on such essential questions as the total amount of capital investment done by the company in the past few years. Anyone who wanted to know the longer-run variability in earnings or stock prices would find it difficult to estimate. Of course, extensive historical information on stocks is in the library.

Stockbrokers themselves are paid according to the volume of stocks they buy or sell, except in certain special cases. Hence, they are likely to tout special deals, or mutual funds that pay them 8 percent, or anything to get you to buy something. There is little evidence that customers switch to brokers who give better advice; in any case, the "advice" is usually packaged by the main office and simply relayed by the broker. Stockbrokers tend to try to sell short-run bargains, so unless you make clear your longer-run investment intentions, you may end up getting hot tips daily from your broker.

The extreme form of the hot tips is a fraudulent practice, largely abolished, of extensive high-pressure touting of certain stocks through offices full of people and telephones (called "boiler rooms"). This effects a kind of self-fulfilling prophecy if people believe the tips and act on them. The money is made by buying the stock before touting it and selling it afterward. Altered forms of this—trading in stocks one is advising others to buy or sell—still exist.

The Securities and Exchange Commission now requires reports on all stock trading by officers of a corporation and on the buying or selling by anyone of more than some fraction of the total shares of a corporation.[2] They are also demanding more and more detailed accounting data from corporations. The annual reports of corporations to stockholders are also required to report the full remuneration of the officers and their ownership of stock in the corporation. And of course, there are rules about stock prospectuses and the issuing of new stock. All this tends to prevent the worst kinds of frauds, although some scandals still erupt. The issuing of stock in new ventures with many shares going to the founders free or cheaply for their "trouble" still goes on abroad. Mail is then used to sell the stock in the United States.

The market for stocks and mutual funds is well organized, with many well-informed large investors. The more nearly perfectly competitive and informed the traders in a market, the fewer the bargains. Some people believe the stock market already reflects future yield prospects and associated risks rather well. You may notice that a company has a great new product, or has been having exploding sales and earnings, but the chances are that many others noticed it earlier and have already bid up the price of the stock. So the only way to do better than average is to know something other investors don't know or interpret incorrectly, and to be willing to invest and wait while its effect shows up. Or if you believe the reason for the depressed price of a stock is temporary, you might get in while others are waiting for clearer signs. There are many books about how to make money in the stock market, but they mostly seem to be saying "buy cheap and sell dear" without explaining how to do it. Indeed, in the present world of massive unexpected events, new government regulation, disruptions of basic supplies, and gyrating prices of basic materials, diversification seems crucial and optimal selection impossible.

Timing of Investments

One more piece of conventional wisdom has to do with stock price averaging. It says that if one puts a constant stream of money into the stock market without regard to short-run fluctuations, one does rather well, getting more shares when the price is low and somewhat fewer when it is higher. In one sense the advice is sound; it does pay to disregard the short-run fluctuations and keep putting

2. Businesses have sprung up selling summaries of what insider trading is going on, on the assumption that insiders are acting on inside information.

money in, because over the long run the stock market has gone only up, reflecting the growth in national income, real as well as inflationary. In another sense it is not sound; one would do better if he somehow managed always to invest during periods when the stock market was depressed. In a third sense it is also good advice; it implies that it is wise to put money in, but not to speculate. The brokers' fees and costs of keeping informed are likely to wipe out any gains from speculation for most people.

There do seem to be waves in the stock market, partly reflecting changing government monetary policy. The stock market competes with other forms of financial investments, and if tight monetary policy drives up interest rates, some marginal shifts of money out of stocks to other investments can be expected. Adjusted for risks and tax advantages, the yields for different forms of investments tend to be comparable. One can even find other investments, such as "riding the yield curve" on a bond, with a similar mix of current yield and capital gain. And, of course, high interest rates depress the market prices of real estate and make it attractive again. (Remember the rule that the price of an asset is the discounted value of its expected future yields.)

It is possible to buy stocks of foreign corporations or funds which invest in foreign corporations. The usual risks are increased by the possibilities of nationalization or of changing exchange rates and by the greater susceptibility of companies in smaller countries to losses of markets when other countries impose tariffs or quotas. There are also complex and changing tax advantages and disadvantages. Remember the rule about the market interest rate being approximately 3 percent plus the expected rate of price inflation. What does this mean about the advisability of investing in stocks or bonds in some other country promising a higher percent return? It might just mean that that country was having a higher rate of inflation, but if they did have more inflation than the United States, they are likely to devalue the currency, which would mean that you would get fewer dollars back than you expected.

All in all, common stocks or mutual funds remain an ideal investment for the household's longer-run savings, providing a hedge against inflation, high yields, relatively small management costs (if one sticks to the larger companies or funds), some liquidity because of the stock exchange, and the receipt of about half the yield or more in the form of capital gains, which can be taken when convenient and which are taxed at lower rates than other income.

Puts and Calls: The Options Market

It is possible instead of buying stock to buy the right to buy it at a stated price. Then if the price goes higher than the stated price, you can take the stock or sell the option for a profit, while if the price goes down you only lose the amount you paid for the right to buy it. These "call options" are sold by stockbrokers operating through the Chicago Board of Options Exchange, which works much like the stock market and publishes closing prices in the newspapers. A call option specifies a regular listed stock, a price per share at which you can buy the stock ("striking price"), and the month the right expires (at the end of the month). The price of the option is the amount you pay now per share for that right, although you must purchase units of 100 shares. The striking price plus the option price per share will always be above the current market price, of course; otherwise you could realize an instant profit. But purchasers hope the price will rise enough to cover the purchase price of the option, the striking price, the broker's commission, and the cost of realizing the option for cash. The periods during which options can be exercised have been standardized to end on the last business day of January, April, July, or October.

So "Ford 40 April at 2⅝" means I can buy the right to purchase 100 shares of Ford stock at $40 per share any time between now and April 30 for 100 times 2⅝ or $262.50, plus commissions. If the price gets above that by more than the cost of exercising the option, I can make a profit, or wait hoping it will go still higher before the end of April.

Buying a "put" gives you the right to *sell* 100 shares of stock at a stated price, and you make money if the price falls so you can buy the stock at a lower price than you can sell it for. If you already own the stock, it is a way of being sure you can unload it on the way down. If not, you can exercise the option, for a fee, without ever buying and selling actual shares.

Obviously, this is a form of legalized gambling, where you can hope for large gains with a small investment, but can limit your losses. Brokers find handling options more profitable than selling stock. There is a $6 charge per option, plus 1 percent, plus a surcharge. If an option is exercised, the broker makes another commission. And, of course, those who write options leave a difference between put and call prices that leave them a profit. There is reason to believe that few buyers make money, but most sellers do because they are hedged, either selling both puts and calls, or selling calls on stocks they hold.

There are many complex combinations of puts and calls with and without owning the stock that allow all kinds of gambling with leverage and some hedging to cut possible losses.

Commodity Futures

Another kind of gambling, requiring somewhat larger sums and perhaps inside information on crops, weather, etc., uses commodity futures. These are essentially the rights to future delivery of some commodity like grain. The buyer of futures bets that the price will go up before he takes delivery so he can sell at a profit. The seller of futures bets that the price will fall. As the market really works, the futures themselves are sold, and the commodities are almost never actually delivered. Such markets perform a useful social function, like that of Joseph in Egypt, inducing less use and more storage today if shortages are expected in the future. Indeed, in spite of the common belief that the market is a noxious exploitation of the farmers, economic analysis shows that the gamblers either improve the allocation of resources or are penalized with heavy losses. If they compete sufficiently, they make only normal profits for their services, so that in a sense the more informed speculation, the better. A well-run grain market reduces the price fluctuations to those reflecting the costs of storage, helping to spread consumption evenly over time in the face of fluctuating supplies. When speculators expect a bad year, they drive up the current price, thereby encouraging less consumption and more storage.

For the ordinary household, commodity futures are closer to gambling; no one is likely to know as much about the expected crops and market demands as the professional traders. Even the proper regulation of these markets to prevent fraud is still far less adequate than with stocks.

Small Businesses

A person can invest in a small business without being directly involved in managing it. A small business often requires more capital than one person has, so that a partnership or a corporation has to be formed. In a partnership each partner is responsible for the conduct of the others, which involves risks that the other partners may be dishonest or inefficient and presents problems if one partner leaves or dies. A corporation limits one's liability to his actual investment and allows postponement of some taxes on undistributed profits, but subjects the earnings to the corporate income tax on profits. A small business can put its resources into real estate, farms, cattle, oil wells, trees, retailing, or even manufacturing. Sometimes businesses grow out of hobbies—photography, saddlemaking, etc. The main difficulty is that any business requires time and energy, and holds considerable risk. A small business is risky for an active partner, and even riskier for a "sleeping partner." Small business failures have been numerous enough to indicate that many people go into unwise ventures or have inadequate experience in accounting and business management. The mortality rate has been highest with retailing ventures, perhaps because they are easiest to get into, relying on rented quarters and an inventory financed by suppliers. And a retail business often arouses the enmity of customers, who exaggerate the gross mark-ups and underestimate the costs.

Preferred Stock, Corporate Bonds, Debentures

There are a variety of other financial investments, generally unsuitable for the ordinary household because they serve other purposes and require substantial amounts of money. Preferred stock has a guaranteed or fixed dividend that is paid before any common stock dividends. The yield is safer for that reason, but, being fixed, it will not go up with inflation or higher profits.

Corporate bonds are elaborately rated as to quality and are most appropriate for insurance companies, which must preserve the principal of their investments because of their obligations to their policyholders. (Insurance companies are not allowed by most state laws to invest more than a fraction of their assets in stock.) The better corporate bonds are safe, and sometimes even provide capital gains when bought at a discount, but they provide fixed yields with little apparent advantage over a savings account. Interest payments on bonds have claim to the company's earnings before even the preferred stock.

The one debenture of some interest to the average investor is the "convertible" debenture often issued by utilities. It is really a bond with the right after a certain period of conversion to common stock of the company. If the price of the stock falls, the debenture can be held as a fixed-yield investment. If the price rises, the debenture can be converted to stock at a bargain. Often there are savings in the transaction costs as well (no broker's fees).

Checking Accounts and Checking-Savings Combinations

Money kept in a checking account can be a kind of investment if it avoids service charges. With combination checking and savings accounts, a relatively low interest rate is paid on the savings account, but if a sufficient balance is kept in the savings account, no charges are made for the checking account or the automatic transfers that replenish it from the savings account. Again, this is really a kind of yield on the funds "invested" in the two accounts, in addition to the interest paid. Whether the total yield is better than alternative investments may well depend on how many checks you write.

Money Market Funds

The inflation of the 1970s which produced higher interest rates, combined with legal ceilings on savings account rates, led to the creation of a new financial instrument, the money market fund. These funds pool individuals' savings and make short-term commercial loans, providing the savers with high yields, high liquidity, and reasonable security through diversification and the short duration of the loans. Some of these money market funds are offered by banks, some by stock brokerage companies, and still others directly from the companies. Minimum deposits, transaction costs, check-writing privileges, and liquidity differ substantially from one fund to another, and are likely to change in such a competitive business. Since the yields depend on what can be earned on short-term government and corporate bonds, and no legal ceilings apply, the yield to the saver is high when short-run commercial interest rates are high, as in any inflationary period. Savings are not insured in such funds, and the yield can change rapidly, but the risk of capital loss appears small, and you can always get out if rates start to drop. Remember, however, that as interest rates drop, there are large capital gains to be earned on longer term investments, including stocks. A stock, depressed so that its yield is quite high, will appreciate when that same expected future stream of yield is discounted at a lower interest rate. If you do decide to save through money market funds, an investment of time spent acquiring information about them may have a high payoff.

Odds and Ends

Beyond what we have listed, the possible places where one might invest savings tail off into antiques, paintings, precious metals, diamonds, or foreign currencies. Most of these require either special skills or inside information if one is to make any money. Many produce nothing, so any yield can come only from an increased demand facing a stable or decreasing supply—often a temporary situation. When one has both time and skills to invest, there is a variety of special investments. Some people purchase old houses, live in them while they fix them up, and then sell them. Under present tax laws there is not even a capital gains tax on such a profit provided the seller buys another house costing at least as much within a year. This means that all the effort put into such a venture would earn tax-free income. The question, then, of course, is whether one could earn still more, even after taxes, by concentrating on his main occupation, because the main return here is not so much on the financial investment as on the labor.

For those with a long time horizon and a love of nature, trees are an excellent investment, aided by a number of special subsidies (including free seedlings in some states) and some tax advantages.

It is important to remember the principles of compound interest, and at market interest rates, when comparing investments. An antique chair that doubles in price in twenty-five years earns less than 3 percent (remember the Rule of 72)!

Some Technical Details

We have already discussed some technical considerations, such as joint tenancy, the cost of trading, trusts, putting assets in the names of children, and partnerships versus corporations. Other technicalities concern state and local taxes and estate and inheritance taxes. Estate planning is discussed more fully at the end of chapter 9.

The "dividends" received from a mutual fund are not entirely current income, at least for purposes of the tax law. Part is considered a distribution of the capital gains realized when the fund sold one stock in order to purchase another. Some funds attempt to maximize the fraction of dividends that is capital gains for the tax benefit of their customers.

A curious provision of the tax law states that if an appreciated asset is given to charity, the full market value can be deducted as a charitable contribution, but no capital gains tax is payable on the difference between that value and the original cost. Anyone who has owned stock for any length of time, and who is making contributions anyway, would therefore be well advised to make contributions in stock rather than cash. It might even be an incentive to weed out stocks which seem to be going nowhere. Strangely enough, even among the affluent very few people do this. This loophole is being restricted by revisions in the law.

The tax advantages of investment in real estate without the management problems are available in real estate investment trusts. In one outstanding case, that advantage has been used to speed up racial integration in middle-class housing. One can purchase shares in a mutual real estate investment trust, called M-Reit, where the funds will be used to purchase, renovate, and maintain apartment buildings that will be operated on an open-occupancy basis. The dividends will be tax-free because of the double declining balance depreciation allowed.

In any investment program, particularly one focused on stocks or mutual funds, there are choices between investing more time or money in information or advice, on the one hand, and reducing the need for it by diversification on the other. Diversification can come through investing in large multi-product firms, or in a large number of different firms, or in mutual funds which invest in many different firms, or some combination of these. There is no best advice here. The choice may depend on whether you want to make detailed choices and follow the fates of several individual companies, or pay a commission to a mutual fund for taking that responsibility.

How does one assess the payoff to more information? If one pays for it (in management fees) by investing in a mutual fund, the payoff is in the expected higher return. If you are thinking of paying for advice from the many firms which offer it, you should ask why anyone who could really predict the stock market would sell the information rather than use it to get rich. And if a large number of investors receive advice from some service, what might happen?

First, it could be fairly obvious information already acted upon by others, so that the stock price would already have taken account of it. Large speculative operators may have gotten the information early and acted on it, only to unload on you at the higher price.

Second, the very price changes predicted might happen, but only because the subscribers to the service took the advice, in which case the long-run movements might be unaffected.

The basic problem for the small investor is that he or she is competing with large professional investors who have a great deal of information and a much wider range of alternative investments. The investors of pension funds, for example, have specialists who follow subcategories of investments.

There are schemes now in which the dividends on stocks or mutual fund shares are automatically reinvested in more stock, and with the right to purchase more stock through the same mechanism. The charges for the automatic reinvestment are not always clearly stated in advance, and the varying purchase prices require detailed records for paying capital gains taxes when the stock is sold. It can be a convenience for stock held in the names of minors for their college education because it avoids dividend checks. The right to purchase more stock for a fee smaller than the usual broker's fee can also be attractive. It might be better, if you have the time, to make fresh decisions about additional investments, but it is an automatic saving-investment device for those who feel they might otherwise spend the dividends. Indeed, making it difficult to spend savings is one way to hold on to them.

When assets are put in trust, there is the problem of who will manage them, and sometimes the regulations seriously restrict the investment options. A trust is essentially a fictitious "person" owning some assets for the benefit of someone else. Because the trustee is responsible for proper management and can be made personally liable for the results of bad management, he tends to be quite cautious about investing the money.

Complex business deals, whether for profit or tax avoidance, often involve tricky legal and tax filing problems. These can absorb time and money, and it may prove difficult to extricate yourself from them. There is an emotional cost in such complications, particularly when one gets older and thinks about turning things over to a survivor. Indeed, any investment that is difficult to sell can prove to be a problem, perhaps more from the uncertainty and worry than from any real long-term loss. This speaks against partnerships, new businesses, real estate in undeveloped areas, and unlisted stocks not sold on the major exchanges.

What People Do

Given the reasons for investing savings and the options open to them, what do people do? Most of them put their money in fixed-yield assets like savings accounts and United States bonds. If one asks them whether that was wise in view of continuing inflation, they say that of course it was, except that they should have saved more. If one asks about common stock as an alternative, they reply that they don't know much about it or that it is risky. This means that for most people their only important hedge against inflation is their own home. Consciousness of inflation has not been accompanied by any insights about investment for most people; instead, it is seen as requiring that one economize and not make new commitments, in order to be able to meet the (higher) food and clothing bills in the future.

Among the more affluent, of course, consciousness of the importance of capital gains is quite salient. On the other hand, even the affluent are not usually actively attempting to reduce their income taxes; they are more concerned with earning money and getting a good yield on their investments than with exploiting tax loopholes. This implies, of course, that special tax provisions available only to the wealthy and used by only a fraction of them are unfair not only as between rich and poor but as between rich and rich, and could be abolished more easily than some people think.

At the same time, the affluent, and particularly the wealthy (those with high assets as well as high income), are quite concerned about passing their estates on to their heirs and eager to escape estate and inheritance taxes. So despite the traditional economist's belief that the heaviest taxes should be on inheritances, popular opinion is against more effective taxation of estates.

The pattern of asset ownership varies with the amount of assets involved, of course; the wealthy are more likely to be in stocks and in business ventures. There are also different patterns between age groups, the young people having a larger fraction of their assets in the home and savings accounts, older people in real estate and stocks.

Most people seek relatively little information or advice, and yet even among the wealthiest, the actual delegation of decisions about investing assets is quite rare.

Given that our estate and inheritance taxes can be relatively easily avoided by various devices, including trusts, one might think that the main source of the wealth of today's wealthy would be inheritances. But in fact, during the last half-century there have also been vast profits made, and vast capital gains on the profits that were reinvested. We tend to pay attention to the inheritances because they are fascinating or irritating.

Most economists would argue that the pattern of ownership of assets is less important than the control over their use. Vast amounts of corporate wealth are owned by widows and orphans, pension funds, etc., but their productive use is directed by managers who are rewarded mostly for their results. From a hard-headed economic point of view, it would be the wasteful consumption of assets one would object to, and not the technical ownership of them, unless that ownership were used for harmful purposes.

CHAPTER EIGHT **Investments in Consumer Durables**

We have already discussed the largest consumable investment individuals make—an owned home. And we have seen that a crucial aspect of financial management and budgeting is to maintain proper levels of annual investment in human capital, physical capital, and financial capital (savings). The depreciation of consumer durables is a large and often neglected part of the cost of living. We even suggested that one method of spacing acquisitions and staying aware of costs was to allocate some annual percentage of income for the combined replacement, acquisition, and upgrading of the house and household equipment.

There are still problems in deciding how much to invest in what durables. Such investments commit the family to a pattern of consumption, costs, and even payments far into the future. The costs of buying or selling are such that we want to minimize mistakes. Having already discussed houses, we focus here on cars, other durables, and additions and repairs to homes.

Theory Again

A new element enters our capital theory with most consumer durables and cars because of their rapid market depreciation, large differences between their purchase price and their selling price as "used" items (trading costs), and the gap between their market value and use value. The first-year depreciation cost of most durables is extremely high, so we legitimately spread costs over expected years of use. Then, when we want to compare such alternatives as buying a new durable versus repairing and keeping an old one, we do it in terms of costs per year. The cost of keeping something one more year must be based on the difference in what it could be sold for now and a year from now. The cost of buying a durable must be based, in part, on the purchase price, which might easily be 50 percent higher than selling price.

The difference between market value and use value can be very large for some appliances which have almost no secondhand market, substantial for an old car ascertainably in good condition, but relatively small for a house unless there is something an individual particularly likes about it that others do not appreciate.

The benefits of most consumer durables are extremely difficult to quantify, so we need good estimates of the costs of alternatives; then we can ask whether a more costly alternative is worth it in terms of benefits.

Two of the most important costs are depreciation and foregone interest. Dealing with the present value of streams of these costs over time may appear complicated at first, but, fortunately, there is a way to shortcut the calculation of the present value of a stream of depreciation and foregone interest costs by knowing one nonintuitive fact: for a depreciating asset with no resale value at the end, *the present value of the stream of depreciation and foregone interest costs is exactly equal to its present cost-to-own, whatever its expected life and whatever the interest rate used.* Cost-to-own here means resale value if I already own an item, purchase price if I do not. Thus, the present value of the depreciation and foregone interest costs of buying an $800 used car and keeping it until it is junked is exactly $800—and that amount does not depend on whether it wears out in one year or ten. If there is a resale value—I intend to trade it in before it is junk—then the total cost is the present cost-to-own minus the (discounted) present value of the trade-in.

An intuitive reason why this is true is that a less lasting durable has more depreciation each year, but less remaining value and fewer years to cost me in foregone interest. If I want to compare keeping an old one with buying a new one, I need only the cost-to-own now, expected life, and any differences in operating costs to get differences in yearly cost that I can compare with differences in benefits or satisfaction.

While this shortcut will prove extremely useful in comparing the costs of alternatives, the following pieces of economic insight will also help:

1. I still must discount other future costs and benefits with a 3 percent interest rate, and use present-day prices. Inflation will increase trade-in values, but it will also raise the rate of interest, so I am safe in using the 3 percent figure. If I have to borrow money, however, the difference

between what I am charged on the loan and what I could receive if I invested the money myself is part of the cost of the purchase.

2. In comparing costs of an owned durable with those of a newly purchased replacement, I cannot consider only next year for the new one, because the trading costs and the pattern of market depreciation are such that it will seem prohibitively expensive. I must calculate an average per-year cost over the expected life of the new purchase.

3. Inflation is no excuse for ignoring depreciation, particularly since inflation simultaneously increases the cost of replacing the durable. Moreover, if I took current market prices, the apparently lower depreciation would be offset by the higher market interest rate.

4. The principle that past (sunk) costs should be ignored applies to decisions about whether to fix up and keep an old car or appliance. It works several ways. A series of high repair bills already paid does not justify keeping a car just to "amortize" the bills, if the car promises to require still more repairs. On the other hand, repairs that would not be recoverable in the trade-in value of the car may still be worth making if they allow the use of the car for another year or two. Careful maintenance usually has less effect on the resale price of a car than on its usefulness to the owner.

5. Finally and perhaps most important, in deciding about replacement, I must be honest with myself about how long I expect to keep the replacement. I cannot plan to trade in a five-year-old car and claim I will keep the new one for ten years without kidding myself. Hence, replacement choices should usually compare one more year of the old one with one-plus-the-age-of-the-old-one years on the new one. If I have a five-year-old car, the comparison must be the cost of keeping the old car one more year with a six-year-average cost of a new car. Or, if I buy a newer model used car, I compare with average cost per year on that one if it is kept until it is as old as my present one will be a year from now.

Automobiles

In applying all this to decisions whether to buy a car, or to buy an additional one, or to replace one, some additional rules of thumb are useful:

1. The costs of trading cars are substantial. Dealer's

margin, sales tax, and title-transfer costs range from approximately 20 percent for a new car up to 50 percent for a low-priced used car. Trading costs also include the time and money costs of shopping. Spreading these costs over several years of use before trading again is obviously economical.

2. Cars depreciate at a rather steady 25 percent per year of their resale value at the beginning of the year. Inflation will reduce the apparent fall in resale value, but the real, inflation-adjusted drop will be about 25 percent. In spite of folklore about popular or durable cars like Mercedes, Volvo, Volkswagen, or Cadillac, the exceptions to this rule are few and far between.

3. If my old car could be sold for $500, but would cost $1,000 to buy from a used car dealer, it is the $500 that I should use in estimating my costs if I keep it.

We can illustrate these principles by working out the costs of the choices I face if I own a five-year-old car and must decide between keeping that car for an extra year or buying a new one. We will ignore inflation for the moment and assume that both cars cost $5,000 new and both have sale prices as shown in table 6. The sale value numbers in that table are synthetic but realistic, and are based on the fact that cars generally depreciate at about 25 per-

Table 6. Depreciation and Foregone Interest Costs on a Car Costing $5,000 New (in today's prices)

At End of Year	Sale Value	Depreciation for Year[a]	Foregone Interest for Year[b]	Present Value of Sale or Trade-in Value[c]
First	$3,000	$2,000	$150	$2,913
Second	2,250	750	90	2,122
Third	1,688	562	51	1,544
Fourth	1,266	422	38	1,124
Fifth	949	317	28	819
Sixth	712	237	21	596
Seventh	534	178	16	434
Eighth	400	134	12	316
Ninth	300	100	9	230
Tenth	225	75	7	167

[a]Depreciation is calculated as the difference between the second column amount and its value at the end of the previous year. If we allow for inflation, the numbers would be smaller, and foregone interest at market rates higher. First year also includes a $1,000 dealer's margin.

[b]Three percent of value at beginning of year.

[c]See the 3 percent interest rate column of table B in appendix 1 (p. 233).

cent per year. The table also shows depreciation, foregone interest, and the present value of sale value—all of which can be calculated directly from the sale value numbers.

The costs of keeping my used car for an extra year include depreciation and foregone interest, as well as operating and repair costs and insurance premiums. As shown in table 6, the depreciation and foregone interest costs of keeping a five-year-old car for one extra year are $237 + $21 = $258. The one-year depreciation and foregone interest costs of the new car are, of course, much higher: $2,000 + $150 = $2,150. If I have to borrow money to buy the new car, then I have to also add in the excess interest charges. This is unfair to the new car, of course, charging the whole trading cost to one year, and it ignores some differences in operating costs. On the other hand, I would be kidding myself to compare the ten-year average cost of the new car with the average yearly cost of five more years of the old one, unless I have some compelling reason to expect to keep the new one much longer than I am thinking of keeping the old one.

So, to keep myself honest, I must compare one more year's cost of the old car with the six-year average costs of a new one. The latter does not require calculating a lot of present values of depreciation and interest; I can shortcut by deducting the present value of the trade-in after six years from the original $5,000 price and dividing by six: ($5,000 − $596)/6 = $734. The question then is whether the style, safety, luxury, economy, new features, and freedom from bother of the new car are worth $734 − $258, or $476 a year.

There would, of course, be some savings in operating and maintenance costs on the newer car. But even major prospective repair and maintenance costs on the old one probably will not amount to more than one or two hundred dollars per year, on the average. In addition, insurance costs would be lower on the older, less valuable car, since collision insurance never covers more than the market value of a car (chap. 9).

All this might seem relatively simple and obvious, except that popular books on family finance tell you to trade in "when the cost of upkeep begins to outrun the cost of depreciation," which is either meaningless or wrong. It is meaningless to look only at the present car and ignore the alternative, and certainly wrong to compare part of total cost with another part. The United States government was also misleading when it wrote:

> The longer he keeps the car, the greater are his savings in depreciation. But after the first two years he begins to face a series of outlays for tire and battery replacements, repairs, and incidentals that more than offset his savings in depreciation.[1]

If the statement means that the difference in operating cost between the present car and (the average yearly cost of) a new one kept the same number of years tends to get larger than the difference in depreciation, then it might make partial sense. But the data given by the publication also include periodic replacements, ignore the cost of the money tied up in the car, ignore the trading costs, and divide by an ever-smaller number of miles driven, which makes the cost per mile look larger.

A number of credit unions, supposedly cooperatives run in consumers' interest, quote the Department of Transportation as suggesting trading for a new model at the end of two years. What is worse, some suggest financing this two-year turnover with a "balloon note" loan where the remaining loan balance owed at the end of two years is as large as the value of the car. What this does is maximize the amount on loan, maximizing the interest costs as well as the depreciation and trading costs. In the case of our $5,000 car, these latter three costs amount to a whopping $1,375 per year.

Calculations similar to those we discussed for trading in for a new car can be used to compare buying a new car with buying a used car. I must again start honestly by predicting how long I shall keep a car. If it is to be six years, then I must compare the six-year average cost of a new car with, say, the three-year average cost of a three-year-old secondhand car. And I cannot use table 6 for the *cost* of buying a three-year-old car. Although I could sell one for $1,688, I am likely to have to pay about $2,200 to buy one in equivalent condition.[2] Subtracting the present value of a $712 sale value three years hence (0.915 × $712, or $651) from the $2,200, I get $1,549, or $516 per year for the used car, compared with the $734 per year we already estimated for a new car kept six years. These calculations take account of both depreciation and interest, except that if I have to borrow, there will be extra interest charges on the new car.

---

1. U.S. Department of Transportation, *Costs of Operating an Automobile* (Washington, D.C.: Government Printing Office, 1972).
2. See any National Auto Dealers Association *Official Used Car Guide* for wholesale and retail prices. The older the car, the wider the difference.

Again, I must ask whether the extra repairs on the used car will more than offset that difference, or reduce it to where the joy of a new car appears cheap. And it depends on how I value my time spent fussing with a car, the cost of repairs, and whether I have another car to reduce the inconvenience of breakdowns.

Remember that the current cost of acquiring or keeping a car minus the present value of what I can get for it when I trade it in is the same as the present value of the streams of depreciation and foregone interest at 3 percent during the period. I can ignore inflation, because if depreciation is smaller in current (inflating) dollars, the market interest rates are higher. Since inflation is erratic and unpredictable, it is simpler to work in "real terms" or "constant dollars," adding only the higher interest costs of borrowing instead of using savings. Annual costs are 28 percent per year, whether that is 3 percent interest and 25 percent depreciation or 13 percent interest and 15 percent depreciation because there was a 10 percent inflation.

With older cars, the differences between buying and selling prices, and between market values and use values, lead to some unusual choices for families with more than one car. It would be good to have one fairly new, large, dependable car for trips and highway driving; but when that car gets old, trading it in for a smaller, used car to serve as the second car would save little or nothing. Yet buying another large new car leaves the family with two large cars. Even high gasoline prices do not change this situation appreciably. Indeed, a simple calculation will reveal that it is hardly ever worthwhile even to buy a new smaller economy car just to save on gasoline. The higher capital costs will swamp the savings in gasoline costs. Of course, once trading is worthwhile, then selecting a smaller car saves depreciation, interest, and operating costs.

A possible alternative to a second car is public transportation. Whether public transportation will appear more advantageous in the future is hard to say. There are other costs and problems with public transportation, particularly the cost of the extra time taken in travel and waiting. It always seems that the bus arrives one minute before I get to the bus stop and every fifteen minutes thereafter! A major deterrent to using public transportation is that once I own a car I need consider only the extra (marginal) cost of driving it to work. And if I pay for parking by the month or year, even that cost is not affected by one trip more or less. Only drastic measures such as a heavy tax on parking spaces and the use of the revenue to provide free, frequent public transportation would have a chance of altering our socially and economically inefficient but personally pleasurable driving habits. The air-conditioned car with automatic transmission makes the contrast with public transportation even more dismal.

When During the Year?

Almost peculiar to cars is the annual model year, with the emphasis on changing at least the exterior every year. Secondhand cars are sold largely by their model year with relatively little attention to how long they have actually been in use. This leads to some implications about the best time of year to buy a car.

A common advertising slogan is "Your old car will never bring as much on a trade-in as it does right now." What the ad does not say, of course, is that the price of a new one will also never be so high again, since it is also depreciating, and by *more* dollars per month. The actual bargained price on a new car is not constant, but falls gradually as the time of a new model's introduction approaches. The recent rapid inflation has caused car companies to raise the sticker prices of new cars several times during the model year, but the inflation-adjusted prices still fall during the year. Regardless of inflation, a car does not start wearing out until it is put in use. So should I buy late in the model year to save money, or early to get a lot of use out of the car before the new models drive down its price?

The answer depends on how long I intend to keep the car. If I keep it for ten years, its market value will be very small and will depend more on its condition than on its model year. So buying late in the model year will give me the same real service at lower initial cost. On the other hand, if I intend to trade in every few years, the model year is more important than mileage, or condition, or the length of time the car has been on the road. In that case, it pays to buy early in the model year, getting as much use as possible before new models reduce the price. To put it another way, end-of-model-year bargains reflect the market's style obsolescence, not a decline in use value. If style is what matters to an individual, those discounts are no bargain.

That the depreciation in market price reflects far more style obsolescence than physical depreciation, particularly with cars, means that those people willing to concentrate on the real services provided (transportation) can reduce their costs by keeping each car a long time, or by buying used cars after their market value has fallen well below their use value. There is always the risk of getting a bad car, and the cost of repairs is going up. Yet many of us consider the irritating and unpredictable repair expenditures to be much more important than they are. It pays to keep track of them to make sure perceptual distortion is not operating.

There are also choices as to how fancy a model to buy and with how many accessories and special features. Price differentials tend to overprice these "extras," a kind of price discrimination that allows those who have money to spend it. Comparing trade-in prices according to special features indicates that the price differential narrows; the extras depreciate faster than does the basic car. The standard remark often made is that the manufacturers make their profits on the accessories, and the dealers on the credit.

Other Durables

Most smaller appliances and durables have little or no resale value, so their total cost is price plus operating costs; the cost per year depends on how long they last. Benefits per year depend on how much they are used. One argument for a gas clothes dryer over an electric one is that the costs of each use are lower, so I am encouraged to use it more, so I get more benefits without affecting how long it lasts.

What can be said about a durable that costs twice as much and lasts twice as long (such as special auto mufflers)? In fact, they are roughly equivalent if you keep the durable for the longer time period. The depreciation and interest cost per year are identical and the average amount of money tied up is the same; the only difference is two trips instead of one to the muffler shop. But if I trade the car in, I may never need the second trip.

The largest potential difference in cost of appliances may well be in the differential likelihood of breakdown and the need for major repairs. In recent years, Consumers Union has been securing repair experience on cars and some major appliances from the readers of *Consumer Reports* and summarizing the results in the *Reports*. Even though the readers are above average in income, education, and probably critical acumen, the differences between brands should not be biased by that. There is the difficulty that data on two years of repair experience are available only on two-year-old models, which may differ from the current models. To reduce this problem, *Consumer Reports* also attempts to check whether major design changes have taken place.

We return in chapter 11 to problems of consumer information, and in chapter 10 to some strategies for shoppers. Of course, all such calculations may be outweighed by the lure of some new piece of equipment. A calculation of the number of likely days of use of a snowmobile per year times its expected life in years would reveal a rather expensive form of recreation for most owners. A tennis racket is likely to get more use, particularly with the explosion of indoor facilities.

Shopping around for durables is likely to pay off, particularly when combined with some watchful waiting, because dealers' margins are substantial, and there are sales. There is a tendency for the "best buys" reported in *Consumer Reports* to be difficult to find, and for the low-rated models to be available at greater discounts. What to look for is the best combination of price (low) and quality (high). In really competitive markets higher prices would indicate higher quality in almost all instances, and the consumer would only need to decide how much quality was worth paying for. But in many markets there are some high-price, low-quality possibilities, which everyone wants to avoid. Once again, a few careful shoppers can improve the market for the rest of us, allowing the best buys to prosper and eliminating the bad buys.

Benefits

We have said little about estimating the benefits that durables provide, because in most cases they are so difficult to quantify that we can only set differential costs of alternatives against their differential benefits. But sometimes the benefits can be given an economic value. An appliance might save time, which can be valued at some hourly rate. It might also save money. One can evaluate a clothes dryer by computing the difference between its total costs and the present value of the savings in laundromat charges and time, and comparing that difference to the differential satisfaction and other benefits.

Sometimes the decision to own an appliance depends heavily on estimated use. A gas clothes dryer costs more to buy but less to operate than an electric clothes dryer. Obviously, the heavier the use over which the fixed (purchase) costs are spread, the greater the advantage of a gas dryer. Rising costs of energy mean that the best design for appliances like washing machines may change. In Europe, where electricity and hot water have always been much more expensive, washing machines are more complex and cost more to build and maintain, but are more economical in their use of hot water and electricity. They allow more alternation of agitation and soaking. With the United States government already requiring that consumers be given information about the energy demands of new appliances, manufacturers may well begin offering consumers a choice between the old models and newer models that cost more initially but save energy. The consumer must then calculate, on the basis of how much the machine will be used, which is the most economical, and then add other considerations such as more concern for future generations than even current high energy prices represent.

The economics of a food freezer are more complex. It reduces the number of required shopping trips, increases flexibility of planning and menus, and allows saving of leftovers. It is often touted as allowing stocking up on bargains. All these savings must be compared with the costs of the freezer—depreciation, interest, electricity costs, and possibility that a family might eat more expensive things by stocking up on luxuries. On the other hand, stocking up on bread and freezing it may reduce trips to the store and the impulse purchases that go along with them, and this might encourage greater use of staple foods. The whole issue of stocking up and of large-size economy packages depends on what it does to consumption as well as to costs (chap. 10).

A philosophical issue arises about benefits when a new appliance or piece of recreational equipment appears. If people find they cannot get along without it, are they better off than before? Or were they "brainwashed" by advertising or by their friends and neighbors? At the other end of the scale, the rapid style obsolescence and frequent upgrading of appliances leaves a supply of old, very cheap ones that are still serviceable, or could be with little work. Repairing an appliance is simpler than it once was, because whole components can be replaced. Repair people frequently suggest replacing an appliance when, with a few repairs, it will serve for many more years.

Shared Ownership or Renting of Durables

Some equipment is used only at rare intervals, and one way to reduce its cost is to share its ownership and use, particularly if the cooperators are not all likely to want to use it at the same time. Lawn mowers and sailboats are likely to be wanted by everyone on the same weekends. There can also be a problem of maintenance and repair, because "everybody's business is nobody's business." The group might well want to pay one member to be responsible for maintenance and repairs.

The organizational problems of owning things cooperatively are apparently larger than the economic and tax advantages. Commercial rental businesses have developed to take advantage of the economic efficiencies, renting power tillers, rug shampooers, power chain saws, party glassware, and hundreds of other rarely used appliances. There has always been a big rental market for such things as boats and summer homes. Some stores even lend a spreader when they sell lawn fertilizer, hiding the rent in the price of the fertilizer. This is still a bargain for the person who fertilizes his lawn once a year and does not have storage space for another piece of equipment.

Do-It-Yourself Repair and Maintenance of Appliances

Most modern appliances come with detailed parts lists and diagrams showing how they are put together. If you save these, it is often possible to locate the trouble, get at it effectively, and replace the offending parts. The cost of labor for diagnosis and repair is so high now that all the repair person generally does is replace whole components, even when only a small subcomponent is broken. In the case of cars, it is often possible to buy the component at a junkyard, or to get a rebuilt rather than a new one.

You can start to learn how to fix things and also avoid some frauds by watching the repair people and by keeping the replaced parts. Examination of the part can teach you exactly what went wrong and assure you that the repair person was not replacing parts just because it is fast and easy and because most people do not object to paying for new parts. It is easy to condemn repair services for replacing parts that were not bad, but a little thought will show that it might actually save money in wages to waste a little in parts. If it costs $16 just to get a repair truck to your house and $16 an hour for the truck and repair person, then putting in $10 worth of parts, only half of which were really needed, might be justified to save half an hour or a second trip.

An advantage of investing in your own skills in diagnosing and repairing is that since you are around when the trouble starts, you often have better information with which to diagnose the trouble and more time to experiment. Indeed, detailed knowledge of a particular appliance and why it stopped working may well allow less expensive repairs. You are less likely to replace a whole appliance when only a new pump motor is needed. Needless to say, it is possible to get in over your head, particularly with complex electronic equipment.

The surprising thing, considering the double taxation on the division of labor and the advantages of being able to fix things without waiting for a repair person, is that there is so little of this do-it-yourself activity. Division of labor and specialization apparently really do make people more efficient and productive.

Additions and Repairs to the Home

Investing in home modernization or repairs involves the same economic calculation of a cost and comparing it with a benefit. The benefits are difficult to quantify but often last for many years and, even when discounted to a present value, can be very great. The costs are likely to involve substantial amounts of time, because there are complex problems deciding just what to do, even if you hire someone to do it, and problems of supervision. Hence, even apart from the advantages of the tax-free income from doing your own work, there is a saving of the cost of the communication and negotiation needed if you were to hire others to do the work. And some of the investment in learning how to do things, or how to get them done, can pay off in greater efficiency in later similar activities. One gets confidence in tackling new tasks, an ability to find out from library or friends or experts how to do it, and the proper balance between caution and courage in making decisions and acting. The best craftsmen are often so busy that they are happy to tell you how to do it yourself.

There are other sources of information. *Books in Print* lists well over a thousand books whose titles begin "How to . . ." and there are many more that will tell you about carpentry or electric wiring or drywall construction, and so on. They must be chosen carefully, because many such books tell you just enough to encourage you but not enough to keep you out of trouble or to allow you to do the job right. Local building codes exist, with the necessity for permits and inspections if the alteration or addition is extensive. Most inspectors are quite considerate of people who want to do things themselves; they even give advice. For very extensive work it may be wise to engage an architect on an hourly basis as a consultant to help with the original plan and even to draw some plans. Given most state laws about architects, however, it is unwise to contract with an architect for a whole job until hourly consultation has at least led to agreement on the plans and scope and a lot of confidence in a good working relationship. Otherwise, you may be obliged to pay the architect a percentage of the amount bid on the work even if it is not within your stated budget limits, the design is unacceptable, or the work is never done.

Additions to a home may or may not improve its sale value. If you intend to stay in the home for a long time, very idiosyncratic changes for your own needs may be worth it even if no buyer would appreciate them. Changes that bring a house up to modern standards—for instance, adding a second bathroom or a whole family room—may seem expensive but are the most likely to be recoverable in the sale price.

Sources of Information

Shopping is one obvious source of information on durables (chap. 10). There are various sources, discussed in chapter 11, of market information and background information on what to look for. There are manuals of used car prices, based on dealers' auctions and other information, giving retail, wholesale, and "loan value" prices on cars by make and year model, with adjustments for special equipment. Dealers do not like to share their copies of the National Automobile Dealers Association manuals of prices (which come out monthly, separately for each region of the country), but the more forthright ones will do so if pressed.

Product testing agencies like Consumers Union have also started reporting evidence on actual as against list prices for appliances, reflecting the confused nature of the market. Sometimes discounts reflect difficulty selling an item, or a manufacturer's policy in setting a published price, or the imminence of new models. For most appliances there is a range of models within each brand with different special features and different prices. It often seems to be the deluxe models that are discounted most. How is the consumer to decide whether the extra features are worth it? Some of the descriptions in the mail order catalogs are useful, but mostly it is a matter of personal judgment. If the washing machine has a way to save the wash water for a second load, will you have a tub to hold it, and is hot water supply enough of a problem so you would use it? Do you want to save on a dishwasher by omitting the feature that adds a wetting agent to the last rinse, and then have water spots on your glassware?

The price structure for smaller appliances is more complex than most people think. Besides the seasonal sales, there are "discount stores" that post "list prices" higher than they actually are, so that their "20 percent discount" is really closer to 10 percent. There are also catalog discount houses with no store costs, shipping from warehouses or even direct from the manufacturer at much larger discounts. This is common in specialties like hi-fi and camera equipment, and the ads usually appear in the specialty magazines. The guarantees are usually honored by the catalog houses, but you may have to ship a defective durable back and wait a long time for a replacement or refund. Some of what you pay for at a retail store—information, advice, and help in securing warranty repairs—may be worth it!

Information about quality and durability is harder to get than information on prices, and may be more important. A washing machine that lasts five years instead of ten and has twice as many repair bills is no bargain at half the price. The consumer may find it difficult to decide whether the fancier appliances are giving more durability and better service or merely special features and style. As mentioned earlier, *Consumer Reports* summarizes the experiences of its own readers with repairs and reports this regularly along with results of laboratory tests on cars and some major appliances.

You may wonder why there is not a detailed account here of some of the tricks used by sellers. It is not because they do not exist, but because they are endlessly varied and constantly changing. For the most part, they rely on carelessness, gullibility, or avarice on the part of the buyer. A modest amount of shopping and the knowledge that really big bargains are unlikely should go a long way.

Students experimenting with the effects of shopping and bargaining report that simply standing and hesitating, or returning after visiting another dealer, often results in some recalculation of the price or special offer that lowers the price. They also report that sellers like to suggest alternative features, muddying up the price comparisons. Or they want you to believe the bargain will not remain available long enough for you to make sure it is a bargain. It is a great help to specify precisely what you want; otherwise, price comparisons get very difficult.

Two tricks, however, are so frequent that they deserve to be mentioned. "Bait advertising" means advertising a huge bargain that the store doesn't have, immediately runs out of, or resists selling, and then switching the customer to something "better." The classic example used to be the $29 used sewing machine. "Low balling" refers to offering a low price which is turned down by "the manager" after the customer is committed emotionally; it assumes that once committed you will stand still for another $100. Whenever you run into the more extreme forms of "bait advertising" or "low balling" it pays to leave immediately and report it to the nearest Better Business Bureau.

There are special problems of low-income families in buying durable goods. This is partly because of the combination of a need for credit and a poor credit rating, and partly because of their concentration in subsidized housing projects or slums and their isolation because of inadequate public transportation and language barriers. The studies made, however, deal with prices, not with profits of the sellers. Given the problems of stores in low-income areas, it is not at all certain that profits are higher there. On the contrary, stores tend to move out of such areas. While it remains true that low-income people do suffer from disadvantages in buying durables, these disadvantages are not *necessarily* accompanied by anyone's profit advantage but are dissipated in higher costs.

The Timing of Acquisitions

Assuming that I have applied the analysis of investment theory to estimate costs and benefits and to establish priorities for my purchases of durables, how do I space the acquisitions so as to avoid spending too much too fast? And how do I compare durables with the nondurable items of current consumption in terms of benefits? Is a Christmas trip to Mexico better than buying a canoe? How do

I value my estimates of future joy from a canoe, or do I discount them heavily for uncertainty?

Survey data show that families spend substantial fractions of their incomes on cars, durables, and additions and repairs to houses, and that the proportion does not vary much with income or with age. By the time the family gets one of everything, it starts replacing things or finding new items that seem attractive. A safe estimate would be that 15 to 20 percent of income should be allocated for the durable goods capital account. Young married people have difficulty in pacing their acquisitions, as evidenced by the fact that a substantial fraction of personal bankruptcies occur when family income is rising but within a few years after marriage. Apparently the desire to acquire everything at once plus difficulty in coordinating two people's plans and desires leads to overcommitment.

The use of some budget total, plus some priority list to determine the order of acquisition, should be sufficient. We have already suggested (chap. 5) that the family might want to have a separate savings or checking account into which they put some fraction of their income and from which they purchase durables. By buying the next one only when the capital account showed sufficient cash, the family would be earning a little interest between purchases instead of paying interest (at a much higher rate) all their lives.

More Information on Durables

There is frequent change in the design and quality of cars and durables, in addition to the stylistic model changes; prices and availability are even more variable. Some information, though not usually naming brand names, can be expected from the Consumer Product Safety Commission and the National Bureau of Standards, and even from the Army specifications for their purchasing. But the most useful quality information comes from consumer-run product testing organizations like Consumers Union, which publishes the monthly *Consumer Reports*.

A great deal of information, for the most part stressing only the positive, is in the articles and ads in various enthusiasts' magazines devoted to cars, hi-fi, trailers, motorcycles, or general mechanical interests, such as *Popular Mechanics*. The ads in these magazines and those in the *New York Times* by New York "wholesale" or "discount" stores provide some indication of the extent to which products are being discounted. Trade association publications are also useful.

CHAPTER NINE **Risks, Insurance, and Estate Planning**

Everyone at some time must make important choices about whether or not to buy the service called insurance, and about what types and combinations are the best. These choices involve substantial amounts of money and require sophisticated decision making. Fortunately, understanding a few simple principles vastly improves the chances of making the proper choices.

Some Principles

Life is full of uncertain events, some of them pleasurable, but many of them potentially destructive or unsettling in their effects. When the uncertainty is regular enough so that we can assign a probability of its happening during some period of time, it is called a risk. When such a probability is reasonably independent between individuals (i.e., when the event is not contagious or does not affect many people at the same time, unlike an atomic bomb or hurricane), then it becomes an insurable risk.

Insurance eliminates the risk for any one person by pooling it with the risks of large numbers of individuals. The insurance company itself bears almost no risk of loss and has ways of coping with what little risk is left, as we shall see. The elimination of risk is possible because the accuracy of our ability to predict probabilities (e.g., the number of accidents or deaths or the amount of average loss) increases with the number of individuals exposed to that risk. Suppose we have an age group that, according to mortality tables, loses 2 percent to death each year. If we took one hundred people of that age, we should expect that two of them would die in a year. However, there is an appreciable chance (one in fifty) that five or more would die, a very large relative error. If an insurance company could increase the pool by selling policies to 10,000 people in that age group, then the chance that 500 or more (5 percent) will die drops from one in fifty to one in five hundred. (In general, the range of likely variation in the percent who die decreases with the square root of the number of policyholders.)

For the individual, then, insurance can be thought of as exchanging the possibility of a large loss for the certainty of a small cost (the insurance premiums). It is clear that insurance is worthwhile when the possible loss from one's own assets is intolerable. We can apply the traditional economist's argument against gambling here. That argument says that even a fair gamble at even odds is not a good idea because the value of money per dollar diminishes as one has more of it. Hence, the added utility from winning $10,000 may be less than the loss in utility from losing $10,000. So a fifty-fifty chance of winning or losing $10,000 has a negative value. In most insurable situations, a few not-so-valuable dollars spent on premiums provide compensation against losses so large that some of those lost dollars are much more important than the premium dollars. It is not only a matter of being unable to bear the entire loss, but also whether the cost per dollar of that loss is greater than the cost per dollar of the premium. To avoid the one chance in a thousand of losing my $50,000 house is worth more to me than a $50 insurance premium.

Major Risks

What are the major risks a household faces that might require insurance?

☐ A major earner might die too early, leaving dependents.
☐ You or your spouse might live longer than you anticipated, and exhaust your savings (see chap. 5).
☐ A major earner might become permanently disabled, requiring care for him or her and provision for dependents.
☐ A mother might become permanently disabled, requiring care for her and care of children.
☐ A child might become permanently disabled, requiring extra care, and for a much longer period than a child is normally dependent.
☐ The house or its contents might suffer from fire, theft, or other damage.
☐ The car might be damaged or stolen.
☐ You might be sued for damages to others done by your car.
☐ You might be sued for damages suffered by others on your property.
☐ Anyone in the family might require extensive medical care, including psychiatric treatment.

Decisions about insurance for these risks, however, must be made against a patchwork background of overlapping and confusing possibilities and programs. Some insurance is already provided by the Social Security system, by semi-voluntary group insurance connected with some jobs, etc. In addition, some losses may be compensable through a civil suit (suing someone else) or through collecting from someone else's insurance company, or through worker's compensation. The problem of insurance, then, is to cover the worst holes in the patchwork of coverage you already have.

How Much Insurance?

Insurance is necessary when the possible loss from one's assets is intolerable. It may be desirable whenever a possible loss is not easy to plan and budget for. But how much insurance? If the possible loss, say of future income in the event of an earner's death or disability, is much greater than the amount that dependents would need to be comfortable, then insurance need cover only the latter, smaller amount. On the other hand, insurance should not attempt to provide more than the potential loss. If it did, the insured would be worth more dead to survivors than alive! Insurance companies do not like to insure for more than the amount of "insurable interest" for this very reason. Life insurance should at most make one's survivors financially indifferent to whether or not one dies; no more. The amount of insurance then should be the smaller of two amounts: the amount to be lost, or the amount required so that the loss does not create suffering.

A common misconception is that insurance decisions should depend on how probable the event is. Actually, neither the need for insurance nor the amount of insurance needed depends on that probability. This misunderstanding is one of the reasons people buy airplane trip insurance, feeling that because the probability of dying is a little higher, more insurance is called for. In fact, the probability has nothing to do with the amount of insurance needed, or with the decision whether to insure at all. If an unbearable loss is possible, beyond the capacity of other resources to cover it, then insurance is called for, provided it is available at reasonable rates. In fact, the cost of special short-term insurance like flight insurance only *appears* reasonable, because the period covered is so short that the probability of death is very low. The premiums cover a great deal of administrative and selling expense spread over very little insurance and also cover the possibility of adverse selection (people taking out insurance when the weather is bad). In fact, nearly three-fourths of the premium for flight insurance is expense and profit.

Availability

Reasonable insurance rates ought to reflect the amount to be paid if the insured event occurs, times the probability that it will occur, plus some additional amount to cover insurance company expenses and a reasonable profit. The following conditions should be met if insurance is to be available at reasonable rates.

1. *There is a clear definition of the event insured.* It is usually easy to define death; it is difficult to define mental illness and disability. Hence, the premium rates for the latter must allow for expensive claims investigation, and even perhaps some fraud, which makes them very high.

2. *There is efficiency and competition in the insurance business.* There are some clues as to the efficiency of the insurance company: What fraction of revenues is paid out each year in benefits? If it is less than half, meaning the expense-profit "loading" is more than half, that insurance is probably not a good buy. Other less conclusive clues are: Does the policy pay only if other sources do not, or reclaim its payments from other sources? If so, it is valuable only if there are not other sources. Is it a fairly standard policy, so that price competition can operate, or highly differentiated by special options? Does it list what is covered rather than what is not covered? It is easy to exclude most of the real risks this way. The best policies cover everything *except* a specific list.

Policies of a type that is renewed regularly will have lower prices than those with high lapse records.

The individual company may have better rates if it sells mostly large economy-sized policies, has good experience and steady growth, and maintains a good balance between low expenses and good individual service.

Group policies avoid agents' fees, reduce administrative costs, may well be negotiated at advantageous rates, and may be an even greater bargain if an employer absorbs some of the costs.

3. *There is no adverse selection.* If only those people likely to collect the benefits carry the insurance, it is not a good buy for the average person.

4. *The probability of the event is not affected by the fact*

of insurance. Are you more careless or more likely to be sued because you are insured?

5. *The cost of the event is not raised because you are insured*. Does the doctor or hospital charge more because you are insured? Do auto repairs cost more when insurance pays? Or will the doctor keep you in the hospital longer when he or she knows it does not cost you anything?

6. *The risk is the same for you as for others in your insurance rate group*. Are you a better driver than most, or younger than most of those in a group life insurance group with fixed premium independent of age? If so, you are paying for others' higher risks.

7. *The cost is as high for you as for others*. If you can repair your own car or get a discount on doctor bills, the loss to you would be less than what it would cost the insurance company.

8. *The cost of repairing the damage is not more than the loss*. If your car is so old it would not pay to fix it if it were damaged, why pay for insurance that provides for such payments? You might enjoy getting the insurance money and using it for something else, but you would be insuring the car for more than it is really worth. Dents reduce use value and even trade-in value by less than the cost of repairing them perfectly.

Even "unreasonable" rates can be worth paying, however. In spite of the many ways in which insurance is priced above the actuarial value of the possible loss, it may still be desirable, particularly for the largest, unbearable losses.

The largest total losses possible are certainly those resulting from the permanent disability, mental or physical, of a main wage earner, since they involve extensive extra outlays for medical care as well as the loss of earnings. Yet difficulties in defining the condition of permanent disability and the fact that insurance itself may affect probabilities and costs make it impossible to insure adequately for these risks. A floor is provided by Social Security benefits for the permanently and totally disabled, covering a fraction of the income loss but none of the medical bills. If the disability is the result of a work injury, the employer's worker's compensation insurance may cover extensive medical costs and some fraction of income loss. But attempts to cover the remaining risk by private insurance are unlikely to be successful. Insurance companies are still wincing from their experience in the depression of the 1930s when a man could get more in disability payments than he could earn.

Life Insurance Needs

When is life insurance called for? When there is some stream of expected earnings that could stop and there are dependents who are counting on part of the future stream for their support. Nonmoney "earnings" from housework and child care are to be included too; we are discussing both parents' insurance needs here.

How much life insurance is called for? Recall that the amount needed is the smaller of two amounts: the amount to be lost, or the amount needed to prevent financial hardship to survivors. In most cases, the smaller of these two will be the needs of dependents, so it is not usually necessary to insure against the loss of the total future stream of earnings. Some part of those earnings would have been consumed by the deceased, and the remainder may well be larger than the dependents need—after other sources of support are considered, especially Social Security survivors' benefits. The needs of dependents, then, should be the basis for calculating life insurance needs. Since these needs are spread over many years into the future, it is necessary to estimate their present value—the amount required at death to assure such a future stream of support for dependents. Future needs must be discounted to present values, but at what interest rate? As elsewhere, we can use a relatively low rate of discount, 3 percent, on the argument that a rate of return any higher would imply an inflation that would erode everything but 3 percent; the real value of assets rises only by about 3 percent per year, on average.

Generally, the amount of life insurance needed is the present value of the dependents' needs less the other financial resources available to cover those needs. Besides the Social Security benefits, accumulated savings and other assets are also available, and these increase with the age of the insured. Needs vary too, depending upon normal living expenses, educational goals for the children, and the one-time costs associated with the death of the insured—funeral and burial expenses, taxes, and legal expenses.[1] How, then, can we calculate the amount of life insurance required?

In a childless household where husband and wife both work and neither depends on the other's income, there seems no purpose in life insurance on either spouse, unless

---

1. For a useful "worksheet" approach to calculating insurance needs, see Consumers Union, *The Consumers Union Report on Life Insurance*.

one or both gave up some career plans on a promise of shared accumulation of assets. But if there is a child or children, one or both parents must devote time to them: a great deal for the first five or six years, somewhat less for the next twelve to fifteen years. If one partner stays home to take major responsibility for the children, it may be difficult for her or him to find a good job even after the children are gone. (Furthermore, if a surviving spouse does go to work, he or she loses Social Security survivor's benefits, though not the benefits for the children.) Thus, there is a need to insure against the difference between what the survivor could earn and the total needs of the survivor and dependents.

There are, crudely, three periods of need for a family with children: one when there are children to care for, offset by some Social Security survivor's benefits; a second after the children have gone but before the survivor is sixty-two, during which period the survivor can work but gets no Social Security survivor's benefits; and a third when the survivor is too old to work but can get Social Security survivor's benefits. Of course, there are possibilities that the needs will be met by the remarriage of the surviving spouse, or with help from the earnings of children; but most partners are likely to want to provide enough to allow the survivor independence.

Surprisingly, the net yearly amounts for these three periods of need are likely to be very similar. Suppose that the total needs amount to $10,000 per year. If Social Security in the first period, earnings in the second, and Social Security again in the third are about $4,000, then unmet needs are $6,000 per year. How much would it take to provide $6,000 a year for a survivor now aged twenty until death? The answer depends upon the interest rate used and also upon assumptions about expected length of life. As before, we use our 3 percent interest rate rule. Life expectancy is not a serious problem; the risk of living too long can be reduced by purchasing a lifetime annuity that provides a constant stream of income until death.

Annuities are based on an average expected lifetime. For example, on the average, a twenty-year-old woman will live another fifty-six years. (Of course, those who survive until they are sixty-five can expect to live until they are eighty-two, rather than seventy-six, because they have already passed certain of life's hazards.) How much would you need now, if it could earn 3 percent interest until you used it, to provide $6,000 a year for fifty-six years? The present value of such a stream can be found in the tables of the value of $1 per year in appendix 1, p. 233, or elicited from inexpensive pocket computers. Again, we assume that if prices increase, you can earn a higher interest rate to offset that occurrence, something which is not always true these days. Small differences in the number of years of expected life do not affect the present value of the need much, because the extra year is added to or subtracted from the distant end of the stream, and the present value of $6,000 fifty-six years from now at 3 percent is only $1,146. Fifty-six years of $6,000 is worth $161,793; fifty-five years would be worth $160,647.

When there is need to provide for children as well as one's self, the amounts per year are likely to vary, but adding that responsibility to the amount of insurance needed now is simply a matter of calculating the present value. To avoid calculating and adding a separate component for each year, you can often take sets of five or more years, calculate the value of the annual amounts at the beginning of the five year period, then calculate the present value of that sum now. Take the five years when a child is expected to be in college, starting fifteen years from now. The value of $5,000 a year for that purpose, for five years, at the beginning of college, is not $25,000 (because you earn a little interest on it till it is used) but $22,899, and to have that amount available fifteen years from now, you need only $14,698, the rest coming out of interest accumulated over the fifteen years.

The Family Life-Cycle Pattern of Needs

At any point in time, the sum of the needs of the surviving parent and each child gives the amount needed to assure support of dependents if one spouse were to die at that point in time. But what happens to insurance needs as both parents survive each additional year? Obviously, the needs go down, because each year completed is one less year of obligation to worry about. But it is not correct to assume that the insurance needed drops each year by the amount that dependents would have required for that year. This is because all the other sums needed in the future are a year closer and consequently have a higher present value.

This does not mean that the drop in needs each year is unimportant enough to be ignored, however. The annual amounts are large, particularly during the early years when support is also needed for children, so the total amount of insurance needed drops by a substantial amount with each year successfully negotiated without death. As we shall see, it is possible to purchase insurance protection which decreases over time to match the decreasing pattern of needs.

It is sometimes suggested that the amount needed does not really drop each year, because of inflation or because family standards of living go up. We have already taken account of the first of these by using a low discount rate. Inflation will raise future living costs but will also increase the rate of return to the investment of death benefits by one's survivors. The second can be allowed for in calculating the amounts needed at later points in time, but it is unlikely that any adjustment in standards would reverse the overall tendency for the total amount of insurance needed to drop with each succeeding year.

Insurance needs depend upon total income needs of survivors, but they fall as other sources of income increase. The only other source we have taken account of is Social Security, but most families accumulate company pension rights and other assets. While these assets may be intended to supplement Social Security retirement benefits, they are available to support the survivor if one partner dies before retirement. *Any savings program that will accumulate enough to support a husband and wife in retirement will have sufficient funds long before the date of retirement to provide for a widow or widower.* (This assumes something that is almost universally true: that any company retirement plan turns over the accumulated contributions and interest to the survivor if the person dies before retirement. It also assumes that the worker has the wisdom to arrange the retirement annuity so that about two-thirds of it continues to the survivor so long as she or he lives.) The implication is that the provision for the risk of living too long also helps provide for the risk of dying too early, and *the net need for insurance drops to zero several years before expected retirement age*. How can this be true when the surviving spouse has years more to live (particularly a wife, who is likely to be younger and has a longer life expectancy)? Because by then the other accumulated savings and rights will be sufficient to take care of the survivor.

The implication of accumulating assets for insurance planning is that the decrease with each passing year in the amount of insurance needed is accentuated by any amounts saved during that year plus the accumulated interest (and employer contributions) to those amounts. If the need for insurance begins when the first child is conceived, reaches its maximum amount when the last child is conceived, and drops to zero by, say, age sixty, then what is needed is an insurance policy or policies which provide this kind of lifetime pattern of insurance coverage. Notice that the Social Security survivors' benefits are in this form—so much per year for the period of need.

Life Insurance Needs for Equal Spouses

The whole set of assumptions about financial responsibility for children and surviving spouse needs careful reexamination, partly because the world is changing—more women working, more men taking day-to-day caring as well as financial responsibility for children—and partly because we have all been guilty of undervaluing housework and child care. Families today vary from the old stereotype of a male earner and female housekeeper to the new, rarer, partnership of two who share everything equally, including child care, housework, and regular jobs. We have already looked at the insurance needs of the first kind of family. Now we will plan an insurance strategy for the equal partnership.

If two parents contribute equal dollar value of work to a family, whatever the mixtures of money and nonmoney, what would a surviving spouse need to maintain the family standard of living? The total real income is cut in half by one partner's death, the needs cut by the value of the needs of one adult. In general, eliminating one adult cuts the cost of living by more than one-fourth and less than one-third, and cuts income by less than half after income taxes. But because income taxes ignore nonmoney earnings, they fall more when the loss is in money earnings; the survivor may want to switch from work at home to work in the marketplace, too.

The question is how much the parent was contributing to the family in money and work, how much of that would need to be replaced somehow, and what sources of help other than life insurance could be counted on. Social Security is one, lower income taxes another. It might seem that a woman's longer life expectancy would call for more insurance on the husband; but her better treatment as surviving parent under current Social Security law works the other way, so the really modern equal partnership probably needs roughly equal amounts of life insurance on each parent. The insurance should provide, with Social

Security and other income from assets, a total family income of about two-thirds of what the income would have been with both partners alive. This means replacing one-third to one-half of the deceased's expected income.

What kind of contractual commitment might embody the implied financial responsibility of each parent to the children? Two eventualities need to be covered: death or departure. The analysis above indicates the amount of insurance required in case of death; this kind of a plan can take advantage of Social Security survivors' benefits and other resources. Divorce or departure requires more extensive compensation, because there is no Social Security or life insurance available. In this case, the amount required for equal protection would be the required life insurance plus the present value of the Social Security survivors' benefits. Since both are based on amounts per month for the remainder of a period, the commitment could be expressed as some amount per month for the remainder of the period until the children are all grown, or so much per month for each child until the child is twenty-one. This would leave the spouse who takes responsibility for the children with flexibility and freedom to work for money or not, and would provide for the children should both parents die or depart.

Given the residual inequities in our laws and customs, a woman in particular would be well advised to insist on such a protective commitment from a man for each child they have. And if it is true that the number of women deserting families is increasing, a man might want a similar commitment from his equal partner.

Types of Life Insurance

The pattern of changing amounts of life insurance needed over one's life span is the sum of a series of separate needs, each jumping to its maximum the instant an obligation is incurred (e.g., by marrying or conceiving a child), and then declining to zero as the period of commitment passes. In a modern family with two roughly equal earners, the commitment to a spouse may not start until there is also a commitment to a child, since it is then that both partners commit themselves to joint support of the child. The result is that the amount at risk is usually at its greatest at the point where the last child is born, declines rapidly as the children grow up and leave home, and declines slowly after that, reflecting the obligation to the spouse who gave up savings, if not some career possibilities, to raise a family. If there is inflation, that may seem to offset some of the decline in needs, but the principle remains.

What types of policies are best to meet these needs? There are two general types available from insurance companies—term insurance and cash value insurance. Term insurance provides pure life insurance: If you die, your survivors receive the "face value" of the insurance policy; if you do not die, then you and your dependents receive nothing. Cash value insurance combines pure insurance with savings. The "face value" of the policy is paid to your survivors if you die. But also a savings fund accumulates during the life of the policy so you and your dependents can receive an increasing fraction of the face amount ("cash surrender value") if you choose to cancel the coverage. "Whole life" is the most widely sold form of cash value insurance.

Term Insurance

Term insurance is pure insurance with no savings mixed in. It can be purchased for one-year, five-year, ten-year, or longer intervals. Rates rise with renewal because you are older and can expect higher mortality. By paying a higher premium, one can guarantee that the term insurance can be renewed for another term, regardless of one's health. The amount of insurance provided by term insurance need not be constant each year. *Decreasing term* insurance, as the name implies, provides a decreasing pattern of coverage. It is the exact analogue to the Social Security survivor's provisions for wife and dependent children; both provide a stream of benefits from time of death until the end of a period. The amount of insurance in a term policy is simply the present value of the stream, so it drops with each passing year as the period to be covered gets shorter and shorter. The premiums can be kept constant during the term because the decreasing amount of insurance for the most part offsets the rising probability of dying, small accumulated reserves offsetting discrepancies.

Some combination of such decreasing term policies can provide exactly the pattern of insurance each year that is needed for a family, leaving them to accumulate their savings some other way, more flexibly and with a better hedge against inflation. To cover the changing needs spelled out in our earlier example, one policy for each spouse, providing $6,000 per year for the remainder of the forty-year period, plus one for each child providing for a twenty-year period, would be sufficient. Why only forty years for the spouse? Because forty years from now you will have reached age sixty, and other accumulated assets plus Social Security should have become sufficient to take care of one spouse. After all, they were accumulated to take care of two people, and only one is left! Remember, the stream of net needs may be sixty years long at the beginning, but drops to zero in forty years.

There may be some situations where heavier needs are expected some years hence, leading to a total need that does not decline much for several years. Renewable level term policies are available to meet this pattern.

Whole Life Insurance

A typical whole life policy with a face value of $50,000 provides $50,000 in life insurance only during its first year. After that, a reserve which is part of what your survivors get if you die builds up and hence substitutes for part of the $50,000. A crucial fact is that the amount of insurance provided by the policy is not the face amount of the policy. Rather, it is the difference between the face amount and the cash surrender value, since the latter is available to you even if you don't die. A great many conceptual errors about life insurance can be avoided by keeping that fact constantly in mind.

The fact becomes clearer if seen from the company's point of view. The aggregate amount they must charge the policyholders as a whole to pay for each one who dies is the face value of the policy minus the reserve, which is the policyholder's own money. The policy has a declining amount of insurance each year, made up for by the policyholder's own accumulated savings plus interest. Does the declining pattern of insurance match the declining pattern of insurance needs faced by most people? Unfortunately not, because the amount of insurance needed drops by far more than these accumulated savings go up. So even if one were willing to have all his savings tied up in a life insurance policy, most policies do not provide the needed pattern of protection. Besides, most people want some of their savings in the form of equity in their house, others want some in a more accessible form like savings accounts, while others want theirs in investments that are more likely to increase in value with inflation. A whole life policy is used as a forced saving program by many, but the money saved through a whole life policy is not likely to earn as high a return as it would if it were invested elsewhere. And, anyway, the *pattern* of insurance provided is not optimal.

Another way to look at policies that combine insurance with savings is to see what happens each year in the life of such an insurance policy. Policyholders make two kinds of payments—an explicit premium payment and, implicitly, the interest earned by the insurance company by investing policyholders' reserves. These amounts are used to cover four kinds of costs to the insurance company:

1. The pure cost of the pure insurance, paid out to the survivors of those policyholders who died. This amount is roughly the probability of dying times the face value minus the cash value.
2. Expenses (including agents' fees) and profits of the insurance company (roughly 20 to 30 percent).
3. Increase in the policy reserve and in the cash surrender value.
4. If the policy is a "participating policy," there is a dividend payment to the policyholder from the company. This, of course, is paid for by the policyholders in the first place. A dividend, then, refunds some of the excess premiums.

A variety of whole life insurance policies is offered, differing chiefly in the rate at which a reserve is accumulated and in the amount the insurance is reduced each year. Ordinary life insurance policies may become "paid up" at age eighty-five, or sixty-five, or in twenty years. "Paid up" means that the reserve is large enough that the interest earned on it is sufficient, without additional premiums, to cover three of the four items just mentioned: the pure cost of the pure insurance, the expenses and profits, and the continued increase in the reserve. The term "paid up" means no more premiums are required, but it is misleading, because the policyholder is still paying, in the form of the interest that the company is earning on his or her own money.

The sooner a policy is to be "paid up," the larger the premiums must be so that the excess can increase the reserve and thereby decrease the amount of actual insurance (and thus, the pure cost of the pure insurance). And the earlier the *age* at which the policy must be paid up, the smaller the total accumulated reserve must be, because the probability of dying is lower. The real cost of insurance is not affected by any of this. It depends on the amount of pure insurance, the probability of dying, and the company's expense-and-profit loading—not on the amount of saving built into the policy. *It is crucial to keep in mind that the premiums are not the only cost of the policy and that the face value is not the amount of insurance.*

Some policies do not just become "paid up" but can be cashed for the face amount after a specified period, sometimes as short as twenty years. These are called endowment policies and simply have such huge premiums that by the end of twenty years the accumulated reserve is equal to the face value, and there is no real insurance at all. Policies taken out on children to provide for their college education are of this sort. They combine a savings program with insurance that drops to none by the time the money is needed for college.

The crucial point about all cash value policies is not that they combine insurance with savings but that they do it so rigidly. The only way the amount of insurance is reduced over time is by building up an equal offsetting savings reserve. To meet this objection, some insurance companies offer "family income" or "mortgage protection" policies which combine the usual ordinary life insurance with decreasing amount of pure insurance. A few have gone the whole way, providing straight decreasing term insurance ("income protection").

New policies combine insurance with a large, flexible amount of investment which can be shifted between a mutual fund and a high-yield, liquid money fund. Such a neat tax advoidance device may well run into trouble with the Internal Revenue Service. Without the tax advantage there seems to be little reason to combine the insurance and investment.

There are a variety of other special provisions in whole life insurance policies, but they are largely selling devices and methods of making it difficult to compare prices. Each provision has an actuarial value that is often difficult to estimate. Some are totally unjustified.

"Mortgage protection" policies, for example, add to the face value of the life insurance an amount equal to the remaining mortgage on the house. But what is there about a mortgage that changes the amount dependents would need for their support? Nothing. This is just one example of the folly of insuring bits and pieces, or treating some needs as different from others, rather than insuring to cover the total need. For a small added sum one can have a "disability waiver of premium" clause, which continues the policy without further premiums if the insured should become permanently and totally disabled. This is not a proper disability insurance policy, but only the small amount of disability insurance needed to pay the life insurance premiums. But what is the point in carrying life insurance on someone permanently and totally disabled? Unless a disability insurance policy replaces some of the lost earnings, there is no longer a stream of future income that will stop if the person dies. Indeed, a stream of *costs* will end if the person dies; the survivors, sad to say, would be better off economically if the person did die. It would make more sense to cash in the policy in the event of disability, unless one felt certain the person would die shortly. But that would be gambling, not insurance, and only emphasizes that keeping such insurance makes the person "worth more dead than alive."

For other (nonproducing) family members, there is no point in life insurance. If children were really expected to repay their parents' "investment" by supporting them later, life insurance on the children might make sense. But the loss occasioned by the death of a child is usually emotional, not economic. Yet many poor families carry insurance on everyone in the family or, worse still, everyone except the main earners. A small amount might be justified as burial insurance, but even this violates the principle that the cost of the event should not be increased by the fact of insurance. Funerals tend to cost what the insurance will pay.

Evidence on Life Insurance Costs

Despite vast assemblages of published details about premiums, dividends, and cash values, the complexities of policies make it difficult to compare prices. The prices of cash value insurance policies are especially difficult because those policies combine insurance protection and a return on savings. It is impossible to price both simultaneously. One can make assumptions about the return on savings and then calculate the implied price of protection. "Twenty-year net cost" figures exemplify this method, assuming a zero interest rate. "Interest-adjusted costs" assume some rate like 5 percent. The alternative is to calculate the return on savings after making assumptions about the price of the pure insurance. Prices of term insurance are used for this purpose. Although the interest-adjusted cost and return-on-savings methods produce a similar ranking of actual insurance policies, the rate of return calculation would seem to be more useful to consumers, who can then compare that return with the return on alternative financial investments.

Twenty-year net cost is arrived at by taking the premiums for twenty years, subtracting estimated dividends (based on past experience or on the present rates), and then subtracting the cash surrender value at the end of the period. It should be clear that this is not a true cost estimate, because the interest earned on the reserve has been omitted. This becomes obvious sometimes when the twenty-year net cost comes out negative! Furthermore, even for the same kind of policy, it is easy to make the net cost figure low by charging slightly higher premiums and thereby accumulating a larger reserve, which earns more interest *and* reduces the pure insurance costs by reducing the amount of real insurance. One can also make net costs look low by paying no dividends for the first two years, which has the same effect without even making the premiums higher. Note that such rapid accumulations of reserves do double duty: they not only earn interest but also reduce the amount of benefits that must be paid out of premiums, because each death benefit has a larger component of the policyholder's own money.

In response to objections to the ignoring of interest in twenty-year net cost comparisons, interest-adjusted cost indexes were developed, tested for consumer acceptance by the Federal Trade Commission, and are published annually by the National Underwriter Company. The particular interest rate used will, of course, affect the absolute and even relative insurance cost estimates of the individual companies. The use of 5 percent for 1979 when market interest rates were 6 to 12 percent clearly makes the insurance look cheaper than it is, and makes insurance policies with larger saving features look better than others. Indeed, the complexity of policies with saving features and dividends allows a variety of manipulations to make them look cheaper, and a continuing battle goes on within the industry about this, particularly through the efforts of Joseph M. Belth and his publication, *The Insurance Forum*.[2]

The insurance cost-adjusted interest rate on the savings in the policy is the alternative way of pricing cash-value insurance policies, less subject to manipulation and more understandable to the consumer. Such estimates of return

---

2. *The Insurance Forum* is published monthly by Insurance Forum, Inc., P.O. Box 245, Ellettsville, Indiana 47429.

on the savings element in cash-value life insurance were proposed many years ago by M. Albert Linton. Recent discussion suggests that even they can be misleading unless carefully interpreted. But most such studies reveal rates of return that are generally, but not always, smaller than passbook savings account rates, particularly over short periods and for older nonparticipating policies taken out when interest rates were lower. (Interest earned on insurance policies escapes income tax, so these calculated rates of return on savings are comparable to the after-tax rates of return of alternative investments.)

A recent (1979) staff report of the Federal Trade Commission reaches very negative conclusions about the pricing practices of insurance companies.

The life insurance industry is a major repository of consumer savings, holding over $140 billion in 1977. Yet in 1977, the industry paid its policyholders less than 2 percent on their savings in a year when the rate of inflation was around 10 percent and in which all other savings institutions were paying higher rates. Life insurance companies paying 2 percent *after twenty years* compete successfully against companies paying 5 percent. Penalties for early withdrawals are remarkably severe but unannounced. We recommend that the life insurance industry be required to disclose the rate of return and several other items of information to their policyholders in a simple and effective manner. Price competition can only be effective when some significant fraction of the market is *able* to compare prices, and this is what the disclosure system is designed to do.[3]

The report points out that the rate depends on how long one holds a policy since various administrative costs are being spread over various numbers of years, but chides the companies for ignoring the service charges entirely when announcing rates of return on annuities. It also points out that the profits of the insurance industry have not been excessive. This raises the question of how more price competition would produce a net benefit for all consumers. Presumably, the improvement would result partly from consumers making better choices to meet their own needs, but largely from driving out inefficient companies and forcing increases in efficiency on the rest. The report also points out that federal regulations have kept interest rates paid by banks and savings and loan associations down to 5 and 5.25 percent when open market interest

---

3. U.S. Federal Trade Commission, Bureau of Consumer Protection and Bureau of Economics, *Life Insurance Cost Disclosure* (Staff Report) (Washington, D.C.: Government Printing Office, 1979).

rates were 9.5 to 10 percent, and even the latter were barely covering the current rate of inflation. Inflation has served to dramatize and amplify the extent to which regulation and lack of competition have injured consumers who saved their money in traditional ways, like insurance and savings accounts.

Rules of Thumb

Some rules of thumb about life insurance needs might be useful, even though they do not apply to all situations. Let us assume that the decision to purchase life insurance is made at the point when a couple is in their twenties. Both partners assume that they are making some commitments and career sacrifices and should have some claim on their partner's future income (or an equivalent amount if the partner dies or departs). Assume also that for each child conceived, the commitment increases by the amount each partner is expected to contribute (in time and money) to the raising of the child.

Each spouse or partner should start with a forty-year decreasing term policy on his or her own life that replaces about a fourth of his or her market and nonmarket income. That fraction is somewhat arbitrary but represents an estimate of the amount that is sacrificed in a marriage or other partnership. Since the present value of a forty-year stream is twenty-three times the annual amount (see app. 1), this means the initial insurance amount in the policy should be about $23 \times 0.25 = 6$ times the person's income. Thus, a spouse earning $20,000 per year should have about $120,000 worth of forty-year decreasing term insurance. For each child, a twenty-year decreasing term policy should be taken out by each parent, replacing some eighth of his or her income. Since the present value of a twenty-year stream at 3 percent is about fifteen times the annual amount, this means the initial insurance amount in the policy should be about $15 \times 0.125 = 2$ times each parent's income. Hence, for a family with two very young children, each partner should be carrying a set of decreasing term policies with starting insurance amounts equal to about ten years' income.

As time passes, the needs decrease, but so does the amount of the insurance provided in a decreasing term policy. Only changed family obligations or inflation will alter the picture. In the case of inflation, additional policies, also decreasing term but only for the remainder of the period, can be taken out periodically. The amounts in the supplemental policies should be enough to provide annual incomes equal to the inflation rate times the annual incomes provided in the original policies. For example, suppose five years after the initial purchase the price level is 20 percent higher. Then each partner needs an additional thirty-five-year decreasing term policy equal to 0.20 times 6 times initial income and an additional fifteen-year decreasing term policy for each child equal to 0.20 times 2 times his or her initial income.

What about real increases in income and in living standards? These can be handled as similar to inflationary increases. But rather than treating inflationary and real income increases separately, we can assume that increases in nominal income reflect both inflation and rising standards of living. Then additional policies (for shorter remaining periods) could be taken in amounts equal to the percentage increase in income times the original income amounts.

Social Security will cover some of these insurance needs. Social Security survivor's benefits are like decreasing term insurance since they pay so much per month until the children leave home or school or reach eighteen. But they assume that after that the surviving spouse needs nothing until retirement, and they provide a benefit based on previous income only up to a modest level. The present value of the expected survivor benefits can be estimated with information from a local Social Security office and subtracted from the total insurance need.

More Details about Life Insurance

One of the reasons so little has been said here about shopping for life insurance is that it is far more costly to buy the wrong type or the wrong amounts of insurance, or to insure the wrong people, than it is to select the wrong company. Insurance companies are heavily regulated, particularly in some states, so that almost any national company licensed to do business in a large state like New York is safe. If you are looking for decreasing term insurance, the problem is more one of finding a company that handles it in proper varieties than of finding the cheapest one. The use of twenty-year net cost figures, even interest-adjusted, tends to make the price differences look dramatic. Yet a careful examination of comparative pricing done in different years shows substantial instability in the ranking of insurance companies over the years. And as we said earlier, even the interest-adjusted rates are imperfect measures.[4]

There are some "bargains" in insurance: GI insurance, savings bank life insurance in a few states, and group life insurance negotiated efficiently and competitively and with minimum fees by an employer or some organization. In a period of rising interest rates, the right to borrow on one's reserves at a fixed low interest rate may be an advantage. Conversely, a policy taken out when interest rates are high may have options to convert it to an annuity at a favorable rate that make the policy worth keeping. Both of these possibilities are more likely with nonparticipating policies, where the company's errors in predicting future interest rates cannot be offset by a reduction in the dividends.

It is important to know that some life insurance agents sell insurance for more than one company and hence may be better able to advise you about their differences. But there is probably no better way than to decide how much insurance you want and of what kind, then to price it with different companies. It also pays to keep in mind that the agent's fee is a substantial part of the first year's premium and a small percentage of renewal premiums, so creating a flexible decreasing term coverage by buying multiple policies and dropping some may well prove to be inefficient.

To summarize the main points again:

1. The amount of life insurance needed is the smaller of two amounts—the amount needed by survivors, or the present value of the amount of income lost less what the deceased would have consumed.

2. Accumulations to handle the risk of living too long also serve in case one partner dies early, and should be deducted from insurance need.

3. Every year passed is one less year of risk, so the amount of insurance needed tends to start high and decrease, usually to zero long before retirement, because savings to take care of two people in retirement are enough for one long before retirement.

4. Life insurance policies with savings features are unlikely to provide the proper pattern either of saving or of insurance with the passing years. Insurance need drops faster than savings can accumulate.

---

4. For a shopper's guide, see *The Consumers Union Report on Life Insurance,* 4th ed. (Mount Vernon, N.Y.: Consumers Union, 1980).

5. Pricing a joint product is always difficult. Combining savings with insurance confuses people, since the amount of insurance is not the face value of the policy but—at most—the face value minus the cash value. Ignoring the interest earned by the company on the accumulating savings underestimates the cost of the policy.

Automobile Liability Insurance

Next to death or disability, the next largest risk an individual faces is probably the risk of being sued for damages to other people's property or persons resulting from negligent operation of his or her car. People feel so strongly that auto accident victims should be compensated that there is pressure to use the damage suit combined with liability insurance as a way of doing this. In fact, laws dealing with damages (tort laws) stipulate that compensation is supposed to be paid to the victim only if the other driver was negligent and the victim was not also negligent (contributory negligence), or if the victim was also negligent, the other driver still had a last clear chance to avoid the accident.

Given negligence, the guilty driver is responsible for property damages, medical costs, lost income resulting from death or disability, and even a dollar amount for "pain and suffering." The present value of a stream of income lost through death or disability is potentially the largest of the amounts. Some delicate writings on the value of a human life arise from such cases, including estimates of the future earnings of young people whose educations have barely begun.

Since few individuals have assets sufficient to cover large damage awards, most carry liability insurance, although very few carry an amount adequate to cover major losses. For this reason, people have exaggerated notions of what they can collect in an auto accident case. Newspapers publish huge jury verdicts, many of which are never paid in full because they are later reversed or modified, or because the guilty driver has inadequate insurance, or none. And most payments made pursuant to court awards are larger than the much more numerous out-of-court settlements. In even more cases, there is no tort claim at all.

Many people have very few assets that can be attached if they lose such a case. Most have their savings tied up in retirement plans, a house, or life insurance. If one attaches (garnishees) their wages, they may well be fired, drying up that source. If a person has only $20,000 in liability insurance, all you can get from a suit may turn out to be $20,000 minus your own lawyer's fee of $5,000 or more. A suit is usually handled by a lawyer who takes a "contingent fee"—if the lawyer loses, he or she gets nothing—so it is difficult to get a lawyer to take a small case. On the other hand, the system does discourage a lawyer from taking on cases where liability is difficult to establish.

Despite this, however, the amount you can be sued for is not exaggerated. Many people innocently say, "Since I have only $10,000 in assets, I need only $10,000 in liability insurance." The absurdity is obvious: *you can lose your own funds if the award is larger than your insurance coverage*, e.g., if you have $10,000 in insurance and are successfully sued for $20,000.

The logic behind applying tort liability to auto accidents seems to be that accidents are the avoidable consequence of negligence, and the negligent should be punished. It does not work that way, of course, since insurance relieves the guilty driver of punishment and spreads the cost among all drivers, including the innocent. The guilty may be punished by higher insurance rates or for negligent homicide, but they are not really made to pay the full costs of their misdeeds. Spreading the costs through insurance was felt to be justified in order to assure that victims would be compensated, and by a system that put the costs of such compensation upon the activity of driving where it belonged. But the logic of this also was faulty. The easiest way to see why is to categorize accidents arbitrarily into two types: avoidable accidents arising from negligence, and unavoidable accidents that are simply the inevitable result of a lot of cars and the combinations of chance events.

Avoidable accidents are often uncompensated, and the largest and most serious ones are the most seriously undercompensated. The compensation comes mostly from insurance charges paid by the good, safe drivers, when it should come in part from a government that does not have the wisdom or courage to keep drunk drivers off the roads.

The unavoidable accidents, on the other hand, are not compensated at all; yet they are obviously part of the overall cost of driving and should be compensated out of charges on all drivers, in proportion to the extent to which they expose themselves and others to risk (mileage, safety of their car). Yet these costs are not put upon the activity of driving at all. Since the tort law applies only to cases involving negligence, the costs of unavoidable accidents are borne largely by the particular victims and whatever other compensation systems come into play (medical insurance, life insurance, disability insurance, welfare). A little is covered by collision insurance and auto passenger medical payments insurance, but not much.

From an economist's point of view, the auto liability insurance system leads to poor pricing and cost allocation and to erratic losses by the victims of most accidents, since guilt is often difficult to prove. In addition, the system itself introduces very high costs—costs of determining guilt, selling insurance, determining amounts of compensation, etc. Only a few cases go to court, and only a few of these go to trial and judgment, but expenses are very high, as in any adversary system. Auto insurance premiums themselves are more than twice the benefits paid out, and there are further court costs borne by the state.

A few states have passed some form of no-fault auto insurance law, but most are compromises and are still being fought by the trial lawyers.[5] A federal law has been proposed, but the outlook for major reform is not good, and the individual household has to face more immediate problems. Auto insurance rates keep rising with increasing costs of repair, of medical care, and of handling claims. Companies are trying to keep premiums down by getting rid of their bad risks—cancelling policies or raising rates of those with any accidents. Since the biggest risk is personal liability for damages and injuries to others, the important thing for the individual is to carry a very large amount of such insurance. The rates do not go up appreciably for the larger amounts. Since it is crucial to keep that coverage, it is obviously unwise to use one's insurance to pay for minor damages done in accidents that do not involve personal injury. In fact, coverage for such minor claims is illusory, since most companies raise rates after a minor claim or two, and can even cancel insurance, leaving one with no liability coverage. The sensible thing to do in minor accidents where one is at fault is to pay the damages directly (asking for three bids as the insurance company would), turning the matter over to the insurance company only when the other driver is unreasonable or the amount is very large (several years' premiums).

---

5. It has also been proposed that the no-fault insurance principle be extended to all kinds of accidents on an elective basis, cutting down on malpractice and product-liability suits.

Insurance for Damages to Your Own Car or Its Occupants

Besides liability, auto insurance policies also include coverage for theft of the car, for medical payments to occupants, and "collision insurance" for accident damage not collectible from someone else. The value of any of these depends on the amount at risk and on one's ability to shoulder the possible loss. It also depends on other sources of compensation. The main reason for medical payments is probably to cover one's sense of responsibility for occupants in those cases when the other driver involved in an accident cannot be made to pay, but the occupants may well have their own medical insurance. Theft coverage is reasonable until a car is four or five years old, at which time its value is not all that great.

The federal income tax law allows deductions from taxable income for casualty losses, so the value of casualty insurance is reduced because an uninsured loss net of tax reductions is less than the full loss the insurance would have to cover. For instance, suppose the probability of theft was 0.01 in a year, the car was worth $1,000, and your marginal tax rate was 30 percent. Insurance, with 50 percent expense loading, would cost about $20, but the actuarial value of the expectation of loss to you is 0.01 times $700 ($1,000 minus an estimated tax offset of $300), or $7, so the insurance would cost not twice its actuarial value but nearly three times.

Collision insurance also fails to meet many of the conditions that determine whether insurance is likely to be available at reasonable rates. Some of the drawbacks are:

1. *Adverse selection.* People who carry it are more likely to have claims than others. Careful drivers who do not expect accidents except when someone else is to blame are less likely to carry it. It is also probably carried more by people with very expensive cars, and the rates are not fully adjusted to the differences.

2. *The cost to the insurance company is affected by the fact of insurance.* Substantially higher costs are likely when the repair job is insured, and three "competing" bids will not solve this problem.

3. *The amount of insurance benefit payable may not represent the real loss.* The insurance must make good the damage (unless the market value of the car before the accident was less than this), but many a driver would prefer to use the money on a new car, or on something

else. If one has an old car, worth say $500, it makes economic sense to leave the dents in it, since they will reduce its trade-in value by far less than the cost of repairing them.

4. *There tends to be cheating on the deductibles, the garage writing a bill larger than its real bill by the amount of the deductible, and then excusing the customer from paying the deductible amount.* The expenses of claims adjustment and of keeping down cheating by repair garages or customers are substantial.

Buying Auto Insurance

There are differences in auto insurance rates among companies, but they are difficult to assess because some companies have a high first-year charge (covering most of the agent's fee), and others seem to have a practice of charging very low fees but raising them rapidly, particularly if there are any claims. Furthermore, you are paying for service as well as insurance. You want the company to be careful and not "taken" by absurd claims, and you need to know whether they pay valid claims promptly and fairly, either to you or to someone else. One source of information about this comes from questionnaires returned by members of Consumers Union and reported at intervals in *Consumer Reports*. They represent a very special group of alert, educated, concerned consumers, but their relative ratings of insurance companies should not be biased by that.

Insurance is also combined with other services in auto clubs. The quality of these clubs varies from state to state, as does the quality of their insurance, since the American Automobile Association (AAA) is really a federation of state auto clubs, each with its own insurance arrangement.

When the children start to drive, it may be necessary to reexamine insurance and shop again, since companies vary in their treatment of teenage drivers. When the family acquires a second car, there should be some discount because the total mileage (exposure) is not doubled by having a second car. (On the other hand, one must remember that with two risks a large loss can happen three ways: a large loss on either car, or a moderate loss on each of them.)

In response to growing public clamor against rising auto insurance rates, group coverage has been proposed, but this can save only a little of the agents' fees. Short of turning all compensation (whatever the cause) over to a single national system and taxing drivers for the costs which auto accidents add to that system, the most appropriate compromise solution seems to be a plan of no-fault, first-person insurance. In the meantime, the driver needs a lot of liability insurance and a skeptical attitude toward the other coverages. No amount of liability insurance is enough, given the open-ended nature of the possible damage claims. A person should carry an amount so large that no one is likely to win a damage award against him larger than that, provided he has anything at all to lose. This means half a million dollars, if one can get it.

Medical Insurance

Hospital and medical costs form a queer statistical distribution, with small costs for large numbers of people (or for most years for one person), but always the small chance of bills large enough to wipe out a family's assets. It is very important to make the distinction between the small, relatively predictable items that should be budgeted for rather than insured, and the large, rarer disasters that are a proper field for insurance. Historically, however, medical insurance has spread rapidly in a form that covered all illnesses but was limited to hospital costs, since these were more easily defined (eligibility being determined by doctors, legitimate costs more easily determined, etc.) A fear of discouraging people from seeking early care restricted the use of deductibles or even coinsurance. In negotiating plans for their members, trade unions stressed the coverage of small items lest their members be impoverished by a series of small bills; they were less concerned about the large catastrophes, since most of their members had no estates to lose anyway.

For anyone with any assets at all, however, and any flexibility to budget for mildly erratic costs, there is a strong case to be made for medical insurance that will cover the very large catastrophic bills, but with deductibles or coinsurance for the more budgetable risks to keep the premiums down. (Premiums are also kept down by reducing the costs of policing and of handling a lot of small claims.) There are problems of defining the unit for a deductible. The most sensible arrangement is probably to have the insurance cover the costs above some stated total in any three-month period, rather than trying to define one illness or incident. The policy should also cover the family as a unit, and not apply a separate deductible to each member. Coinsurance, where you pay some fraction (perhaps 20 percent) of bills beyond the deductible, is also suggested to motivate economy.

The familiar problems arise also with medical insurance: the amount used and the price may both be enlarged by the fact of insurance. Even where the doctor determines the length of hospitalization, he or she can easily be influenced by the presence or absence of insurance in making recommendations. There is evidence both that the uninsured get less care than they should have and that the insured sometimes get more than they need. Both the likelihood of needing medical care and the likely length of hospital stays increase dramatically with age, so insurance that does not adjust premiums with age may well be a bargain for older people and overpriced for younger ones.

The complexity of medical care and the open-ended nature of some risks have led to attempts to cut insurance premiums by excluding specific illnesses from policies. One might think that a policy which lists exclusions is bad. In fact, a policy which lists what it covers may well be worse. There are so many things to be covered that a policy covering "all medical costs except" will resolve all uncertainties in your favor and include all those things you would never have thought to look for in a list of covered illnesses or conditions. Of course, explicitly excluding the large risks is also likely to be disadvantageous, whether by name or by limits on the number of days in the hospital, or by the total amount payable. As in any insurance, a critical question is what fraction of the premiums (plus interest the company earns on them) is paid out in benefits. In the case of medical malpractice insurance, this fraction has been estimated to be 16 to 17 percent; Blue Cross group plans pay out around 97 percent.[6]

Worker's Compensation Insurance

You have no choice to make about it, but since worker's compensation insurance covers some of the same risks as other insurance, it deserves a brief discussion. Worker's compensation insurance is the earliest social insurance in this country, being introduced state by state starting early

6. A pamphlet on the loss ratios of 327 of the largest health insurers is available from the Research Institute for Quality Health Plans, 1611 Foster Street, Lake Charles, Louisiana 70601 ($1.50).

in this century. The state laws generally required employers of more than some minimum number of workers to carry insurance, or prove capacity for covering their own risk, to cover medical care and partial replacement of lost wages for workers injured in the course of employment.

What these laws really did was remove the right of a worker to sue his employer for negligence (e.g., unsafe equipment) in return for guaranteeing him a more limited compensation without question of fault. It was felt that employees would not dare sue their employers anyway, or could not afford the loss of income during the trial. It was also argued that it would be efficient since there would be no expensive court determination of either guilt or the amount of compensation. (It has not quite worked out that way, since workers often engage lawyers to fight about whether the injury was compensible—arose in the course of employment—or about the amount.)

On a broader scale, it was argued that such insurance properly placed on each industry the costs of its work accidents and saw to it that they became part of the price of that product. Experience rating by the insurance companies—raising rates on companies with bad records—was expected to induce companies to install safety devices.

The details vary from state to state, with the poorer states tending to have less adequate levels of compensation. Medical care is covered, but only some fraction of the lost wages is paid, in the belief that this will encourage return to work. There may even be a dollar limit on the compensation payments, which tends to become more and more inadequate as prices and real wages continue to rise. With increased coverage from other forms of compensation such as medical insurance, unemployment compensation, and liability insurance, state legislatures have been reluctant to improve worker's compensation benefits, particularly in the face of anguished cries that the rising insurance costs would put that state's insurance industry at a competitive disadvantage. Such worries demonstrate the difficulties of state responsibility, and attempts to promote uniform national standards have not succeeded.

Household Insurance

Like auto insurance, household insurance covers personal liability for damages sustained by others on your property—from slipping on your sidewalk, for instance—and compensation to you for casualty damage sustained from such causes as theft, vandalism, fire, wind, and hail. In addition to the usual rules of liability, householders with swimming pools or nice trees to climb face a doctrine of "attractive nuisance," under which one is responsible for what happens to young children even if they have been warned to stay away. Even so, the probability of being sued is low, except in our three most litigious states of New York, Florida, and California, so the cost of liability insurance is quite low. The amounts to be lost in house and furnishings are large enough to justify casualty insurance.

The other coverages are straightforward enough, usually including theft of such property as bicycles and lawn mowers and theft of personal belongings while traveling (within the United States). There are two complications. Many policies have a coinsurance clause, which says that if you insure for less than 80 percent of the current replacement cost of the property, then the insurance company will pay only the fraction of 80 percent that you insured. For example, if you insured your house and its contents for 50 percent of its market value, the company would pay only 50/80 of your losses. (This should not be confused with two other uses of the term coinsurance: where you pay, say, 20 percent of the costs, as with 80 percent coinsurance in major medical insurance; or the practice of insurance companies of dividing large risks among themselves, several companies jointly insuring each.)

A special risk is connected with buying or building a new house. The title to the land may be faulty, in which case the real landowner ends up owning your house as well, without having to pay for it. You can take out title insurance to cover this (see chap. 4).

In an attempt to cut selling costs and perhaps paper work, insurance companies have been selling "package policies," which cover several things at once. Whether they are bargains depends on the individual situation, but as in most package sales, it is difficult for the customer to make price comparisons and to know how much he is paying for what.

Household Behavior

There is evidence that many of us behave irrationally when risks are involved, overestimating likelihood of some events, underestimating the chances of other events. There is a lack of symmetry in our behavior toward the events with bad outcomes or good outcomes, and it would help us all to plan insurance if we understood our own foibles. Most people underinsure the largest risks, such as death of a main earner with many children, which explains why the survivor's benefits were added to the Social Security system rather early. Among those under forty-five and with children under six, who have the maximum risk, not one in ten carries as much as a few years' income worth of life insurance. At the other extreme, a substantial number of people with no children or who are retired still carry life insurance. Even with the example of Social Security survivor's benefits tailored to needs, many people still tend to accumulate more insurance as they grow older and more affluent even though their insurance needs are dropping. And many still purchase high-priced airplane trip insurance.

Gambling

Sometimes people purposely increase the risks in a situation rather than avoid, or insure, or bear them. There seem to be two reasons—the lure of a very large possible gain which might totally alter one's life, and the sheer excitement, often combined with a belief that one can beat the system. Even if one gambles for fun, the notion of "loading" (expenses and profit of the "house") is still appropriate. What fraction of the money bet ever gets won by someone, rather than appropriated by whoever is running the game? Except in a few areas where gambling is legalized (on-track betting on horse races, state lotteries), that fraction is difficult to find out.

Why should anyone gamble and carry insurance at the same time? Perhaps some believe the odds are better than they are, or that they have a system, or that they know a lot about horses. Perhaps the lure of a very large gain prevents people from seeing that, multiplied by a very low probability, it has a very modest "expected value." Some of the lure, as with bingo games, is social, plus a feeling that the profits are going to a church or other worthy cause. In American colonial days, churches were often built with the proceeds of lotteries.

More Information on Insurance

Libraries have compendiums of insurance companies listing their premium schedules and other information—Best's *Insurance Reports*, for example.

General treatments by Joseph M. Belth and by Consumers Union combine technical precision with good sense and readability. Insurance texts sin by omission, being directed toward selling insurance; the passionate critics are frequently careless and even incorrect.

A general agent who handles more than one insurance company, particularly if the firm also handles mutual funds, Independent Retirement Accounts, and other investments, is likely to be a less biased source of information about differences in companies and about policies with and without saving-investment features. If you know exactly what you want, it might be interesting to ask how much the agent gets out of the first year's premium, in case it might be shared with you, directly or in some other way.

Your state insurance commissioner has a list of approved insurance companies, and keeps a file of their reports giving total benefits paid versus total premium and other income; the ratio of the two should be of interest to you.

The Institute of Life Insurance serves the insurance companies but is a useful source of general information.

Funerals

Part of the cost of death and of the need for insurance is the cost of the funeral. Recurrent muckraking aside, it remains true that grief-stricken survivors often make decisions they would not have made in a calmer moment, and spend more than the deceased ever wanted them to. Religious institutions exist in an uneasy truce with the funeral directors, wishing their members would use the church or equivalent, but unable to intercede. There are even laws in some states making it illegal for a minister to negotiate a funeral with a funeral director.

In this situation, many concerned people advocate pre-planning and the depositing of instructions with some minister or burial society. Legally, these desires are not binding on the survivors, who may do anything they want, but they are likely to be useful. The instructions may include donating one's body to a medical school for research and teaching, or parts of it to eye or ear banks.

Over the years, laws have been passed in many states making it difficult for people to economize on funerals and impossible for them to engage in do-it-yourself burials. (One state passed a law making it illegal to bury someone within two days of death, in case an autopsy might be required to check for foul play, and then a week later passed another law which said that if the body was not buried within twenty-four hours, it had to be embalmed!) Bodies cannot be transported except in licensed vehicles; cremation may be illegal except in a casket; the list goes on and on.

Within all these limits and restrictions, it is still possible, particularly with a small cooperative society, to work out arrangements with cooperative undertakers. The important thing is that the plans be made by each individual in advance. Some burial societies arrange to take most of the burden of arrangements off the hands of the survivors. Others, formed in religious groups, actually arrange memorial services far more personal and appropriate than the commercial ones, often with testimony by the deceased's friends. The Seattle office of the Federal Trade Commission issued a handbook on how to do a local survey on the costs of burials, cemeteries, and grave markers.

Prepare Now, Go Later

Assuming that you have an adequate combination of assets and insurance to provide for survivors, and have made some plans or commitments about how your funeral is to be arranged, there are still some things that can be done to save taxes and to make things easier for those you leave behind. However small your "estate," the state laws will require some accounting and probably a formal probate to see to it that everything is accounted for and properly distributed. Everyone should do at least the first few things on this graduated list; the later ones should also be done by the wealthy:

1. Leave a set of financial records, including the location of will and other records, names of insurance agents and companies, stockbroker, lawyer, etc.
2. Leave a proper will for each adult on file with your lawyer, burial society, or bank—but *not* in a safety deposit box, which will be sealed when you die.
3. Have an agreement with one or two people to serve as executors of your estate, including their fees.
4. Make sure that the ownership and the source of funds for acquisition of every asset is clear.
5. Set up one or more trusts.

Before taking these up in order, some general remarks are needed. There is a federal transfer tax on the deceased's estate and on gifts during his or her lifetime, plus state taxes on the heirs' individual inheritances received and sometimes also on the estate itself. Since the state inheritance taxes are smaller and partly deductible as a credit against federal taxes up to a maximum of about 10 percent of the taxable estate, it is wise to ignore them at first and to try to minimize the federal transfer tax. The laws about ownership of assets, however, are state laws, so that we cannot be too specific about dealing with the federal tax.

Estate and gift taxes are not a worry for most people. By 1987, there will be no estate taxes for estates valued at less than $600,000. For those with estates larger than the limit, estate taxes can be minimized with gifts to children ($10,000 or less per child per parent per year) or with trusts. We will not detail the bewildering array of trusts that can be set up, although it is useful to distinguish "living" trusts, which entail management fees and tax reports before death, from a residuary trust that is set up before death but does nothing until the will places the estate into it. Trusts usually do avoid substantial estate taxes and some probate costs, but do cost something to set up and require expert legal help. Any active trust requires management charges and compensation for the trustee. Most advice about trusts and estate planning comes from trust lawyers, insurance salesmen, or "estate planners" (who are usually insurance agents). All of these types have something to sell, so the consumer needs to be certain that it is really needed.

In general, the whole process of estate settlement can be regarded as a ghoulish scramble for your assets after you die. Burial and legal expenses and executor's and probate and appraisal fees all come out first, and so reduce the estate tax; in a sense they come out of what the federal government would otherwise get. Since the marginal estate tax rates go up to 50 percent on estates over $2.5 million, it is easy to see why people billing an estate might feel that the federal government would pay much of the bill. State laws are often designed to maximize the amount of state revenue that is taken by reductions in the federal estate tax revenue rather than out of the net estate. Since state taxes are deductible before calculating the federal tax, this is easy.

Elaborating on our list of possible preparations:

1. Financial records are crucial for those who administer the estate. And the mere act of systematically recording transaction dates and sources of assets may uncover

gifts subject to tax, or allow proof that they were within the limit prevailing at the time. Prior tax returns are most useful, since they contain lists of assets producing income.

It is also important for survivors to know where your birth and marriage certificates are, the names and addresses of living relatives, and where your most recent will is. Your burial instructions and commitments or even prepayments should be where they will be found in time, even though they do not legally bind the survivors. (Survivors can take your money and give you any kind of funeral they like.)

2. A will is universally advised, even if it simply appoints an executor or executrix and makes sure that the surviving partner gets enough of the estate (tax free) to minimize taxes. A simple will is not expensive, and the recent changes in regulations regarding lawyer advertising has introduced some price competition into the legal market for routine services such as wills. Without a living executor/executrix appointed (often a resident of the same state is required), the state will appoint an administrator to do the same job and fix a fee for it. There will be an added cost of bonding the appointed administrator.

The main argument for a will is that without it state law specifies the distribution of the estate. Parents take precedence even over spouses, and a surviving spouse with children sees half or two-thirds go directly to the children. The court will appoint a guardian if funds go to minor children, and when one of the children dies, its *natural* parent inherits its money—even an estranged or divorced spouse!

3. There are fees set by the state for the executor/executrix or administrator, as well as for other things, but the former can be replaced by a more modest prearranged fee. This is particularly useful if a family member is made co-executor with a lawyer and there is an agreement with the lawyer about fees for legal services.

4. Given the possible liability for transfer taxes from an innocent act of buying some asset and putting it in joint tenancy, and the fact that assets in the name of the surviving spouse are entirely outside the estate, it is important to have a clear set of records. The fact that the source of a family's savings is ambiguous, and that the total could be attributed (at the margin) to either spouse, will probably be increasingly recognized by law; but in the meantime, the law can treat women badly by assum-

ing that all the money to purchase the house was provided by the husband.

The mere act of sorting out assets and ownership now may make it clear that something needs to be changed in order to reduce potential transfer taxes. It used to be that so few people had to pay estate taxes that they were hardly worth mentioning; since the deduction and exemption levels have been raised to allow for inflation, that time has returned. Merely distributing assets in the names of husband, wife, husband and wife jointly, and children, may be enough for most people, without the need to become involved with trusts at all.

There are many people in the United States who have accumulated substantial wealth in the last decades, without much, if any, help from inheritances. Many of them have doubts about the wisdom of bequeathing large sums to children, as distinct from investing in their education and training and initial ventures now. For these people, charitable bequests are an attractive option, again because such bequests are tax free. This means that a favorite charity can get a great deal more than the family would be able to keep after estate taxes. A wealthy man with a wife and no other close relatives can give half to the wife and half to charity and pay no estate taxes; or he could set up a charitable trust to support the wife until she dies, with everything going to charity afterward. Charity "bargains" may be even greater than those from giving now and saving on income taxes.

CHAPTER TEN **Meeting the Cost of Day-to-Day Life**

We have discussed the decisions households make about education, work, residence, saving, investing, and the major expenditures. As we go down the list, the things we spend money on involve smaller and smaller amounts of money and less commitment to the future, and so are worth discussing only if interesting or useful applications of economic principles are involved. We shall therefore not discuss every item in the consumer budget, but some important categories—medical care, food, clothing, transportation, recreation, recreational equipment, philanthropy, and repair services. Once again, some introductory discussion of principles is in order.

Priorities and Shopping

Having decided upon the amounts to be invested in self, durables, and savings, the household has an available sum of money to be allocated among its remaining consumption needs. A clear economic principle mentioned frequently earlier is that the cost of any expenditure is the value of the best alternative use of the money. Hence, I should push the expenditure in any one area up to the point where the added satisfaction from the next (marginal) expenditure in that area will produce less added satisfaction than an expenditure somewhere else. (The competing alternative of spending at some later time has already been taken care of in setting savings goals, although it may reassert itself at times.)

This way of looking at the choices is really simpler than asking "Is it worth the money?" because that shorthand rule assumes I always know what money is worth. But particularly in periods of inflation with differentially changing prices, I may have a distorted notion of whether something is a bargain. And besides, our rule places the decision to buy into a *choice* context, which properly deals with the opportunity costs involved.

The implication of this application of the principle of opportunity cost is that it is extremely useful to keep a rather comprehensive priority list of family needs, so that the priorities are set with forethought, and not by thinking about one need at a time. Indeed, opportunities for bargains are common enough that if one has a list of several high-priority next-needs, slight alterations in the order of acquisition may save substantial amounts of money. This is quite a different way of using sales from buying at bargain prices things that one had not even considered buying at all. Nothing is really a bargain if you do not need it.

A systematic listing and ordering of priorities also allows time to accumulate information on prices and qualities easily and efficiently in the course of other shopping, reading, or talking with friends. Setting such priorities, and even making sure that all the needs are simultaneously considered, will require some family discussion and collaboration. Adequate solutions to the problems of priorities among expenditures, and the compromising of the desires of different family members, probably make more difference in the total family satisfaction than shopping around for the best combination of high quality and low price. But shopping matters too. The ideal situation is to see something you need on sale, of a brand you have already decided is acceptable, and at a price you recognize as substantially less than has been available even at discount stores. A little systematic planning and a good memory can help make this happen.

Shopping includes the acquisition of information about a possible purchase, which, in turn, involves costs and benefits, not all of them easily measurable. Shopping costs are mostly time costs, plus some travel costs and perhaps the costs of books or magazines with information about the product or service in question. How much it pays to invest in shopping depends on expected benefits. The benefits may be partly psychic (e.g., the satisfaction of knowing that you got the lowest price), but even achieving the concrete economic benefits of a better quality or price requires the solution of a complex problem. By altering my idea of the actual quality and price variability, each additional bit of information I acquire can change the expected payoff to still more information. If I find that the first four stores I visit quote the same price, then I may decide that there are no bargains to be found and further search is not worthwhile. If I find a wide variety of prices, I may decide it is worth looking still further for an even better bargain.

In a classic study of shopping activity it was found that visiting more car dealers produced high but diminishing expected savings. More important, that study indicated that the bargaining skill of the purchaser had little to do with it. The implication is that it pays to shop around even if you are not good at haggling—and in the car market at that, where the conventional wisdom is that haggling is required.

There are a few general principles about when it pays to assume that large variations in quality or price exist. It always pays to shop around when other people typically buy a particular item or service in a hurry or in desperation (film), or on expense accounts (restaurants, hotels), or infrequently and without much expertise (cameras, hifi components), or where there is low turnover and great variety and hence high markups (furniture). Sometimes shopping does not help even here, if the demand fueled with other people's money (expense accounts) has simply driven up all the prices.[1]

We turn now to some important categories of expenditure.

Medical Care

Medical care is not the next-largest item of consumer expenditure after housing and durables, but it is one of the most troublesome for a number of reasons. Medical care has aspects of both current consumption and capital investment, since some of it is investment in one's future health. It involves both insurance problems and budgeting problems, the former already discussed in chapter 9. The household has problems of information and of strategy, not only in paying for medical care, but also—perhaps more important—in reducing the need for medical care, in getting proper care when it is needed, and in handling the income loss that may also be involved.

Reducing the Need For Care
A great deal of illness and disease is preventable, often at lower cost than the cost of cure. The most obvious exam-

1. For an enthusiastic but analytical study of how to shop and get redress, see E. Scott Maynes, *Decision-Making for Consumers* (New York: Macmillan Co., 1976).

ples of preventive care are vaccinations, inoculations, periodic checkups, and early diagnoses. People with very tight budgets or particularly bad eating habits also could benefit from improved nutrition; moreover, attention to proper nutrition is important even among the affluent.

Nutrition

Nutrition is too complex a subject to cover thoroughly here, but it is important to remember that a wide range of diets is still nutritionally adequate; the human body has a remarkable ability to adapt to variety. Also, there are complex interactions among nutritional elements which make it difficult to specify absolute ideal levels for each one. Often several elements must be present simultaneously for the body to receive the full nutritional benefits of each. In addition, it is difficult to know the nutritional composition of some foods, since it depends heavily on just where they were grown, how they have been treated since then, and how fresh they are. (Indeed, there is evidence that food grown in tropical climates is deficient in B vitamins.) A wide distribution of both food types and colors may be more important to adequate nutrition than a detailed, prescribed diet, because vitamin content is often revealed more by color than by food name, and variety minimizes the chances of imbalance. Most experts claim that for those who eat well and with some variety, supplementary vitamins are unnecessary and even wasteful.

Despite some fantastic claims to the contrary, there is no convincing evidence of unique health benefits resulting from the ingestion of a large excess of any one nutrient. In fact, nutritional deficiencies are encountered primarily in populations with a limited choice of foods, indicating that variety is important.

An individual who wants to get a proper protein intake with foods less expensive than red meat must do some complex planning and problem solving. The body can use protein only if the protein is properly balanced as to essential amino acid components, and some of the most popular substitutes for meat, such as soybeans, are quite inadequate by themselves. There are twenty-two different amino acids, eight of them essential in that they must be present in the right proportions if the protein is to be fully usable. Some can be manufactured in the body. What this means is that achieving a proper diet efficiently is a complex task requiring knowledge of what combinations of vegetable protein sources will provide a "complete protein" balance. Adequate supplies of vitamins, minerals, fats, and carbohydrates can be provided cumulatively, but protein balance must be at the same meal. The simple rule about combining a grain with a legume or milk product in the same meal is a handy shorthand way of remembering how to do it. Grains, nuts, and seeds are all low in some of the amino acids that are plentiful in milk and in legumes (soybeans, lentils, other beans). The grains—wheat, rice, barley, oats—are like the nuts and seeds, so the "beans and rice" combinations offer a wide range of possibilities for protein balance, as well as some fun in the experimenting.

The leading proponent of such diets has been Frances Moore Lappé, in her book, *Diet for a Small Planet*. Lappé gives recipes as well as the theoretical explanation. Using the less expensive sources of protein, rather than eggs and meat, has other advantages. It reduces fat intake and also helps reduce world pressure on land and resources; it takes several pounds of grain to produce a single pound of meat. However, lest you think that it is enough to know the chemical analysis of amino acids and the food combinations that provide a balance chemically, there is a substantial discrepancy among the chemical analysis, results of nutrition experiments on rats, and experiments with human beings. Foods that appear excellent chemically may perform poorly in practice, and vice versa. (For those who like peanut butter, it can be said that it is one food that seems to produce better nutrition than its chemical analysis would indicate!) The more general point is that nutrition research is not all that definitive yet. There is even reason to believe that individuals differ as to what they can metabolize effectively. We know, for example, that some of us lack the enzymes to digest cow's milk properly, and that some entire tribes manage to survive on apparently inadequate diets. Better diets may be made easier to attain by a number of new scientific developments. One is a cross between rye and wheat called Triticale, which contains more total protein and more of two essential proteins, lysine and methionine. Another is a cross between a cow and a buffalo that produces meat with less cholesterol. Some new animal feeds do the same thing.

Great attention has been given to reducing cholesterol in the diet because of its apparent association with heart disease. Unfortunately, many of the nonmeat protein diets proposed by conservation enthusiasts are high in cholesterol because of their reliance on cheese and eggs. Luxury foods like beef, butter, blue cheese, crab, and shrimp also tend to be high in cholesterol. On the other hand, it is the more expensive oils like safflower, sunflower, and corn oil that contain less saturated fat than the other vegetable oils. The hydrogenation necessary to solidify oils into hard margarine or shortening increases the proportion of saturated fat in all vegetable oils.

If you have solved the complexity of balanced proteins, there are still the minerals and vitamins, and the need for enough calories for energy. Calories come from carbohydrates, fats, or proteins and are of real concern only to those who need to gain or lose weight. But there are some twenty-three minerals, sixteen of them needed only in trace amounts (that includes iron), the other seven in less microscopic quantities, the most familiar being calcium. Obviously, a variety of foods is the only way most of us can be sure of receiving all those elements.

There are twelve important vitamins, some with two names, like ascorbic acid (C), thiamine (B_1), riboflavin (B_2), and pyridoxine (B_6). The four fat-soluble vitamins (A, D, E, and K) can accumulate in the system, and overdoses can be dangerous, whereas huge doses of vitamin C (as recommended, with inadequate evidence, by some) tend to flush right through. Again, eating a variety of foods seems the only way—without a large household computer—of assuring adequate nutrition. Experts like Jean Mayer recommend variety, moderation, exercise, and lower salt intake. The reason for cutting sodium is that it is associated with hypertension and heart disease and is certainly no longer necessary for food preservation, as it once was. Most of the other spices are safer and can substitute for salt.

The amount of each nutrient needed varies according to age and sex, and standards are recommended by two groups of experts, who give slightly differing advice. The United States Department of Agriculture's "Recommended Daily Allowances" are used in the Food and Drug Administration's dietary labeling regulations. The other "Recommended Dietary Allowances" provides more detail. It is issued by the Food and Nutrition Board, National Research Council, National Academy of Sciences.

Exercise
There is a growing belief that exercise may be even more important than diet in maintaining good health. High cholesterol may result from excessive intake of saturated

fat combined with nervous strain, but only when exercise is inadequate to burn it up. Of course, one should consult with a doctor before beginning any program of vigorous exercise.

The accumulating body of evidence about the beneficial aspects of exercise is impressive. There are even extreme examples of people overcoming handicaps of one sort or another by persistent effort. But single case studies are less persuasive than large-scale scientific studies. Perhaps the most interesting of these was a longitudinal study of London bus drivers and ticket takers, who worked for the company for many years and who were issued uniforms, requiring records of their weight and girth. Over the years, the ticket-taking "squirrels," who went up and down stairs on the double-decker buses collecting fares, remained slim and healthy. The drivers, who sat, got heavier and suffered far more heart attacks and other illnesses. One could argue that the London traffic caused the drivers a lot of nervous strain, but the "squirrels" also suffered strain, keeping track of a changing mix of passengers, dealing with unruly ones, and answering questions.

Another result of lack of exercise is "back trouble," variously referred to as lumbago, slipped disc, pinched nerve, neuralgia. Poor muscle tone or deterioration of the discs allows the fibrous discs between the vertebrae to slip and pinch the nerve fibers that run down through the vertebrae. The nerve then causes various muscles to go into spasm, which usually increases the pinching in a reinforcing cycle. The standard prescription—aspirin, heat, rest, and mild exercise when it is possible—is not only for comfort but to break the cycle. Most doctors say that a regimen of relatively simple exercises, regularly adhered to, will usually prevent the problem or a recurrence. It turns out that the prescribed exercises for lower back problems mimic those of pushing a lawn mower or hoeing a garden!

Older people tend to be plagued with circulatory problems, also made less serious with regular exercise. Analogies with animals are always imperfect, but there are very impressive studies of rats showing that they live a great deal longer when they are hungry and active much of the time.

One of the perils of affluence is that we tend to pay machines or other people to do all the things that exercise our muscles, leaving us with the tension-producing tasks like fixing things or earning the money to pay for them.

Even power steering and automatic transmission, for all their convenience, remove most of the mild exercise that driving used to call for. Substituting tennis or jogging or other sports tends to produce too much strain at irregular intervals, or for only selected muscles. Some real planning and discipline may be called for, particularly for those in "sedentary occupations."

Safety, Prevention, and Strategy

Avoidable accidents account for some medical costs, because people seem to undervalue the probabilities that they will occur, or the possible costs if they do. The evidence on the value of seat belts is clear, but apparently not convincing. People still leave overturned boats to swim for shore, go boating without life preservers, and live with frayed electric cords and other hazards. Would they buy a lawn mower that is safe but costs twice as much? This raises the tricky question of whether laws should mandate expensive safety.

Preventive medicine is proving especially necessary for world travelers, particularly when they leave a highly sanitary society, and the germs from which they have developed immunity, and expose themselves to new dangers. Virulent strains of malaria, typhoid, amoebic dysentery, and hepatitis are the main examples of diseases arising from travel in countries with less concern for sanitation.

Much is written about checkups and preventive medical care, and they are important. Yet going through a full inventory of available tests is difficult, expensive, and perhaps not even necessary. Some tests are costly or even dangerous and might be used more selectively. As to symptoms, after sixty years of age, the usual medical signs do not predict accurately, so specialists in geriatric medicine are needed to decide what to test for. The proper strategy has to be based on some assessment of the probabilities of various illnesses or diseases and the costs of not finding them early. In many cases there are early warning indicators which can increase the precision of probabilities and lead to more effective choices. What the public needs is a strategy: which symptoms should indicate which further investigation? At what ages should there be assessments looking for certain common troubles?

In the case of a bad back, there are remarkably clear and unambiguous indications as to whether the problem is a simple muscular strain or involves a pinched nerve (slipped disc), because in the latter case the pain travels along the nerve down a leg or arm. The potential problems are serious, and medical care is essential; yet there has been no attempt to educate the public on how to recognize the symptoms.

In small children, symptoms of illness are often dramatic, but the doctor usually cannot produce a useful diagnosis until a fever has persisted for at least a day or two. The error of waiting too long needs to be avoided, but so should the error of running for help too early. Self-education in medical matters needs to focus on knowing enough to know when one needs a doctor, and when one does not.

Mental Health

Avoiding the need for medical care has the highest payoff in the area of mental health, where the potential costs are immense and mostly uninsurable. There are books, a proliferation of them, on methods for staying sane, achieving inner peace, or just being happy. There are also organizations, movements, and cults. That few of them have any scientific credentials or evidence, and that most of them are highly profitable to their founders or managers, has apparently not stifled their growth. The quantitative evidence on the beneficial effects of legitimate psychotherapy is not much better, although some of the biofeedback people and meditation experts can show some physiological changes produced by their methods, with at least some selected individuals.

Some of the traditional psychology books may be useful in suggesting ways of staying out of emotional trouble and listing "early warning" signs that indicate a need for help. There are two main indicators to watch for in yourself and your friends: *overreacting*—responding in intensity or manner out of all proportion to the stimulus, and *stubbornness*—continuing some pattern of behavior in the face of repeated experience that it does not produce desired results. The very emotional difficulties that call for help may make it difficult for us to realize we need it, however. Indeed, there is evidence that even spouses, close relatives, and friends tend to overlook or excuse obvious indications of trouble until it is too late for therapy to be effective, or some damage has been done. People who end up on shooting sprees or who require institutionalization frequently have a long known history of bizarre behavior, covered up by loved ones.

One other common strain running through much of the

literature on mental health is a generalization that too much concern with oneself and one's own feelings, and too much isolation from others, can itself cause or accentuate emotional difficulties. The Russians claim that during the 800-day siege of Leningrad during World War II, when millions died of bombs or starvation, there was not a single recorded case of suicide. People were too busy trying to keep the invaders out and trying to survive! But others insist that organizations require, perhaps for efficiency, that people conform and give up some individuality and freedom, and some people find this difficult. The great efficiencies from division of labor and specialization also require that we cooperate and conform even in such mundane things as working regular hours.

A third line of explanation of emotional difficulties focuses on guilt and conflict between values we were supposed to have and things we ended up doing. Whether openly rejecting the values of the past eliminates this problem without substituting others is unclear.

For a person who realizes that help is needed with mental or emotional problems, however, there is no buyers' guide to good psychiatric care. A psychiatrist, who has an M.D. degree as well as some psychiatric training, may be more likely to distinguish organic medical problems from emotional ones. Psychologists are licensed to do clinical work in some states, and degrees in clinical psychology, guidance and counseling, or social work indicate the amount of formal training. More and more ministers and staff people in social agencies are being trained in guidance and counseling, and they are presumably responsible and competent. Beyond that, there is the proliferation of self-accredited experts, gurus, etc., who may well be excellent—one just does not know. Occasional scandals indicate that there are problems. These can occur even with well-trained counselors, but (it is hoped) not as often.

Getting Medical Care

When the symptoms call for medical care, or there is good reason for a checkup, how does the individual know where to go and what to do? There is no consumers' protective league that rates doctors and hospitals. In fact, the only policing of the medical profession is by the profession itself, and even when problems are recognized, they are handled quietly and privately. There are "academies" and societies which accredit hospitals and specialists, and most libraries have copies of *Directory of Medical Specialists*.

But the consumer's main aid must necessarily be an expert inside the system, which means a good general practitioner. The value is not only the care the general doctor provides in ordinary illnesses, but the skill in diagnosis and referral to competent specialists when one needs them. Unfortunately, most consumers do not appreciate the value of diagnosis and referral; the big rewards in fame and money go to the specialists. It is proving difficult to get doctors to go into general or family practice and stay there for this reason.

It is against the ethics of the profession to solve this problem by allowing the specialist to remit part of his fee to the doctor who referred the patient to him (fee-splitting). The reason is obvious—how can one trust a doctor to refer a patient to the best specialist, and only when necessary, if the referring doctor receives a payment only upon referral, and perhaps a larger split if the specialist needs the business? Perhaps people will begin to realize the value of good diagnosis and expert referral (and follow-up), demand more of it, bid up its price, and, as a result, induce more doctors to go into general practice.

How is one to select a general practitioner? Word of mouth tends to get many patients for the popular doctors. But do people really assess their doctors on the basis of their care in diagnosis, careful records, and frequent updating of their knowledge? One can assess for oneself on the first visit whether a doctor takes a good medical history, collects symptoms methodically, and explains things adequately. Since it is difficult to change doctors, and since good care requires that the doctor be familiar with your medical history, the initial selection process is crucial. To avoid having to repeat the process, or being turned over to another doctor one did not select, it may be wise to select a doctor not much older than oneself.

One also wants a reasonably priced medical care. It avoids worry and some unpleasant surprises to ask about the likely cost of any treatment or special examination before it is undertaken. A good doctor considers it proper medical practice to discuss fees beforehand.

More and more doctors are practicing in groups, so the consumer needs to consider the quality of the whole group. The best group situation is the one in which each member of the group has primary patients and takes others only when their main doctor cannot. The older, more autocratic group of one senior doctor and his (sometimes exploited) assistants is not so good.

Drugs

A major part of the cost of medical care is drugs, particularly prescription drugs. There is a long history of controversy over retail price maintenance and the use of the law to increase the power of producers over the retail prices of their products. Substantial retail markups were buttressed by the various licensing regulations on pharmacists. Legal breakthroughs that make the posting of prices permissible or even mandatory are helping, as is the growth of mail-order companies selling even prescription drugs (except narcotics) at much lower prices.

It is difficult for an individual to shop around for drugs, particularly when he is in pain and anxious for relief. Some groups have conducted local drug price surveys in an attempt to increase competition and decrease prices. *Consumer Reports* published a list of the most frequently used drugs, four of them nonprescription insulin preparations used continually for diabetes, with illustrative amounts and prices from the Chicago area, revealing the wide spread in prices. The Seattle regional office of the Federal Trade Commission issues a handbook for use in community drug price surveys with instructions and a list of twenty-five drugs with quantities, three of them generic—that is, not brand names restricted by patents. They also suggest checking on nine services that might affect costs and what you get for your money, such as delivery, acceptance of checks or credit cards, and discounts for senior citizens. Consumers are often urged to get their doctor to prescribe by generic drug name rather than brand name, and some states have passed laws allowing pharmacists to substitute generic drugs if asked. There are, however, a substantial number of new drugs still available only as brand-name drugs.

Food

We discussed the complexities of nutrition for health earlier. Nutrition is a subject that repays further study, not just for health, but for lowering the cost of achieving it. The more one knows, the wider the range of substitutes possible and hence the more the bargains of the day can be seized.

When people begin to keep track of their expenditures and worry about economizing, it is usually food and clothing which get the most attention. Food seems to take the most money, and visibly each week. Clothing seems the most discretionary and postponable. On the other hand, food habits seem to be solidly fixed in childhood and appear difficult for most people to change. Thus it is fairly easy to predict future food budgets for a family, because standards do not change much, and because volume needs (calorie and protein requirements) change dramatically with the changing ages of family members (particularly boys).

Because most people's food preferences are relatively inflexible, there are real savings for those who are willing to be more flexible, not only in using less common foods, but in changing menus as prices change. Of course, this requires a good memory for prices. A good memory is in any case absolutely necessary in food purchasing. It is certainly not economical to visit several food stores each week looking for bargains, particularly if it turns out that the lowest prices are sometimes in the first store. What may pay, however, is to go to a different supermarket each week, buying what is cheaper in that particular store (memory again). Some investment in learning the layout of several stores is required to cut the shopping time costs. Food retailing profit margins are quite narrow, but there are differences between stores as to where they are reduced the most. Since margins are so narrow, it is quite unlikely that any one supermarket will consistently charge substantially less for a whole market basket than other supermarkets doing the same volume of business.

Savings on the food bill, beyond those from finding the lower prices and adapting the menu to prices, depend heavily on the family's general mode of living. Some families do not plan ahead or manage carefully, and for them it pays never to buy more than is actually needed for the week. On the other hand, those who have a lot of willpower (or, rather, "won't power") can save by stocking up when prices are low, and buying economy sizes. It probably pays, however, to stock up mostly on necessities, not luxuries. In fact, one of the wisest things with which to fill a freezer is bread, which may even improve on freezing, can be toasted frozen, avoids the necessity for a trip to the store (when one usually ends up buying more than bread), and avoids the temptation to stock up on prime steaks. There are also costs of storage, of course: electricity and depreciation and foregone interest for the freezer, and foregone interest on the money invested in the stock of food. If food prices rise faster than the rate of interest on savings, there is no *real* foregone interest.

The price-shopping issue and the bulk-buying issue are interrelated. One can take substantial advantage of bargains only if one is willing to stock up on things when they are cheap or when one happens to be in the store which sells them more cheaply. But it pays to stock up only if one is not then tempted to use food more wastefully or live more luxuriously than one intended. For many families, the solution may be to stock up on bargains in necessities like bread, sugar, flour, etc., but never to stock up on luxuries, even at good prices, unless the family has some other control system for regulating its consumption of luxuries. Remember that in hoping to stock up on temporarily cheaper food, you are competing with large commercial operators whose storage costs are lower and whose knowledge of probable future prices is likely to be more accurate. The best economy may be to eat less, and there is evidence that you may also live longer eating less!

Both the growing and preparation of food offer opportunities for direct home production, economically speaking. But unless one values the exercise, or the recreational aspects, or particular qualities connected with fresh produce, the savings from growing one's own food, calculated as hourly earnings on the time spent, are likely to be rather low. For some of us, it is fun, and we do need the exercise, and the whole thing is a worthwhile challenge.

The same comment, with the added payoff that it may allow an expression of creativity, goes for investing more time in preparing foods at home rather than purchasing prepared things which already incorporate a lot of labor. The hard-headed economic way of looking at the investment of added time for preparation is to figure out how much you earn per hour by saving on the cost of food and to compare that with the value of alternative opportunities. Of course, if a parent cooks while watching the children, the opportunity cost of the time may be nearly zero. Or if one feels a need for variety in one's tasks, one might argue that the opportunity cost is really low, or that there are other benefits.

As we said earlier about other do-it-yourself projects, the payoff depends on amortizing the investment in equipment and in learning how. In deciding whether to start, one must guess the learning costs and the potential use. In deciding whether to continue, the past investment costs should be ignored, so the returns per hour may well be quite high.

Going in the other direction, another way to buy your

own time for leisure or fun is to eat in restaurants. Upper-income people and multiple-earner families do this a great deal, restaurant expenditures being highly "income elastic." Presumably one also gets entertainment and service as well as freedom from cooking and doing the dishes. At today's wages, it is still much cheaper to eat out than to have a hired cook at home. In response to the needs of people who are most interested in saving time, the speedy service drive-in has arisen, its major attraction being that one can get extremely rapid service and the low prices that production line food preparation makes possible. When a single chain can advertise that it has sold more than fifty billion hamburgers, it must be serving some need! It is quite possible, however, that the time saved is more important to the customers than the money saved.

Clothing

The budget item most often robbed when things do not come out right is the clothing budget. We can postpone buying clothing if spending money is scarce, and it is difficult to predict clothing needs because they come in waves with the seasons. The distinction between depreciation and obsolescence (becoming out of style) is crucial in this area. If the only problem were physical depreciation, we should all buy the best quality clothing for the money, i.e., the most months of wear per dollar. But with most visible items, styles change with blinding rapidity. In this situation, it is hard to avoid the feeling that clothes need not be durable, since they will be out of style before they wear out. On the other hand, most people are convinced that the really expensive clothes by good designers do not go out of style so quickly and so are a good buy, having both low depreciation and low obsolescence. We might also feel good in them because we know they are well made.

Clothing labels tell the content of the fibers or furs, but nothing of the quality of construction and nothing of the quality of the materials, which can vary within each type. Again, the household learns by experience, word of mouth, and occasional articles. Most articles on new fabrics appear in magazines which accept advertising from producers and sellers; for this reason, they tell what is good about each new product, but not what is bad. The customer has to learn through experience that 100 percent synthetic fabric shirts wear like iron but may also feel like it, that synthetic socks foster fungus infections of the feet, or that the "wash and wear" cotton and dacron-cotton fabrics are also impregnated with resin or similar substances and are quite uncomfortable for anyone with a tendency to perspire. What is needed is a better system for circulating information on what is wrong with new products—the producers will tell what is right with them—so that each household need not pay to find out for itself.

Another problem is that manufacturers, particularly of men's clothing, have a tendency to produce the same limited set of styles and colors, changing them systematically as though a conspiracy existed to increase obsolescence as well as to make all men look alike at any point in time. For instance, men's raincoats come in black (which shows the dust) or light beige (which shows the dirt) or green (which is often ugly or clashes with suits). Only in the most expensive, custom-made lines is there real variety. Women sometimes face the reverse problem, with so much variety that a particular item is not available in their size when they want it.

The regular seasonal sales of clothing, particularly men's clothing with its slow style changes, are hard to explain. How can the stores sell at *other* times, when customers know that if they only wait a few months for the next sale, they can get at least 20 percent off? Apparently there are enough people who simply have to have something, or are afraid that the one item they like for color or style will disappear before it goes on sale. Smart buyers do a little scouting, then pick up what they want at the sales. The prior scouting also helps them avoid being "taken" by sales specials (bought or brought in for the sale and often not the same quality) or fictitious mark-downs.

Sales of men's clothes usually provide genuine bargains; for women, it is often a sign of change in style or season, so somewhat more risky. A woman with a sense of style, capable of guessing what will look right a year later, is thus better able to save money.

Children wear out some clothes before they outgrow them, and whether the optimal quality (durability) is worth the price differential may depend on whether there are younger siblings to take over the outgrown items. The large chains and catalog houses are an excellent place to buy children's clothing, because they are clear about what is in the fabric, offer a range of qualities, and deliver the purchase to your door. The larger catalog houses also test some of their clothing and will make good if things wear out too fast. Proper accounting for the costs in time and money of shopping locally may show that catalog shopping is cheaper, even with some mistakes to be returned and high postal rates.

Home production of clothing was for many years quite uneconomical. Clothing was being produced by mass production methods at relatively low wages. Recent years of climbing wages and rising distribution costs have driven many people back to the fabric shops and their own sewing machines. A big business in "simple" patterns fuels the drive. It may still not be worth investing in the skills to tailor men's clothes or such items as suits and coats, so it may pay best to make children's clothes—dresses, shorts, etc. Many a family has found it wise to provide a convenient place for the sewing machine. Skills at alterations and repairs are also handy in these days when it is difficult to get anybody to do anything cheaply (or at all).

An added advantage of some do-it-yourself home production is that in addition to providing tax-free income it may also save time. Altering clothing is an example, like repairing one's own appliances, where the alternative might be to take it somewhere and pick it up later. The extreme example is cutting the children's hair, where the job itself takes far less time than taking the children to the barber, and the equipment and training costs to be amortized are small.

A more complex economic consideration when one thinks of doing it oneself is the investment in equipment and training involved. It is not just a decision to invest time and materials in an individual act of sewing or gardening, but a decision to accumulate equipment and know-how, the return on which comes over many years of productive activity. The sewing machine, and learning how to use it, is a good example. The investment really pays off only if one continues to make use of the machine and the skills. In fact, since the necessary standard of style and quality of clothing goes up as one gets older, most people are unlikely to make much of their own clothing after age thirty, unless they have by then acquired a rather high level of skill. The investment of time in learning the skills may well be larger than the investment in capital equipment, particularly since the equipment can often be rented.

One difficulty in learning skills is that the available printed materials telling how to do many of these productive activities are seriously deficient if available at all. The printed instructions on clothing patterns make sense only to those who already know pretty well what to do. A book on home gardens is not always adequate. Perhaps the best-written instructional books are the cookbooks.

Finally, even though one may enjoy creative work as recreation, it pays to take the hard-headed economic view first, then introduce these other considerations.

Transportation

In the United States, the dominance of the automobile makes it necessary to consider transportation and recreation together. If the family needs a car for transportation, then that same car is available to reduce the costs of recreation, especially the vacation needs of large families. Indeed, the decision to buy a car, or to buy a newer one, involves an estimate of the payoffs both in transportation to work and stores and schools, and in making some kinds of recreation a great deal easier and cheaper.

The fact that cars can fulfill both transportation and recreation needs causes some budgeting problems, particularly if one attempts to keep separate account of transportation and recreation expenditures. The gasoline purchased on a pleasure trip belongs in the latter category, but the rest of the gasoline bill in the former. And how should one divide the other car costs, including depreciation and foregone interest, between the two uses? Perhaps we should allocate almost all of the costs to transportation, so that our recreation expenditures look smaller. Then we are induced into "economizing" by using the car, rather than airplanes, for vacations. It is correct economic analysis to consider only the marginal (added) costs in deciding whether to use the car for each purpose, of course, once the car is owned. Rising energy prices will affect all transportation, leaving choices still to be made, especially if gasoline taxes are raised to discourage the use of private cars.

The major transportation decisions have to do with the journey to work. Most people prefer to drive; except in the largest cities, they find they can get there faster and more conveniently by car. The convenience includes comfort, speed, privacy, and flexibility in timing. But the car costs more than alternative methods, particularly if one charges the full capital cost of the car to transportation, and the margin is greater when parking must be paid for. Most American families have more than one car. In households with two earners going to work in different places, the pressures are obvious. Even if the one car in a family is used for work, this leaves the other parent and children needing transportation to school, stores, etc. Given what we have already seen about the importance of depreciation and interest in the cost of a car, and the fact that a second car does not have to be used for highway travel, many families sensibly have one reasonably old car just for in-town transportation. The difficulty is that for family vacations a good, large car, usually a station wagon or van, is best, while for transportation to work, a smaller car, less expensive to operate and easier to park, seems optimal. Yet the cheapest way to get an older car initially is to keep your own old one when buying a new car. It costs a lot in trouble, risk, and dealer's margins to trade in a larger car on a more "economical" one. The result of this situation is that a lot of large cars are being used for driving to work. The inefficiency is only apparent, not real, for the individual family. Those large cars were originally the good, "family" car.

At various times, attempts are made to reduce the cost of the trip to work by the use of car pools, and various pressures will surely come to do more of this, but these pools tend to be inconvenient unless the members agree pretty well on time schedules and other details. If the schedule of drivers does not need constant adjustments, and if the driver phones each rider just before he leaves the house (not waiting for an answer), and if each rider then comes out promptly, the whole operation can be quite efficient. It avoids the need for two cars per family, and lowers the cost of getting to work every day. The sight of innumerable cars during the rush hours, a single person in each, testifies to the difficulties of cooperation and economy through car pools, and the value placed on privacy and flexibility.

One of the difficulties in any cooperative arrangement is keeping account of the relative contributions and preserving equity. Since car pools are essentially barter operations, there is bound to be some feeling of inequity, if not actual maldistribution of costs and benefits, unless prices are put on things and balances kept. One solution, used mostly in babysitting cooperatives, is to use "token" paper money designed for the purpose. Each member is given an initial sum of "token" paper money, and the services are then paid for in the "token" paper money at an agreed price or system of prices. This acts, just as real money does, as an automatic method of balancing out; so long as you do not run out of the paper money, you know things are in balance. All that is needed in addition is a rule against accumulating too much of the money and hoarding it, which would cut off trade altogether. A similar system might be possible for a ride-sharing cooperative in cases where it was impossible for each rider to provide the pool car for the same fraction of the time.

The cost of public transportation cannot be directly affected by the individual consumer, but he can influence the cost of his own car and its operation in a number of ways. The simplest, already mentioned, is to keep each car longer, cutting the yearly cost of depreciation and interest. A second is to buy a secondhand car. Another is proper maintenance, a difficult thing when manufacturers' instructions vary so much and tend to suggest excessive caution and care.

Do-it-yourself maintenance and repairs, for those with some skill and interest and a place to do it, can save a good deal. Perhaps even more with the car, there is an investment in equipment and in learning the necessary skills. Charges for simple things that have been getting simpler have been rising as wages rise and labor gets scarce and as fewer people think of doing it themselves. What used to be a complex job—greasing a car—now consists of applying grease from a pressure gun in less than a dozen places. A hand pressure gun is inexpensive and adequate. Changing oil and oil filters is an extremely simple, if dirty, task which costs dearly in labor charges plus inflated prices for the oil and filter. As it becomes increasingly inconvenient to have a car serviced or repaired, shops having moved out to the edge of town where land is cheaper, the net benefits from doing it yourself get bigger; it may take no more time to do it yourself than to get the car to the garage and back again. Indeed, it is difficult to see the advantage of having the service garages so far out, thus requiring extra driving and time by each owner. Perhaps it is assumed that the owners will not take account of their time. But it is entirely possible that the garages which do try to save their customers' time will end up with most of the business.

Manufacturers issue a shop manual for each car they make, and these manuals can be purchased, making it easier to maintain and even repair your own car.[2] Secondhand parts from junkyards can often be used at great

---

2. Indeed, more and more manuals are appearing which spell out a step-by-step strategy for diagnosing the causes of trouble.

savings; on the other hand, repair garages get discounts on the parts they use, so some of the savings get dissipated in heavier charges for parts.

A substantial number of people do some work on their own cars. They are mostly middle-income people. The highest-income people are too busy, and the opportunity cost of their time is too high; lowest-income people may not have the confidence, skills, or ability to use written instructions easily, or may be working such long hours at such hard work that they cannot take on more tasks.

One major cost of any car is the tires, and they present one of the most confused and cut-up markets of any major consumer product. There are seasonal sales, and special cheap lines, and "discount tire stores." There are also places which recap tires with new tread, or sell such tires. The cheap tires are frequently no bargain, wearing through most of the tread in a year or a few thousand miles, and having such a weak carcass that they puncture easily. On the other hand, some of the most expensive tires can be justified only for high-speed, long-distance trips over bad roads, and perhaps even then a somewhat less fancy tire would do. The tubeless tire, a great product for good roads, has turned out to be a nightmare for anyone using a car on bad roads. It develops small leaks around the rim and elsewhere, and is difficult or impossible to patch. The steel-belted radial tire does wear longer, doesn't heat up in use, and increases gas mileage. It is still something of a luxury and should not be mixed with other tires on the same car since its dynamic properties are quite different. When it comes to buying tires, little can be said that is not obvious. Of course, it pays to shop around, and yet to stick to known brands of known quality, and to try to identify the quality lines of each brand when their names keep changing.

Another tire problem in areas requiring snow tires is the twice-a-year changing operation. One solution is to purchase a secondhand rim and then to change wheels, not tires, which can easily be done at home. One of the wheels with snow tire serves as a spare in summer, and one of those with a regular tire as a spare in winter. Again, it may take no more time to switch the two wheels oneself than to take the car somewhere, have it done, and pick it up. At present charges, a consumer could save several dollars a year and some time, minus the cost of an extra rim, plus the savings of not keeping an unused spare tire. (One needs only four regular tires and two snow tires.)

More complex car repairs often need extensive equipment. Rental businesses have sprung up all over the country that will rent such equipment, including portable hoists with which you can remove a motor or transmission. And since some specialized repair services often operate independently of the general repair garages, one can remove a piece, have it rebuilt or repaired, and replace it, without much skill.

While a few individualists will get around on bicycles, motorcycles, boats, or even on foot, most of us use either our own car or public transportation. Public transportation for the journey to work is only rarely adequate, and then mostly in cities which became large before the advent of the motor car. Even in those, and even with subsidies in some of them, it has a difficult time competing. For longer journeys, the railroads, once the favorite or the only method of travel, are on a persistent decline, reinforced by reductions in frequency and quality of service. One might think that with expressways, the long-distance buses could compete with private autos, with all the economies and convenience of their size. But getting to and from the center-of-town terminals remains a problem. At present, buses tend to serve the people who live in the center of town, have low incomes, and perhaps do not have cars.

For more extensive travel, the consumer faces greater unknowns as to the costs and quality of the alternatives. Car rental costs vary widely, and can be quite deceptive if they are quoted as so much per day plus so much per mile or kilometer. The quality, and even prices, of hotels is difficult to determine in advance, except in Europe, where relatively complete guides are published. Guides on how to get along cheaply in foreign lands are often useful, but quality can fall and prices rise between the time they investigate and the time the reader gets there; this is a common problem with something in limited supply. Better information about quality can rapidly eliminate the bargains. The ordinary traveler should be happy for such better information even if he does not use it, because it makes it less and less likely that he is missing any bargains, or hitting any bad buys.

What complicates the picture most is the growing use of package vacation tours, which not only can afford to invest in better information, but can negotiate bargains unavailable to the individual traveler. For the lower price, one trades the freedom to select schedules or activities, and gains freedom from worry and from having to do a lot of individual negotiating and decision making.

As hourly earnings rise, the opportunity cost of vacation time also rises, and the natural tendency is to find recreations which use more money relative to the time they take. The rapid rise in vacation air travel can be interpreted in this light.

The choice between car and bus or airplane involves tradeoffs between convenience, speed, and cost, which vary with the size of the family and the distance traveled, and whether each end of the trip is near a major airport. For a single person, air travel costs per mile are roughly equal to the real costs of travel by car if one includes depreciation and wear and tear. Remember that time is valuable, so one should not compare only out-of-pocket costs.

Even when the trip is a vacation trip, it consumes both time and money to produce enjoyment, and calculations should involve both. If the trip is by car, the drive itself may be enjoyable, depending on where it is and on the individuals. Children seem to find long drives boring. But some people manage to break up long trips so that the trip itself, and the activities along the way, are part of the vacation and not just a cost of getting to it and back.

Recreation

More and more recreational activities involve not only time and money but the use of equipment. Part of the cost, then, is either the rental cost of such equipment, or the depreciation, interest, and maintenance costs of owning the equipment. People own or rent boats, tent trailers, vacation trailers, snowmobiles, skis, summer cottages, fishing equipment, and so on. The advantages of owning such equipment are obvious. But to own a piece of equipment that is used only for a week or two of the year is clearly an expensive luxury, compared with renting it. The costs per use depend on the amount of use and the length of time over which the fixed costs can be spread.

The industries producing recreational equipment have innovated rapidly, produced a bewildering and changing variety of items at the cost of never achieving the major economies of mass production. There is mass production of some components, but until the consumers settle on a few standard lines and concentrate on looking for better prices, the situation seems unlikely to change. It is particularly chaotic in recreational vehicles.

In deciding whether or not to own a piece of recreational equipment, the rate of depreciation is clearly important. Things like tents and canoes and trailers, properly cared for, depreciate very slowly, since there is little to wear out and little obsolescence. So they may be worthwhile owning even if used only a little each year.

One compromise is joint ownership in some cooperative arrangement with one or more other families. Differences in standards of upkeep and conflicts over scheduling may be tolerable if the savings are substantial. A more common procedure with a large item like a summer cottage or a motor home is to rent it out during the times when the owner is not using it. This leaves the responsibility for maintenance in one place.

Remembering again that a vacation requires both time and money, one can interpret the advantages of various kinds of camping equipment in those terms. For instance, as one goes from a regular tent to a tent trailer and then to a camper, trailer, or motor home, the amount of time required to unpack, set up, break down, and repack, gets smaller and smaller. (And it is also smaller than staying in motels.) For people on long trips, staying at a different place each night, the difference in free time for enjoying the scenery or fishing may be substantial. Of course, some people enjoy the work and think it gives the family something to do together, although casual observation of American campgrounds reveals father and mother doing most of the work. A trailer or camper or motor home saves time also in food preparation, since everything is available in cupboards, and there is water at the sink and a protected table at which to eat. With children, there are added advantages: stops for lunch can be made when convenient, next to a park or playground.

Philanthropy

Giving can be considered a consumption expenditure, without denying the virtue and benefits of altruism and compassion. Like any other expenditure of time and money, charity can stand some thought and planning and even shopping. There may be little choice about gifts to relatives or individuals in need, but with charitable organizations one might like some comparative information.

There is an organization set up to provide that information, telling you whether a charitable organization meets certain minimum standards and roughly what they are doing with their money. For a small annual fee, you have the right to ask for evaluations of charities to which you are thinking of giving (The National Information Bureau, 419 Park Avenue South, New York, New York 10016). If a charitable organization does not have audited financial statements, uses unusually large amounts of money for management and fund raising, has no unpaid board of directors, or simply shows little evidence of getting anything done, the National Information Bureau will so inform you.

The United States Treasury has a large catalog listing all the organizations deemed charitable so that gifts to them are deductible from your income for tax purposes—if you are itemizing deductions. The Treasury accepts or rejects applications for such status, and there is no independent review or appeal procedure. Organizations can qualify as nonprofit, with some tax advantages, but only a subset of them also qualify as charitable so that gifts to them are deductible by the donor. The general rule is that organizations primarily engaged in political activity or lobbying do not qualify as charitable, but the boundary line is hazy; some organizations avoid the problem by setting up a separate foundation that can qualify for exempt status. So we have the Sierra Club and the Sierra Foundation, or the Southern Christian Leadership Conference and the Southern Christian Leadership Foundation.

As we saw in chapter 1, tax considerations have important implications for philanthropy. If your marginal tax rate is 35 percent, then it costs you only $65 to give $100 to charity, but $100 if you give it to a needy friend or relative. There are partial tax savings if you provide more than half the total support of the relative for a year, and are paying taxes and itemizing. In addition, gifts to charity of appreciated assets (within limits) allow you to deduct the current market value of the asset from taxable income without paying any capital gains tax on the appreciation. Hence, anyone with appreciated assets such as stocks is well-advised to give them, instead of cash, to charity. Appreciated assets are often owned in amounts larger than you might want to give to any one charity. Fortunately, some stockbrokers have set up accounts for a number of local charities so that you can have the brokers divide your shares of stock among several charities, letting the charities decide whether they want to keep the stock or have it sold and take the proceeds. Technically, you have given the stock to charitable organizations and can consider its market value as a tax-deductible contribution.

Other Expenditures

There is little more that can be said about the other kinds of expenditures, except that it is useful to distinguish, both in your mind and in your record keeping, those which are deductible or potentially deductible for tax purposes. The Internal Revenue Service provides average amounts for state sales taxes, by income and family size, which you can use without keeping records, but records may prove that you spent more than that. You may even want to bunch certain deductible expenditures in alternate years, if you are close to the boundary where itemizing pays, so you can take the standard deduction every other year, and have lots of deductions in the alternate year. For example, you could make one year's charitable contributions in January, the next year's in December of the same year, then skip a year.

You may also want to keep track of certain luxury expenditures, like vacations, in order to keep them under control, and to know how much you could save for other urgent purposes by cutting out some discretionary items.

Services (Particularly Repairs)

In many respects, consumer products are much easier to deal with than consumer services. With consumer products, there are sources of information about quality, enough continuity so that one can learn from experience, and some standardization. When it comes to services, the problems are much worse. We have already discussed the need for a personal doctor who can serve as a guide to whatever other medical services one needs. And we indicated that the likelihood of finding a good advisor on financial affairs and investments is slight.

In spite of all the advice about seeing your lawyer to avoid trouble, selecting a lawyer and deciding when to use one are difficult problems. There is a *Martindale-Hubbel Directory* available in most libraries, which lists most of the lawyers in the United States and gives some ratings. There may be conflict of interest problems if you ask your insurance agent or banker, so it is often suggested that you rely on friends' or clergy's or relatives' advice about a lawyer. This has the disadvantage of piling the business on a few well-known lawyers who are already too busy and perhaps expensive. The standard advice is to ask beforehand what the charges will be, but you are likely to be told an hourly charge (plus expenses), so only some initial consultations or small jobs will reveal what costs are actually like. It is probably somewhat easier to change lawyers than doctors, but there is cumulative benefit from a lawyer who knows your situation. What most of us would like is a lawyer who will tell us when we do *not* need his or her services.

Many elaborate devices for making money or saving taxes involve heavy use of lawyers, often repeatedly, so that their net benefits depend heavily on whether the gains outweigh the legal fees. At any rate, there are some books to help the innocent layman use lawyers and the law more effectively, such as Martin J. Ross's *Handbook of Everyday Law* and Virginia Lehmann's *You, the Law, and Retirement*. Even these books, however, are written by lawyers and seem to the layman to encourage more use of legal counsel than is economically sensible for many people.

What can be said about repair services for the car or appliances, carpentry, plumbing, or electrical work, and the like? Here there is no branded item, no professionalization, no simple standard of quality, no *Consumer Reports* magazine. And yet substantial amounts of money are involved, and there is a suspicion that there must be a wide variety of prices and qualities, not highly correlated with each other. There are some national franchises for things like muffler replacement and automatic transmissions, and at least one of the latter engages in some of the most unscrupulous practices since the Holland Furnace Company racket of years ago—and the same way. They disassemble your transmission instead of your furnace, then announce that it needs complete rebuilding or else a large charge to reassemble it.

An economic analysis, however, often shows that it is far better to repair than to replace something in which you have little money tied up (if it has little market value) but which has large potential use value. Many of us replace things partly because of the difficulties of finding trustworthy repair service, and qualified repair people are so busy that they themselves frequently suggest replacement, or replacement of major parts, rather than simple repair. (Some are so busy they will happily tell you how to do simple repairs yourself.)

All of this speaks for investing at least in your own diagnostic skills and perhaps also in repair skills. It also speaks for watching the repair person and asking to keep any replaced parts. But it still leaves the problem of how to select the outfit to do the repair. It is not much help to have occasional reports of tests that show the variety of charges made for a simple repair, or the variety of repairs made on the same simply disabled test car or TV. It makes us uneasy but does not tell us what to do. Those who reveal the problems usually call for licensing, or bonding, or other regulation. In fact, the sorry history of most such legislation should give us all pause:

> Though most government regulation was enacted under the guise of protecting the consumer from abuse, much of today's regulatory machinery does little more than shelter producers from the normal competitive consequences of lassitude and inefficiency.[3]

The history, which will probably be repeated in the case of state licensing of auto mechanics and television repair people, is that the bonding and licensing requirements serve to keep people out, not to police the honesty or effectiveness of those who are in. And the regulations are enforced by those in the business, whose motives are always mixed between assuring quality and restricting competition. It seems clear that better information and more competition would do much more to improve the correlation between price and quality in repair services. But single market tests of the sort commonly run are not fair or adequate information for judging individual vendors, and it would be inordinately expensive to expand them until they were. Relying on consumer complaints does not offer much hope either. They include a large component of misunderstanding and human relations, and tend to reflect the problems of the intellectual affluent rather than the poor, who do not complain much.

I can always just ask a lot of friends and neighbors where they have their repairs done, or by whom, and what their experience has been. I can then weigh this information by knowing how demanding, perceptive, critical, and similar to me each informant is. Even if they are satisfied or dissatisfied for various reasons, including the

---

3. Lewis A. Engman, "Inflation and Regulation," *Antitrust Law and Economics* 7 (1975): 38–39.

personality of the repair personnel, I am likely to be satisfied or dissatisfied for the same reasons, so the information may even be better than the impossibly costly precise information on the mechanical quality of the service.

Indeed, it should be feasible to systematize the collection of the kind of information I erratically collect from friends and neighbors, and make it available to improve the working of the local market mechanism for repair services. If I knew that a significantly larger fraction of customers of Shop A were satisfied with the price and quality of the repair work than the customers of Shop B, and if I knew the difference was persistent and not associated with a particularly demanding or hostile collection of customers, it would be enough to help me choose where to have the item repaired. Indeed, this is the one place where information might be a salable commodity, since continual updating would be necessary. Only if vendors improved so rapidly (by using the same information) that price and quality became very highly correlated, would it cease to be worth my while to pay for the information; and in that case the justification for subsidizing such a service out of community funds (tax money) would be clear. The reason such experiments have not been tried is that they required a substantial initial investment simultaneously to assemble a large mass of information, process it, and develop dissemination techniques so that people can use it. A crucial element would be probability samples of people, not reliance on potentially biased volunteered information or special groups of reporters. But the same process that repeatedly surveyed a community for its experiences could also find out how the information was affecting the market, and the efficiency of service outlets. The increased confidence of consumers might well expand the total amount of repair business substantially.

In the meantime, you can read the "how-to" books, accumulate neighborhood intelligence informally, and find your own reliable repair services, or do it yourself.

With appliances, some careful attention to symptoms can ease the diagnosis problem substantially. Indeed, with the diagrams and parts lists that come with most appliances, one can often locate the offending part, send for another, and replace it.

With more complex things like additions and repairs to the house, a process of negotiation about details, and securing bids, is often involved. The difficulty is that bids almost never really specify the details, and there is often a great deal of leeway. A good outfit will tend to do a little extra if things go well; any outfit will cut corners and omit little things if things have gone badly or cost more than expected. All this is usually obfuscated by the likelihood that you may want to change things or add a few extras in the middle. All changes should have a separate bid to prevent the contractor from charging whatever extra he likes for them. Indeed, any questions about detail as the work progresses should be clearly sorted by agreement into those that change the work and the price and those that do not.

CHAPTER ELEVEN **Consumer Information and Decision Making**

So far in this book very little attention has been paid to either of the two main topics found in most consumer economics books—wise shopping and consumer protection. The application of good economic analysis to setting priorities and budgets and deciding what to buy is more important and more difficult than mere shopping, although shopping has been discussed where it seemed appropriate. It is most important that we understand how we make decisions, and that we understand our own departures from how experts say decisions should be made. We also need to know why consumer information and consumer insight are crucial if a market economy is to function properly.

Motivation and Family Decision Making

The great conceptual contribution of economics to the discussion of decision making has been the focus on choices among alternatives. The value of any one alternative has meaning only when compared with the next best choice. The second best choice measures the opportunity cost—i.e., what must be given up to get the best. But in the discussion of the value of any single alternative, economic theory is relatively empty, assuming that there is some unique utility attaching to that alternative, or some pattern of preference among various alternatives, without going beyond the notion of a single-dimensioned utility.

A theory of consumer decision making is needed to predict consumer behavior, analyze it, or assess the quality of actual decision making, our own or someone else's. Such a theory must be based on knowledge of what the consumer is doing. The simplest assumption is that consumers maximize satisfaction. If so, a theory based on that assumption needs to be based on knowledge of the sources of satisfaction.

We can borrow some notions from psychology to make

the discussion more realistic. First, there are at least four main motives, or potential sources of satisfaction:

1. Power over the environment, that is, the right to the basic physical needs like food and shelter. In a money economy this usually means money.
2. Power over other people, and independence from having to do what they say.
3. Affiliation, the giving and receiving of affection. We get satisfaction from seeing other people happy.
4. Achievement, the sense of accomplishment from the overcoming of obstacles through one's own efforts.

There is an elaborate literature in social psychology about such motives, particularly the last one, since it is in many ways the most interesting and the most crucial for the progress of the world.

Each of these motives can be thought of as a source of satisfaction to the individual, the amount of satisfaction depending on the general level of the motive and on how fully or recently it has been satisfied. In the case of physical needs like food, the notion of incentive value is obvious: the more one has eaten and the more recently, the less motivating is any current activity directed at eating more food.

In an uncertain world, where the choices are actions that are expected to lead to satisfaction of the various motives, a third dimension enters: the probability (subjective) that a particular action will actually lead to the desired result. Will working harder at some task actually make success more likely? Psychologists use the term "expectancy" for this notion of subjective probability. The final attractiveness of some alternative is then stated to be the product of the strength of the basic motive, the incentive value (marginal utility), and the expectancy (the probability that the desired outcome will occur).

We now have a complex theory, which says the total incentive value of a single alternative choice is the sum of its potential values in satisfying each of the four basic motives (power over things, power over people, affiliation, and achievement). Each of the values is affected by the current level of satisfaction of that motive, and by a subjective probability that the choice will have the desired outcome. The same calculations are required for the competing alternatives if one is to select the best.

These motives do not always lead directly to actions. There is a great deal of inertia in human behavior, so that we mostly continue to do what we have been doing until some alternative develops sufficient incentive value to overcome that inertia. A person has to become aware of some problem or better alternative; before he is willing to go through the complex and demanding process of decision making, he has to pay attention to the problem.

Furthermore, many constraints narrow the range of alternatives. There are limits on one's financial power (income plus assets plus credit); limits on one's time (twenty-four hours a day); laws and institutions and customs; and ignorance of facts, of alternatives, or of the way things work. Major differences between countries and cultures may well result not from different human motivations at work, but from different restrictions placed on people's choices by law, custom, and institutions.

In addition, one's own major decisions can put constraints on one's minor decisions. There is a hierarchy of choices, and it is frequently possible to make sure that many minor decisions are at least passably good by making certain major decisions that constrain them. For instance, the choice of house and neighborhood will tend to establish one's general living standards, and a carefully chosen location will make it easier to stay within the budget on other things. A decision never to stock up on luxuries may assure that a conscious choice must be made each time a luxury item is consumed and needs replacement, and thus make it easier to avoid excessive indulgence. The use of installment credit as a self-disciplining device to keep one conscious of depreciation and to encourage spacing of expenditures on durables is another example.

Finally, in a dynamic situation, social psychology makes another contribution to the theory of consumer choice, pointing out that individuals learn and can therefore change their preference patterns. There is some disagreement about whether experience can change people's basic motives. Some argue that the level of a person's achievement motivation is a stable dimension of personality, determined mostly by early training in childhood and not much altered after that. Others argue that basic motives can be changed through experience or education.

Whether or not basic motives can be changed, people's subjective beliefs, about the kinds of satisfactions to be derived (and with what probabilities) from some choice of action, can certainly be altered by experience, information, and new insights. If a person tries hard and succeeds, the assumption that hard work pays off should grow stronger. If one tries a new product, or observes someone else using it, and likes what it does, one's notion that it will satisfy needs is likely to be affected. The belief in the payoff to avoiding risk, planning ahead, deliberation, and information-seeking in making choices, all are learned from successful experiences (or perhaps from the punishment when one fails to plan, avoid risk, or be deliberate). As we suggested in proposing money-handling procedures, effective learning requires early rewards, so long-term planning probably comes after some success at short-term planning.

Even the best theory of individual decision making does not tell us what a family will do. A family is made up of individuals with different personalities and needs and, consequently, different sets of personal preferences. Ideally, each one gets some satisfaction from expressing affiliation (love) and hence considers some of the desires of the other members of the family. In spite of the fact that the preferences of family members may conflict, families make decisions all the time, and most of them do it well enough so that the family stays together, reasonably content. How do they do it?

We must remember first that family decisions are not simple conflict resolution. There are advantages to a family in staying together, even if the benefits are not shared equally, and even without the legal sanctions that hold them. There are economies of scale in feeding and housing. It takes two parents to produce children, and it helps to have both parents raise them. The actual solutions, then, may be sloppy, but solutions nevertheless.

Social Optimum

Given that families can reach a consensus on the goods and services they want, under what conditions will the economy provide them efficiently? Most economists are fond of pointing out that, under certain conditions, firms in a profit-oriented, competitive environment will produce exactly the amounts of goods and services that people want, and at the least possible cost! It is startling to think that thousands of firms, acting with no central direction whatsoever and motivated by the desire for profits, will benefit anyone. And yet economists contend that the result of these independent actions is a situation in which it is impossible to reallocate labor, machines, or raw materials among firms to produce more of one product or service without cutting back on another, or to redistribute the goods and services among consumers so that some are better off without making others worse off.

The key to this result is that all consumers respond to the prices of the goods and services they consume and that firms respond to the product and input (factors of production) prices that they face. How do consumers respond to prices? They are assumed to purchase goods and services to the point where the added utility or satisfaction from spending one more dollar on any given good or service is equal to the added satisfaction from spending that dollar on something else. How much that dollar will buy depends, of course, on its price, so an alternative way of stating this result is to say that the ratio of the added benefit to the price is equal for all goods and across all consumers. If prices change, then consumers will reallocate their income, and will generally tend to consume less of the goods that have become relatively more expensive. By responding to prices in this way, consumers act so that the prices of goods and services reflect the added benefits that consumers attach to them, i.e., price = marginal (social) benefit to consumers in general.

In a competitive economy, producers are seen as slaves to the desires of consumers and to competition in the product market. Profit-maximizing firms will produce to the point where the production of one more unit of goods or services will add as much to their costs as to the revenues from the sale of that additional unit of the goods or services. (If these marginal costs were *less* than the marginal revenue, then firms could add to their total profit by expanding output; the reverse is true if marginal revenue is less than marginal cost.) Since the additional revenue from the sale of one more unit of output is just the *price* of that output, we have price = marginal revenue = marginal cost. Consumers "police" firms, in the sense that firms attempting to charge more than the going price will lose business and be forced to reduce prices back to competitive levels. Firms in industries with above average profits will find that the entry of new firms will drive away excess profits.

Finally, we must assume that firms compete with one another for the inputs to production, i.e., the man-hours of labor, the machinery, and the raw materials needed to produce the output. Each firm will want to produce its output at least cost, and so will respond to changes in the prices of inputs and rearrange its use of these inputs just as consumers rearrange their purchases in response to product prices. The result of many firms competing against each other for the various factors of production is that these factors are used in accordance with the value placed on them by consumers demanding the products that use these inputs. The resulting cost of producing the good or service will reflect the opportunity cost to society of using those inputs instead of letting them be used to produce something else. Combining these results with the others, we have the following set of equalities:

1.	2.	3.
Marginal Social Benefit	= Price of the Product	= Marginal Revenue to the Producer	= Marginal Cost to the Producer

4.	5.
= Resources Used in Producing One More Unit of the Product	= Marginal Social (Opportunity) Cost of One More Unit of the Product

That a competitive market system produces this result leads many people to recommend competition in markets as a better form of consumer protection rather than regulation. But before discussing such policy matters further, let us examine the conditions under which the equalities really hold.

1. When is the marginal social benefit reflected in the price people will pay?

☐ When families make optimal decisions for all the individuals within the family.

☐ When they are well-informed, know what they want, and can compare prices and qualities.

☐ When the income distribution is sufficiently fair that we are willing to count dollar power as a measure of utility, whoever is spending.

☐ When there are no "externalities" in consumption, i.e., when the costs or benefits to others of consuming the goods or services are included in the price. If the costs of cleaning up my litter are not reflected in the price I pay for a can of soda pop, then the price of soda pop overestimates its social benefits.

2. When is the price equal to marginal revenue?

☐ When there is enough competition in selling the product that no seller restricts production to get a higher price and higher profit.

☐ When product differences that keep sellers inefficiently small reflect real preferences for variety and not artificially created "monopolistic competition."

3. When is marginal revenue equal to marginal cost? When each firm maximizes its profits. This is the easiest assumption of all to make, and it is hard to find believable exceptions.

4. When is the price of the extra resources equal to the marginal cost of producing one more unit? When there is competition in the purchasing of factors of production. Associations of employers, on the one side, and labor unions, on the other, may lead to departures from this equality. A union, for example, may drive wages above the level that would prevail in the absence of a union. A one-company town may have very low wages.

5. When does the price of the extra resources used in production reflect the marginal social cost of the increase in production?

☐ When the same first four equations hold in all other lines of production, so that the competing demands for each resource also reflect their contributions to social benefit.
☐ When there are no "cost externalities," that is, when all the social costs of production are included in the private costs. When a firm is not charged for the pollution of air or water that it causes, the total cost to society of expanding production exceeds the private (input) costs to the firm.

It can be seen that there are a number of ways in which the market system may not lead to optimum resource allocation. Economists have given a great deal of attention to some of them—particularly to the failure of competition through various restrictive practices, and to the externalities in costs or benefits which accrue to others than the producer or consumer of the particular product. And economists have been quite aware of the critical importance of a reasonably fair distribution of disposable income, after all the tax deductions and transfer supplements.

But far less critical attention has been given to the assumption that the market purchases of a household actually reflect the benefits received. This requires not only reasonably good solutions to the consensus problem within the family, and adequate decision-making processes, but it also requires that households have good economic information and insights. They must understand the kinds of economic principles discussed in the rest of this book and have the current information with which to apply them. Hence, we now turn to the problem of household economic information.

Household Economic Information

There are some commodities which cannot be produced and sold in the marketplace because they can be enjoyed by additional people without cost. These are sometimes called social goods. Clean air is an often-cited example; I cannot benefit from antipollution expenditures without sharing the benefits with my neighbor. As a result, there is no "market" for clean air, in the sense of everyone paying for the clean air that they want. The shared benefits create a "free-rider" problem; if left to individual decision, there would be too little aggregate antipollution spending. Consumer information is another example of a social good, because it can be given away without being given up, i.e., you can give information to another person and still have it yourself. As with spending for clean air, a free-market approach to information would result in too little of it being purchased.

Since it is important that consumers be well informed, the problem is how the necessary information can be assembled, interpreted, and disseminated to them. Discussion of this problem will be easier if we distinguish consumer insights and permanent information from various kinds of current consumer information.

Permanent Insights and Facts

Some of the things households need to know are relatively permanent items of understanding, insight, or facts that do not change rapidly. Most of this book has been devoted to this kind of information and insight. Households need to be able to use facts and to know what facts they need. The necessary understanding requires working through some rather complex problems. The number of books that focus on the selection of facts and the sophisticated analysis to understand them is relatively small, and they do not sell well. There are many more books that rail passionately against the mendacity of sellers or the stupidity of consumers, but while muckraking may sell books, it is doubtful that it produces consumers with insight or information.

Judicious use of the library can, however, produce a great deal of useful information, and the search appears more nearly worthwhile if one remembers that this lasting sort of information and insight accumulates. It is a kind of capital investment that may pay off in a number of future decisions. Some of the sources are likely to give only one side of the story, such as the official or unofficial journals of various business or labor groups (*Printer's Ink, Tide*, labor union periodicals). Magazines with advertising tell the good points of new products, but information on their drawbacks is harder to acquire.

The *Journal of Home Economics* reflects a more direct concern with household economic problems. Its annual review of research may lead the reader to more extensive studies, often published in obscure places like the agricultural extension service bulletins or research bulletins of the agricultural experiment stations. These government publications are not adequately indexed, although references to them do appear in the United States National Agricultural Library *Bibliography of Agriculture* and in publications of the United States Office of Experiment Stations. There are also technical journals of nutrition, medicine, and public health.

Legal information is more difficult, since a professional association jealous of its prerogatives is involved. But articles in law journals are often useful. The technicalities and variation from state to state are such that the admonition to see a lawyer rather than trust a book may be justified. Do-it-yourself books on legal problems, one of the more popular being Norman Dacey's "classic" *How to Avoid Probate*, do appear from time to time, in spite of the illegality of practicing law without a license. The technicalities of garnishment, repossession, and bankruptcy are unlikely to interest those of us who do not think we shall ever need to know them; but for those who do need to know, the literature is quite deficient.

Medical information, in spite of many publications, is still a problem because the technical journals are not written for the layman. Books on insurance abound, and some of them, such as Joseph M. Belth's *Life Insurance: A Consumer's Handbook*, and that published by Consumer's Union, are quite good.

Perhaps the highest quality informational material for the household is in the cookbooks, although even they have not kept up with progress. For instance, they generally give times and temperatures from a period when things were cooked as fast as possible in order to minimize the time spent watching them. Now that we have good temperature regulators, people might prefer to cook things longer at lower temperature in order to get a moister roast or to adjust work schedules, so it would be useful to know how one can trade a lower temperature for a longer cooking time. Actually, a good cook understands how to handle interlaced tasks so that their timing is right; in industry, the same problem is dignified with titles like "systems analysis" or "critical path analysis."

There are thousands of specialized "How to . . ." books available. Much of the general, permanent consumer information we have been discussing probably belongs in the curriculum of the secondary schools, and some is already there. Since it is a social necessity that consumers be intelligent, and since information is difficult to market and often complex, society owes it to itself to see that it is taught to each new generation. Some parts of it are salable in the marketplace, although sometimes the books that sell do so because they provide convenience, or scapegoats, and not primarily information.

Current Information

When we come to the more perishable information about quality and prices of the goods and services on the market, we cannot depend upon the public schools, or on books which would quickly become obsolete. It is difficult for governments to get involved at all, since it is the fates of private sellers which may be affected by better-informed consumers. Our government's inability or unwillingness to deal with clearly harmful products like cigarettes, and the conservative, even secretive, history of the National Bureau of Standards, are not encouraging. Yet France, Sweden, and Germany all have government-aided consumer information publications.

What households need is information about the choices they are currently about to make, up-to-date information on the alternatives available and their prices and quality, and some renewed insights on how to interpret the information. Unemployment and low incomes, or high and rising prices, usually stir up waves of concern about the plight of the consumer and new attempts to do something about it. In the depths of the Great Depression this led to books like *Your Money's Worth, 100,000,000 Guinea Pigs, Eat, Drink and Be Wary,* and also to the formation of Consumers Research, devoted to testing products and reporting their qualities. Disputes about labor standards (whether to allow the employees to organize, and whether to report the labor conditions under which the tested products were made, since there was no Fair Labor Standards Act then) led to a schism and to the formation of Consumers Union, which answered both questions "yes." Consumers Union's *Consumer Reports* magazine has since far outstripped Consumers Research *Bulletin* in circulation and in quantity and quality of information.[1]

With circulation of three million, *Consumer Reports* has a substantial effect on consumers and producers. The benefits spread far more widely, because there are many more readers than subscribers, because the news travels beyond readership, and because the increased price-quality correlation makes it more likely that even the uninformed consumers will get what they pay for.

In this respect, it should be stated clearly that there is a great difference between buying clubs, which secure benefits for their own members, often at the expense of other consumers, and consumer information services, which increase competition, make it possible for better producers and retailers to survive, and improve things for everyone. If price were a perfect reflection of quality, then I would need only to decide how much quality I wanted (and could afford). And I would not need to shop around. In fact, price and quality often have a surprisingly low correlation with one another. Informed buyers will increase the correlation in the market between price and quality. A common way sellers take the sting out of consumer information organizations is to offer discounts to their members. After a short time, such organizations usually lose their drive, and the sellers can quietly remove the privilege. Even if it remains, other consumers do not benefit.

But what product testing and other market information organizations sell is as much convenience and a sense of belonging as it is information. A consumer could always get the same information by borrowing a copy of *Consumer Reports*, or reading it at the public library. Even that convenience is useful only for those with long memories, long horizons, or the ability to keep a library of journals and look up the relevant parts when some choice has to be made.

Technically, the problem is that the magazine format forces the information to be batch-processed, printed, and allowed to get out of date before the same subject is taken up again. The consumer thus finds that the information he wants is neither easily accessible, nor up to date, nor well tailored for his needs. He may be interested only in

---

1. This happened in spite of the fact that for some years the former was on the House Un-American Activities Committee's *List of Subversive Organizations*. It was formally removed from the list in 1953, and never was on the more carefully prepared Attorney General's list.

a particular type or a particular price range. Or he may want to scan the options.

An easy, but inadequate, solution would seem to be to keep all the information in a computer and allow consumers to address their questions to the computer. Experiments with this procedure have revealed that such interchanges take up time and energy unnecessarily. Something intermediate is required, with continuous updating of the information bank, not just so that the information is as fresh as possible, but so that it is salable. People will not then rely on getting the information secondhand, because it would be just old enough to be possibly inferior to the latest information. Such a system of providing selected subsets of information from a constantly updated file is potentially a self-supporting and economically viable way of using the marketplace to sell consumer information of the more perishable sort. There would be substantial development costs in getting the procedures set up for assembling, processing, and selling the information, particularly since it would all have to be developed simultaneously.

Local Consumer Information

There is a third kind of consumer information: facts about the price and quality of locally produced goods and services. Here, none of the economies of scale of a national organization will help, for the information is not only perishable but local. Yet some of the lowest correlations between price and quality are at the local level. There have been some magnificent examples of what can be done among the local groups of the British Consumers Association. They have examined and rated the sanitation practices of local restaurants and collected information on catering services, laundries, etc. All of this takes work, not simply the pooling of already available information. Many local groups form and enjoy immediate benefits from sharing the pool of knowledge the members already have. But lacking any procedure to stimulate the production of more information, they soon deteriorate. It is worth reconsidering a consumer information system, sharing information rather than expanding consumer protection systems and grievance-handling machinery. Consumer information systems can lead to several possible outcomes in terms of the fortunes of the sellers. Depending on the capacity of the "best" vendors to expand without sacrificing quality, they may either take over larger market shares or gain little. Depending on the capacity of the worst to improve, they may either go out of business or improve and expand.

A local consumer information system also provides three levels of benefits to consumers:

1. To the individual using information he asked for and paid for
2. To others who got the information free, by accident, or because it had hit the rumor mill
3. To others who still operate without information, simply because the correlation between price and quality has improved

So the social value is considerably larger than the market value of the information to the seller of the information. Indeed, if the third effect is large enough, the value of information to the individual drops to zero, because the buyer can go into the marketplace uninformed and still do well.

Information for Consumer Records

There is a fourth type of consumer information useful for record keeping, taxes, and watching trends in prices, namely records of one's own transactions and related flows. The consumer interest in modern computer developments toward a cashless, checkless society is thus far more in the information possibilities than in some small loss of free interest provided by present delays in billing and paying. Consumers need better records of where their money is going, and if the new systems pay attention to that need, they can provide it at little or no cost.

Once all the relevant information is computer-readable anyway, it should be easy to provide the consumer with a detailed, itemized billing that would make his own record keeping much easier. Employers could provide banks with information on employer direct contributions to Social Security, pension funds, insurance, etc., as well as payroll deductions; this information would be passed along with the bank report on other bills paid by the bank or on a bank credit card. In the same way, utility bill information on dates, physical consumption, and rates could also be transmitted, and even the grocery store or department store bill could be itemized, since the information is entered for inventory control anyway.

This would enable consumers to keep proof that particular bills were paid or particular items purchased from a particular store on a particular date. It would allow price comparisons between grocery stores at leisure, and watching for trends in utility bills. Instead of a welter of check stubs, grocery and sales slips, utility bills, payroll check stubs, and scribbled notes, the consumer would have one systematic monthly list.

Sellers as a Source of Information

Those who market goods or services want to provide a selected kind of information to potential customers, ranging from the relatively complex individual counseling of the insurance agent through the newpaper ads for sales to the demure listing of professionals by speciality in the Yellow Pages. Properly balanced with other information and a consciousness of the special interests, such information can clearly be useful.

One of the justifications for advertising is that it provides consumers with market information. Certainly, the local food ads and notices of sales do provide price information. Combined with a good memory, that information can be quite helpful. Advertising that economists regard as unproductive is the more competitive sort, touting one of several similar products and forcing competitors to spend money to do the same. The total result may be no larger sales, no greater competition, but higher costs.

It is useful to note where "sales" are advertised, the sales may be of several different kinds:

☐ Getting rid of things that would not sell because of overpricing or lack of customer interest.
☐ Getting rid of seasonal items to avoid having to store them until the season comes around again.
☐ Spreading sales over the year by keeping the store busy during slack seasons.
☐ Keeping profitably high prices for those more interested in style, or having what they want right away, but cutting them during seasonal sales to pick up the more price-conscious buyers—a form of price discrimination. Those who buy at the sales get it at less than what they would have to pay if there were no sales, thereby benefiting at the expense of those who buy when they need it.
☐ Enticing customers into the store with a "bait bargain," then getting them to buy something else, or something more, that provides some profit.

Government as a Source of Consumer Information

There is a variety of consumer information available, much of it in the form of free or inexpensive pamphlets, from many government agencies. Although some new activities of interest to consumers spring up in the most unexpected places, result in a few publications, and then wither away with a change in personnel or administration, there have been a number of relatively persistent sources issuing information. The United States Department of Agriculture, the Food and Drug Administration, and the Administration on Aging are three. The state agricultural extension services and their experiment stations also issue bulletins. Recently the General Services Administration has been issuing two indexes of selected government publications, one called *Consumer Product Information*, and the other *Consumer Information*. The President's Office of Consumer Affairs issues a variety of publications. The *Monthly Catalogue of U.S. Government Publications* of the Government Accounting Office is also helpful, although not everything government agencies publish gets listed.

There is a bewildering variety of Congressional committees that solicit reports and research and publish them. In general, however, the government seldom gives information about products by brand name, and this includes even the armed services and the National Bureau of Standards, both of which buy or test many products. Attempts have been made (but with limited success), particularly since the Freedom of Information Act, to pry from the government information it has that would be useful to consumers. For example, under the Aging Americans Act, nursing homes must be inspected at least once a year in order to qualify for Medicare or Medicaid. Attempts to secure access to these inspection reports has been discouraging. Similarly, it took a protracted suit by Consumers Union to secure the results of hearing-aid tests from the National Bureau of Standards, and then the information was out of date. It seems likely that the government will continue to be a better source of general consumer information than of information about individual brands.

There are a number of other agencies, mostly private, which provide a mixture of consumer information and protection: the American College of Surgeons; the American Dental Association, Council on Dental Therapeutics; the American Medical Association, Council on Pharmacy and Chemistry, Council on Physical Therapy, Council on Foods and Nutrition, Committee on Advertising of Cosmetics and Soaps, and Bureau of Investigation; the American Institute of Laundering; Better Business Bureaus; Underwriters Laboratories (which test the safety of electrical appliances); and the Major Appliance Consumer Action Panel (with a "hot line" for complaints).

There is probably more consumer information in the Sears, Penneys, and Wards mail order catalogs, and more protection through their testing programs and refund policies, than many other sources offer. Certainly the "seals of approval" of magazines that accept advertising from producers (such as *Good Housekeeping*) are of dubious value. The difference between a magazine like *Consumer Reports*, whose revenue comes solely and directly from consumers, and one whose main revenue is from sellers' advertising is important to remember.

Another procedure tried by consumers to protect themselves has been to form cooperatives. In some areas they have been moderately successful, as in credit unions and the newer burial cooperatives. In food retailing they have been unable to do much better than the large chain stores. With consumer durables, they have usually ended up becoming buying clubs for the exclusive benefit of their members. It is probably not a solution to consumers' problems to attempt to go into business, except in rare situations of insensitivity to consumer wants or restrictive practices and very high margins. We discussed housing cooperatives in chapter 4.

Shopping and Bargaining

One of the great historic advances in merchandising, often attributed to the United States, is the open posting of prices. Economists as well as ordinary consumers applauded it because it increased competition, made it easier for consumers to know the choices they faced, and seemed fairer. Even where prices are posted, however, bargaining still goes on in many places. It is easy to locate examples of substantial savings from careful shopping and from bargaining, and we have already mentioned the price-quality frontier that one tries to approach.

Whenever I need to buy something, I have to add to my accumulated stock of general knowledge about quality and past prices some up-to-date information about what is available now, at what prices, and whether any bargaining is going on. The bargaining may take the form of variable trade-ins, even on useless broken-down things that the seller simply scraps. Or the seller may "throw in" something extra. There is a vast difference, however, between shopping and open determination of best buys on the one hand and secret negotiation for the best bargains on the other. The former increases competition, rewards the most efficient producers and distributors, and improves things for all consumers. The latter makes the market less effective and less equitable for customers who do not have the skill, patience, and fortitude to bargain. The more we individually demand special deals, the more we move back to the haggling system of the Middle Ages, which made the most profits for the shrewdest and most cunning sellers, not for those with the lowest prices for the quality.

Just as there are few economies of scale in settling individual complaints and disagreements, so it is unlikely that the advantages of bargaining would generalize. If every customer haggled about the price, the total costs of distribution would certainly go up because of the time and manpower involved!

With this in mind, I must still attempt to obtain the best price and quality I can, but I can at least attempt to broadcast all the information I get about the actual (bargained) prices, so that they tend to become the market norm, available to everyone. This is why we have stressed the information-getting aspects of shopping throughout this book rather than the bargaining aspects, and proposed more systematic methods of assembling and redistributing the information about prices and qualities. The same principle applies to services, even though the definition of the "service" is less precise.

Research on Consumer Behavior

Research such as product testing, designed to serve the consumer, needs to be based on some prior understanding of the consumer, his wants and desires, and his habits. Product evaluation requires measuring various attributes, and then weighting the scores on each attribute according to its importance. If I do not care about small differences in electricity consumption, but have a lot of difficulty keeping the vegetables crisp in the refrigerator with attendant expensive spoilage, then I am interested primarily in buying a refrigerator with good moisture control, not merely with low electricity consumption.

Some basic research on consumer attitudes and behavior, properly translated, is also relevant to understanding consumer problems. We have already talked about learning and the process by which success leads to rising aspiration levels, and perhaps higher expectancies of future success, and wider horizons. On the negative side, we know that we are all subject to two problems, self-deception and a tendency to conform. The major example of the former is our failure to be critical of our own past decisions; originally called rationalization, it is now more appropriately called "dissonance reduction," the process of making the world seem congruent with our own past decisions. Of course, it is healthy within limits not to spend time regretting past mistakes, but it is not healthy to ignore them entirely or to distort reality in order to make them fit. Indeed, a revealing difference between people who are careful consumers and those who are not is the willingness of the former to admit their mistakes and profit from them.

Conformity is more difficult to discuss, because the evidence is less clear and the interpretation more subject to dispute. Dramatic experiments, in which pressure was put on one individual to agree with the judgments of the rest of the group, all of whom were stooges, show that people will disbelieve even the evidence of their own eyes. But in real life, the people we associate with are not stooges. If we behave the way others do, it can be argued that this is not really their influence, but a reflection of the fact that we have common backgrounds and interests (that is why we associate in the first place), or a result of a flow of information (we found out about the product by seeing it in use, or we figure that if Jones, whom we know to be a knowledgeable and careful buyer, picked that brand, it must be a safe selection).

This is not to say there are not pressures to conformity, but that they are mixed up with other things, and demonstrating influence is much more difficult than showing that groups in fact act or think alike.

Survey Research

While it is possible to find data about consumer behavior, sometimes in individual market areas, or before and after some change in prices or income, such semi-aggregated data do not carry us very far in understanding consumer behavior. The most powerful tool for this purpose is survey research. The results of such research are used in marketing and in helping decide issues of public policy, so it is important for the informed consumer to understand a little about the process to be able to spot poor quality research, and to interpret research findings sensibly.

The big advantage of survey research is that information from a small representative sample can tell us much about a whole population. Survey research on human populations is a relatively recent addition to our arsenal of scientific tools. Any research method becomes scientific only if it produces quantified and reproducible findings. And it can have its findings extended beyond its immediate data only if those data come from a representative sample. Three innovations have converted the process of asking people questions from a journalist's art to a scientific method.

First, one must have an unbiased representative sample in order to use survey results to talk about some whole population or subpopulation. Completely random selection is not crucial. Rather, the key is to know the probability of selection of every eligible respondent, family, or unit being sampled. There are unbiased ways of selecting probability samples which are far more efficient and less likely to vary from the true population than a simple random sample. It is crucial, of course, that a high proportion of the sample be interviewed successfully, because even the best sample can become biased through differential nonresponse.

One important fact about sampling is counterintuitive: the precision of survey results depends on the actual size of the sample and on its design, but hardly at all on the size of the population being sampled or on the percent of the population interviewed! This means that it takes nearly as large a sample to say something about one small town as it does to speak about the whole country. As sample size increases, the variability of sample estimates falls roughly in proportion to the square root of the number of cases, so doubling a sample size reduces sampling "errors" by about 40 percent.

Second, obtaining reliable information requires methods of interviewing and analysis that are reproducible and not biased by the procedures or the attitudes of the interviewers. The basic requirement here is to ask the same question of everyone in the same words, and controlling the interpretation of the responses. Responses other than "yes," "no," some amount, or a choice of a few stated alternatives require that answers be written down and analyzed in a central office under controls, including recoding to assure consistency. When this is not done, there is a disturbing tendency for the replies to questions on attitudes or public policy to vary depending on the sponsorship of the study or the kind of organization doing the work. It is useful for the ordinary reader of survey results to know just what questions were asked—biases are sometimes apparent in the questions—and something about how the answers were treated.

Third, analysis of survey data requires finding relationships that are not spurious. Are women paid less than men even if we take account of education, years of experience, and age? Modern computers and statistical analysis make it easier to tackle such questions. The basic procedure is simple, however. If one looks separately at many small groups with the same age, education, and job tenure within a group, are the men paid more than the women within each group? If the wage differences between men and women remain until we take account of the exact job being done, then disappear, we know that it is access to jobs (or self-selection to jobs) that is crucial and calls for investigation.

For the user of the results of survey research, an assessment of the quality of the data requires answers to questions like:

1. Was there a probability sample, and of what population? (A large sample of a limited population may not be generalizable, e.g., a probability sample of people in one city or state.)

2. Were the questions asked exactly as they appear on the questionnaire and do they seem to be reasonably unbiased? (A request to agree or disagree with some statement or opinion is not unbiased, because people tend to agree to anything, particularly if they have little education or are authoritarian.)

3. Are the relationships shown a possible spurious artifact resulting from joint relationships with some third factor, like age or income?

4. Are the findings "statistically significant," that is, unlikely to have arisen from pure chance? (Even if statistical tests are used, or sampling variances given, the results may still be deceptive if the authors made a large number of tests. But aside from that, the concept of sampling variance is based on the notion that if one had a whole set of similar samples, there would be a range of findings, of which the sample at hand is one. The variability of that range of findings tells us something about the meaning of the one we have.)

How Survey Research Can Benefit Consumers

There are three different ways in which information elicited from consumers can benefit them. One, already discussed, is the redissemination to consumers of sampled experience of other consumers with local repair service and quality, with local price and availability of products, or with quality of products nationally.

A second use of survey data informs producers or retailers about problems consumers are having, or desires that are not being met. While it is true that most market research is an attempt to discover how to sell something, some of it does (and more of it could) focus on improving product design or service.

A third use is to inform elected representatives and government administrators about the quality of what the government does and about people's needs and desires that might call for new government initiatives. As more and more of our resources are allocated by decisions to tax and spend on social priorities, rather than by individual purchase decisions in free markets, we can no longer rely on prices and sales as indicators of what people want and what satisfies them. Elected representatives have to make decisions, and systematic, genuinely representative information from the voters would help. An occasional election is not enough. Where governments or large bureaucracies like the public utilities are serving consumers directly, surveys can even monitor the quality of that service. Wherever consumers have no choice of alternative services, they need a way of letting people know whether they are satisfied, or whether some new services are needed. To each consumer there is only one Internal Revenue Service, Social Security system, welfare department, Postal Service, electric company. Systematic survey evidence would seem a more powerful way of improving such services than occasional incidents or dramatic journalism.

APPENDIX 1   **Consumer Decisions Involving Costs and Benefits at Different Times**

No man acquires property without acquiring with it a little arithmetic also.
   Ralph Waldo Emerson

Decisions involving the future require comparing costs and benefits that happen at different times. If one can settle on some reasonable interest rate, the simplest way to compare alternatives is to calculate their "present value." On the other hand, particularly when widely different amounts of money are involved, estimating the internal rate of return on each alternative investment makes it easier to compare them.

The present value of a future stream of benefits is calculated by adding up the "discounted" present value of each future sum. At an interest or discount rate r, the present value of an amount D, n years in the future, is $D/(1 + r)^n$. When the annual cost or benefit is the same for many years, tables can be set up which allow you to calculate the present value of an annual stream without doing it for each year separately. The present value of $100 a year for ten years at 3 percent, for instance, is 8.53 × $100, or $853. In other words, if you put $853 in the bank, you could withdraw $100 a year for ten years; the difference between what you put in and what you withdrew ($147) is interest earned on the remaining balance.

The numbers in tables A–C, plus a few useful rules of thumb, provide the basis for calculating present values in a variety of situations. The simplest situation is that in which a sum, D, is available in x years. The second column of numbers in table A shows how to discount D back to the present. At a 3 percent interest rate, the present value of $10,000 to be received twenty years from now is $10,000 × 0.554 = $5,540. Table B gives this same information in greater detail for interest rates of 3, 6, 9, and 12 percent.

The "future value" of an amount can be calculated from the numbers shown in the third column in table A. For example, in twenty years $1 will grow to $1.806; during the same period, $5,540 will grow to $5,540 × 1.806 = $10,000.

A constant stream of costs or benefits over time can be converted into a present or future value by using the final two columns of numbers in table A. The present value of $1 per year for twenty years at 3 percent is $14.877; the present value of $10,000 per year for twenty years is $148,770. Since an annuity is nothing more than a stream of annual payments, the fourth column shows, in effect, the cost of an annuity of $1 per year for x years. Table C gives a more detailed listing of these conversion numbers and also shows what they are if the interest rate is 6, 9, and 12 percent. The general formula at the bottom of the fourth column in table A can also be used to show that the present value of $1 per year forever is simply $1/0.03 = $33.33 or, more generally, the present value of a stream of D dollars per year at an interest rate, r, is D/r. This is helpful in chapter 4 when we convert certain constant costs or benefits of owning a home into an increased house price. A $100 per year lower property tax payment, for example, ought to increase the house price by $100/0.03 = $3,333.

Table A. Now and Then at 3 Percent

X (Years)	Present Value of $1 if Only Available After X Years	Future Value of $1 in X Years if Invested Now	Present Value (Cost of an Annuity) $1/Year for X Years[a]	Value at End of Period of Accumulation Plus Interest (Value of an Annuity) $1/Year for X Years
1	$.971	$1.030	$ .971	$ 1.030
5	.863	1.159	4.580	5.309
10	.744	1.344	8.530	11.464
15	.642	1.558	11.938	18.599
20	.554	1.806	14.877	26.870
25	.478	2.094	17.413	36.459
30	.411	2.427	19.600	47.575
35	.355	2.814	21.487	60.462
40	.307	3.262	23.115	75.401
45	.264	3.782	24.519	92.720
50	.228	4.384	25.730	112.797
n	$\dfrac{1}{(1+.03)^n}$	$(1+.03)^n$	$\dfrac{[1-(1+.03)^{-n}]}{.03}$	$\dfrac{[(1+.03)^n - 1]}{.03}$
			Amount Now Amount Per Year	Amount Then (at end) Amount Per Year

[a] For a mortgage, this column gives (Amount of Mortgage)/(Yearly Payment).

Table B. Present Value of $1 in *n* Years at *r* Percent

	Value at r%					Value at r%			
n	r = 3	r = 6	r = 9	r = 12	n	r = 3	r = 6	r = 9	r = 12
1	$.971	$.943	$.917	$.893	41	$.298	$.092	$.029	$.010
2	.943	.890	.842	.797	42	.289	.087	.027	.009
3	.915	.840	.772	.711	43	.281	.082	.025	.008
4	.888	.792	.708	.636	44	.272	.077	.023	.007
5	.863	.747	.649	.567	45	.264	.073	.021	.006
6	.837	.705	.596	.507	46	.257	.069	.019	.005
7	.813	.665	.547	.452	47	.249	.065	.017	.005
8	.789	.627	.502	.404	48	.242	.061	.018	.004
9	.766	.592	.460	.361	49	.235	.058	.015	.004
10	.744	.558	.422	.322	50	.228	.054	.013	.003
11	.722	.527	.388	.287	51	.221	.051	.012	.003
12	.701	.497	.358	.257	52	.215	.048	.011	.003
13	.681	.469	.326	.229	53	.209	.046	.010	.002
14	.661	.442	.299	.205	54	.203	.043	.010	.002
15	.642	.417	.275	.183	55	.197	.041	.009	.002
16	.623	.394	.252	.163	56	.191	.038	.008	.002
17	.605	.371	.231	.146	57	.185	.036	.007	.002
18	.587	.350	.212	.130	58	.180	.034	.007	.001
19	.570	.331	.194	.118	59	.175	.032	.006	.001
20[a]	.554	.312	.178	.104	60	.170	.030	.006	.001
21	.538	.294	.164	.093	61	.165	.029	.005	.001
22	.522	.278	.150	.083	62	.160	.027	.005	.001
23	.507	.262	.138	.074	63	.155	.025	.004	.001
24	.492	.247	.128	.066	64	.151	.024	.004	.001
25	.478	.233	.118	.059	65	.146	.023	.004	.001
26	.464	.220	.108	.053					
27	.450	.207	.098	.047					
28	.437	.196	.090	.042					
29	.424	.185	.082	.037					
30	.412	.174	.075	.033	70	.126	.017	.002	.000
31	.400	.164	.069	.030					
32	.388	.155	.063	.027					
33	.477	.146	.058	.024					
34	.366	.138	.053	.021					
35	.355	.130	.049	.019	75	.109	.013	.002	.000
36	.345	.123	.045	.017					
37	.335	.116	.041	.015					
38	.325	.109	.038	.013					
39	.316	.103	.035	.012					
40	.307	.097	.032	.011	80	.094	.009	.001	.000

[a]Using this line as an example of how the table works, we see that $1 available 20 years hence is now worth only $.55 if the interest rate is 3 percent or $.31 if the rate is 6 percent. (At 6 percent $.31 now will increase to $1.00 in 20 years.)

The final column of numbers in table A shows the future value of a stream, rather than its present value. Thus, a $100 annual deposit will grow, at a 3 percent interest rate, to $2,687 in twenty years.

Future interest rates are unpredictable, and one might fear that they will render present value calculations worthless. Fortunately, this is not the case. Inflation not only drives up the dollar amounts of the future costs and benefits, but also the interest rates that are used to discount those inflated amounts. Since the free market interest rates tend to be about three percentage points higher than the rate of inflation, a 3 percent rate is appropriate for discounting streams of costs or benefits that can be expected to increase with inflation. To see this important result, recall that the present value of an amount D, n years in the future, is $D/(1 + r)^n$. An inflation rate of g percent per year will cause the D dollars to grow to

Table C. Present Value of $1 per Year at r Percent Compound Interest per Year for n Years

	Value at r%					Value at r%			
n	$r = 3$	$r = 6$	$r = 9$	$r = 12$	n	$r = 3$	$r = 6$	$r = 9$	$r = 12$
1	$ .971	$ .943	$ .917	$ .893	21	$15.415	$11.764	$ 9.292	$7.562
2	1.913	1.853	1.759	1.690	22	15.937	12.042	9.442	7.645
3	2.829	2.673	2.531	2.402	23	16.444	12.303	9.580	7.718
4	3.717	3.465	3.240	3.037	24	16.936	12.550	9.707	7.784
5	4.580	4.212	3.890	3.605	25	17.413	12.783	9.823	7.843
6	5.417	4.917	4.486	4.111	26	17.877	13.003	9.929	7.896
7	6.230	5.582	5.033	4.564	27	18.327	13.210	10.027	7.943
8	7.020	6.210	5.535	4.968	28	18.764	13.406	10.116	7.984
9	7.786	6.802	5.995	5.328	29	19.188	13.591	10.198	8.022
10	8.530	7.360	6.418	5.650	30	19.600	13.765	10.274	8.055
11	9.253	7.887	6.805	5.938	31	20.000	13.929	10.343	8.085
12	9.954	8.383	7.161	6.194	32	20.389	14.084	10.406	8.112
13	10.635	8.853	7.487	6.424	33	20.766	14.230	10.464	8.135
14	11.296	9.295	7.786	6.628	34	21.132	14.368	10.518	8.157
15	11.938	9.712	8.061	6.811	35	21.487	14.498	10.567	8.176
16	12.561	10.106	8.313	6.974					
17	13.166	10.477	8.544	7.120					
18	13.754	10.828	8.756	7.250					
19	14.324	11.158	8.950	7.366					
20[a]	14.877	11.470	9.129	7.469	40	23.115	15.006	10.757	8.344
					∞	33.333	16.667	11.111	8.333

[a]Using this line as an example of how the table works, we see that $14,877 now will provide $1,000 per year for 20 years if the interest rate is 3 percent.

$D(1 + g)^n$, but will also cause the interest rate to increase to $r + g$. Since $(1 + r + g)^n$ is approximately equal to $(1 + r)^n(1 + g)^n$, the present value formula in the presence of inflation is $D(1 + g)^n/(1 + r)^n(1 + g)^n$, which reduces to the original formula of $D/(1 + r)^n$. Thus present value calculations that use inflated dollars and inflated interest rates are virtually identical to present value calculations that use noninflated dollars and a real 3 percent interest rate.

Since the free market interest rate tends to be about three percentage points higher than the rate of inflation, a 3 percent interest rate is appropriate for discounting streams of costs and benefits that can be expected to increase with inflation. Notice, however, that the expected *market* interest rate must be used to discount streams of costs and benefits that won't increase with inflation. Suppose, for example, that the inflation rate is 6 percent and is expected to remain at that level for some time, and that the market interest rate is 9 percent. If I win a lottery and must choose between receiving $100,000 now or $15,000 per year for the next ten years, then I must discount the stream of $15,000 payments at 9 percent rather than 3. (If the payments were automatically increased to keep up with inflation, then the 3 percent rate is appropriate.) From table C the present value of $1 per year for ten years at 9 percent is $6.42, so the present value of the payment stream is $15,000 × 6.42 = $96,300, and the $100,000 is preferred. Most of the future costs and benefits relevant to consumer decisions (e.g., income, house value, operating costs) can be expected to increase with inflation. A 3 percent interest rate can be used to discount these future amounts without having to predict future rates of inflation. Occasionally, however, the costs or benefits are fixed in value (e.g., a fixed pension payment) and must be discounted with expected *market* interest rates.

Sometimes some costs and benefits are not measurable. Then the best one can do is to calculate the present values of the measurable parts of two alternatives and ask oneself whether the nonmeasurable differences justify the measurable ones or more than offset them.

When one is purchasing an impermanent, or wasting, asset such as a car or appliance, it is not necessary to calculate the present value of the stream of depreciation costs and the stream of foregone interest on the money invested in the thing. It turns out that *whatever the interest rate and whatever the length of life of the asset, the present value of the stream of "capital costs" is exactly equal to the present price of the asset.* (More on this in chap. 8.) There may be other costs, of course, such as repairs, taxes, or operating expenses, which would have to be "discounted" to present values.

If the present value of the capital costs of a $1,000 wasting asset does not depend on the length of its life, the present value of the benefits clearly does. Consequently, the longer a durable lasts, per dollar of cost, the more likely it is to be a preferred alternative. Another way to think of it is that the annual costs are less.

The most important use of the basic tables of annuity value is in understanding saving for retirement. If one starts working and saving at age twenty-five, then for each possible retirement age there is a relationship between the amount saved per year and the fund available at retirement. Then, given a life expectancy, there is a relationship between the fund available at retirement and the annual retirement annuity purchasable with that fund. By specifying the fraction of the preretirement consumption level desired after retirement, we can estimate the fraction of income that needs to be saved to meet the goal (see chap. 5).

Finally, life insurance needs can also be calculated using the same basic table, this time discounting back to the present the future streams of income needed. A varied pattern can be converted into blocks of years, and the "present value" of the stream at the beginning of each block estimated and converted to a value now (see chap. 9).

The most important compromise or assumption in this whole analysis is that the real rate of interest is 3 percent so that if there is an inflation rate of 4 percent, there will be a market rate of 7 percent. We must assume that it is possible to earn the market interest rate if we are saving rather than borrowing.

APPENDIX 2 **FTC Buyers Guide No. 7: Fair Credit Reporting Act**[1]

If you have a charge account, a mortgage on your home, life insurance, or have applied for a personal loan or job it is almost certain there is a "file" existing somewhere that shows how you pay your bills, if you have been sued, arrested, or filed for bankruptcy, etc.

And some of these files include your neighbors' and friends' views of your character, general reputation, or manner of living.

The companies that gather and sell such information to creditors, insurers, employers, and other businesses are called "Consumer Reporting Agencies," and the legal term for the report is "Consumer Report."

If, in addition to credit information, the report involves interviews with a third person about your character, reputation, or manner of living, it is referred to as an "Investigative Consumer Report."

The Fair Credit Reporting Act became law on April 25, 1971. It was passed by Congress to protect consumers against the circulation of inaccurate or obsolete information, and to insure that consumer reporting agencies exercise their responsibilities in a manner that is fair and equitable to consumers.

Under this new law you can now take steps to protect yourself if you have been denied credit, insurance, or employment, or if you believe you have had difficulties because of a consumer report on you.

Here are the steps you can take.

You have the right:

1. To be told the name and address of the consumer reporting agency responsible for preparing a consumer report that was used to deny you credit, insurance, or employment or to increase the cost of credit or insurance.

2. To be told by a consumer reporting agency the na-

---

[1]. U.S. Federal Trade Commission, *FTC Buyers Guide No. 7, Fair Credit Reporting Act*. Washington, D.C.: U.S. Government Printing Office, 1975. Permission is granted to reprint this leaflet, in whole or in part, in a legal and nondeceptive manner.

ture, substance and sources (except investigative-type sources) of the information (except medical) collected about you.

3. To take anyone of your choice with you when you visit the consumer reporting agency to check on your file.

4. To obtain all information to which you are entitled, free of charge, when you have been denied credit, insurance, or employment within 30 days of your interview. Otherwise, the reporting agency is permitted to charge a reasonable fee for giving you the information.

5. To be told who has received a consumer report on you within the preceding six months, or within the preceding two years if the report was furnished for employment purposes.

6. To have incomplete or incorrect information reinvestigated, unless the request is frivolous, and, if the information is found to be inaccurate or cannot be verified, to have such information removed from your file.

7. To have the agency notify those you name (at no cost to you) who have previously received the incorrect or incomplete information that this information has been deleted from your file.

8. When a dispute between you and the reporting agency about information in your file cannot be resolved, you have the right to have your version of such dispute placed in the file and included in future consumer reports.

9. To request the reporting agency to send your version of the dispute to certain businesses for a reasonable fee.

10. To have a consumer report withheld from anyone who under the law does not have a legitimate business need for the information.

11. To sue a reporting agency for damages if it willfully or negligently violates the law and, if you are successful, you can collect attorney's fees and court costs.

12. Not to have adverse information reported after seven years. One major exception is bankruptcy, which may be reported for fourteen years.

13. To be notified by a business that it is seeking information about you which would constitute an "Investigative Consumer Report."

14. To request from the business that ordered an investigative report, more information about the nature and scope of the investigation.

15. To discover the nature and substance (but not the sources) of the information that was collected for an "Investigative Consumer Report."

The Fair Credit Reporting Act does not:

1. Give you the right to request a report on yourself from the consumer reporting agency.

2. Give you the right, when you visit the agency, to receive a copy of or to physically handle your file.

3. Compel anyone to do business with an individual consumer.

4. Apply when you request commercial (as distinguished from consumer) credit or business insurance.

5. Authorize any Federal agency to intervene on behalf of an individual consumer.

How to deal with consumer reporting agencies

If you want to know what information a consumer reporting agency has collected about you, either arrange for a personal interview at the agency's office during normal business hours or call in advance for an interview by telephone.

The consumer reporting agencies in your community can be located by consulting the "Yellow Pages" of your telephone book under such headings as "Credit" or "Credit Rating or Reporting Agencies."

If you decide to visit a consumer reporting agency to check on your file the following checklist may be of help.

For instance, did you:

1. Learn the nature and substance of all the information in your file?

2. Find out the names of each of the businesses (or other sources) that supplied information on you to the reporting agency?

3. Learn the names of everyone who received reports on you within the past six months (or the last two years if the reports were for employment purposes)?

4. Request the agency to re-investigate and correct or delete information that was found to be inaccurate, incomplete, or obsolete?

5. Follow-up to determine the results of the re-investigation?

6. Ask the agency, at no cost to you, to notify those you name who received reports within the past six months (two years if for employment purposes) that certain information was deleted?

7. Follow-up to make sure that those named by you did in fact receive notices from the consumer agency?

8. Demand that your version of the facts be placed in your file if the re-investigation did not settle the dispute?

9. Request the agency (if you are willing to pay a rea-

sonable fee) to send your statement of the dispute to those you name who received reports containing the disputed information within the past six months (two years if received for employment purposes)?

For more detailed information on the Fair Credit Reporting Act or to report a violation of the Act contact the FTC in Washington or the nearest regional office. The FTC offices are located in the following cities:

Atlanta, Ga.; Boston, Mass.; Buffalo, N.Y.; Charlotte, N.C.; Chicago, Ill.; Cleveland, Ohio; Dallas, Texas; Denver, Colo.; Detroit, Mich.; Honolulu, Hawaii; Kansas City, Mo.; Los Angeles, Calif.; Miami, Fla.; New Orleans, La.; New York, N.Y.; Oak Ridge, Tenn.; Phoenix, Ariz.; Portland, Ore.; St. Louis, Mo.; San Antonio, Texas; San Diego, Calif.; San Francisco, Calif.; Seattle, Wash.; Washington, D.C. area field offices; Upper Darby, Penn.

Look under "Federal Trade Commission" in the telephone directories of these cities for the addresses and telephone numbers of the field offices.

Glossary

Abstract—A summary of the history of the legal title to a piece of property.

Actuary—An expert in the mathematics of risk, probability, life expectancies, and insurance. It takes a special examination to become a licensed actuary.

Administrator of an estate—A person appointed by a probate or surrogate court to manage and distribute the assets of an estate if the decedent (one who died) did not leave a proper will appointing a proper executor or executrix.

Adverse selection—A propensity for those with a higher than average probability of collecting to carry insurance. It makes the insurance a bad buy for the average person.

Amortized loan—A loan repaid by a series of constant payments which repay both a portion of principal and interest on the remaining balance.

Annuity—A stream of annual payments, either accumulating with compound interest, or being repaid with interest on the remaining balance, or both.

Appraisal—An evaluation of the market value of a property (house and lot).

Assessed value—An administratively assigned "market value" assigned by the property tax assessor for tax purposes; often some fraction of true market value. It must be multiplied by the property tax rate to find the property tax, which can then be related to market value of the house.

Assigned risk—A high-risk person who is assigned to an insurance company at random. Some states do such assignments to assure that insurance is available even to high-risk people.

Assignment of property—The transfer of a right or interest in property by one person to another.

Attachable—Subject to being taken to pay debts.

Attractive nuisance—A legal concept making you liable for damages if you have an attraction, e.g., swimming pool, even if you post a sign, "No swimming."

Balloon note—A loan with some amortizing payments, but a substantial balance to be paid off at the end of the period.

Bankruptcy—A legal procedure under federal law for distributing remaining assets among the creditors of a person or business and wiping the slate clean of indebtedness. Cannot be repeated within seven years. *See* Title 13.

Beneficiary—One who receives property that someone who dies has willed to him or her.

Bequeath—To give property upon the death of the giver.

Binder—A receipt for money paid to secure the right to purchase real estate upon agreed terms.

Book value—The value of a business according to its accounting records. Since assets are valued by purchase price less accrued depreciation charges, current market value is often much greater than book value in inflationary periods.

Call—A right to purchase shares of a specified stock at a specified price at any time within a specified period.

Capital—Something purchased or created at some present cost that provides a stream of services, benefits, or output in the future, usually depreciating in the process. Sometimes used casually to refer to assets.

Capitalized value—The present value of a future stream of net benefits. For a constant everlasting stream of $X per year at interest rate r, it is X/r.

Cash surrender value (of a life insurance policy)—A prestated amount, in a policy with a savings feature, that is returnable to you if you cancel the policy. It is smaller than the amount you can borrow on the policy if you keep it in force, and smaller than the cash reserve (of your money).

Certificate of title—A paper signifying ownership of a house, usually with a legal description tion of the house and its land.

Chattel mortgage—A loan with personal property given as security for repayment of the loan, transferring title to the property if the loan is not paid.

Closed-end fund—A mutual fund that does not accept additional investments and reinvest them in the stock market, but merely manages the original fund. Shares are usually bought and sold like any other stock, rather than through agents or through the fund. *See* Open-end fund.

Closing costs (or settlement costs)—Costs in addition to the price of a house, including

title search and insurance, transfer of ownership charges; so called because they are paid when the sale is "closed," i.e, when the actual transfer of money and property takes place.

Clustered sample—A multi-stage survey sample where subareas are listed and sampled for sequentially smaller fractions. The result is a saving in travel and cost greater than the loss in precision, and no bias is introduced.

Codicil—A change or addition to a will, added separately.

Coinsurance—1. A provision of an insurance policy by which you bear some fraction of the cost of loss, to provide an incentive for economy. 2. In fire insurance, if you insure for less than the market value, the increase in the fraction of a loss you must pay (or coinsure). 3. Sometimes, sharing by insurance companies of a large risky policy.

Commodity futures—Rights to buy or sell commodities (e.g., wheat, cotton) at some future date.

Compound interest—A form of interest which pays on previously-earned interest as well as on principal.

Condominium—One of a group of apartments or houses, owned by an individual, along with an undivided shared ownership of common areas and facilities.

Conflict of interest—A situation in which economic self-interest may distort a person's decisions or judgments in another area.

Contingent fee—An arrangement in tort law by which a lawyer is paid only if he or she succeeds in securing a damage award for the client.

Contributory negligence—A defense, if you are sued for negligence, that the other person was also negligent.

Cooperative housing—A group of apartments or houses owned in common by the residents. Individuals own shares of stock in the total enterprise.

Cost—A real using up of assets; or expense; often confused with the financial amount in some transfer, such as the cost of welfare.

Credit bureau—An organization keeping records on individuals to establish their credit rating, i.e., the likelihood that they will pay their debts. Businesses pay bureaus for checking whether it is safe to lend to a customer.

Credit life insurance—A small amount of life insurance sufficient to pay off a debt if you die. This protects the lender.

Custodian account—Assets given to minors and managed by a responsible adult (custodian) until the children are eighteen years old.

Decedent—A dead person.

Declining balance depreciation—A bookkeeping method whereby an asset is depreciated by a fraction of the current value rather than a constant amount each year.

Decreasing term insurance—A policy which pays a stated amount per month for the remainder of a stated period, hence an amount of insurance that drops to zero value over time.

Deductible—An insurance provision where you pay a stated portion of a loss, the insurance company the rest.

Depletion allowance—A tax provision allowing deduction from taxable income for depletion of an exhaustible resource; often cited as a tax loophole.

Depreciation—The wearing out and using up of a piece of capital in the course of producing goods or services.

Devise—To give real property, as in a will.

Disability waiver of premium—A small amount of disability insurance added to a life insurance policy sufficient to pay the life insurance premiums if you become disabled.

Discount—To convert a future sum to the present amount that, with interest, would cumulate to that future sum.

Diversification—In investment, the spreading of risk across a variety of investments to reduce the overall risk.

Dividend—1. A distribution of a share of a company's earnings to holders of its common stock. 2. The return at the end of each year of part of an insurance premium, in "participating" policies.

Double declining balance depreciation—A rapid depreciation charge allowed for tax purposes on investments including rental real estate, converting income into capital gains. The depreciation is a fraction of the remaining value, so is largest at the beginning, and is twice the usually allowed rate.

Earnest money—A deposit by buyer to seller, usually of real estate, applied against the purchase if the deal goes through and otherwise forfeited.

Easement—The right of a land owner to use the land of his neighbor, as in common driveways, or any right to use another's property, view, etc.

Efficiency—The allocation of resources to produce the desired output in the most effective way.

Efficiency frontier—The best available combinations of price and quality.

Elasticity—The percent change in something, e.g., output or sales, resulting from a 1 percent change in something else, usually price or income.

Eminent domain—A legal right of governments to condemn and purchase property for public use, at a court-determined price.

Endowment insurance—A policy that rapidly accrues a cash value equal to its face value, so that it can be converted to cash.

Equity—In accounting, a right to ownership of part of something; in economics, the fairness of the distribution of income or rights to the goods and services of society.

Escrow funds—Funds given to a third party to hold until all conditions in a contract are fulfilled.

Executor, Executrix—Someone named in a will to take charge of the estate and distribute it. *See* Administrator of an estate.

Expected value—The probability that an event will occur times its value (positive or negative) if it does.

Expenditure—A paying out of money, which may or may not involve an expense (cost).

Expense—A using up of goods and services, or incurring of obligations or costs, which may or may not involve expenditures.

Face value—The amount paid to a beneficiary upon the death of the holder of a life insurance policy.

Family income (insurance) policy—A combination of ordinary life insurance and a decreasing term insurance policy, with the face value declining to a base which is then constant.

Fee splitting—A payment by a specialist to the person who referred the customer to him or her. Clear conflict of interest.

FHA loan—A loan approved and insured by the Federal Housing Administration.

Fiduciary—A person who because of his or her position or relationship owes a duty of trust and confidence, as a guardian or trustee.

Garnishment—A notice or proceeding which requires an employer to pay part of an employee's wages to the employee's creditor.

Generic drug—A drug that is not patented and may be sold under brand names as well as (more cheaply) by its generic chemical name.

G.I. insurance—Life insurance available to veterans of the armed services through the government.

Group insurance (life or other)—Insurance, usually handled by an employer who makes a single payment to cover a large group, that allows economizing on costs and sometimes compromising on rates paid by employees with different risks.

Group practice—A sharing of location, records, referrals, and equipment by a group of doctors, for greater efficiency.

Growth stock—Stock in a company that reinvests most of its earnings, and for this or other reasons is expected to grow also in size, earnings, future dividends, and the price of its stock.

Guardian—A person appointed to protect the interests of a minor.

Health Maintenance Organization—A combination of group practice and prepaid health care intended to focus on the maintenance of health rather than the care of illness.

Hedge—An investment with a risk opposite to a risk already being borne, so the two risks cancel.

Hire purchase—British term for installment credit.

Holder in due course—The purchaser of a commitment to pay, such as an installment credit contract, who is usually held to have a right to collect regardless of problems with the original product or service.

Holographic will—A will in the handwriting of the maker.

Human capital—Skills (education, on-the-job training) acquired through a process of self-investment. This concept views a human being like a piece of capital in the sense that investments increase future productivity.

Imputed income, interest, rent, or consumption—Estimated flows, when no cash expenditure or receipt occurs, representing real earning or consumption. Depreciation is an imputed consumption, included in the imputed rental income and rental consumption of an owned home. Interest cost of money tied up in a car is an imputed consumption.

Income—A real flow of accrued rights to goods and services resulting from labor, ownership of capital, or transfers.

Indemnity—A reimbursement for a loss sustained.

Inflation—A general increase in prices and thus in the cost of living.

Insider trading—Purchase or sale of stock in a company by officials of the company that must be registered with the Securities and Exchange Commission. Some think such trading gives the investor clues about future earnings.

Interest—Payment for the use of money, as when money is loaned by passbook account holders to banks or when money is loaned by the bank to its customers.

Intestate—A person who dies without leaving a will.

Insurance—A contract in which, in return for a small fee, a company pooling the risks guarantees to reimburse you for losses from specified causes.

Investment—1. The financial act of purchasing securities or other rights to capital. 2. The real act of using resources to create or improve capital.

Investment trust—A financial arrangement which invests your money in a diversified portfolio of things, usually stocks. Same as a mutual fund.

Joint tenancy—Equal ownership interest in the same property. Usually specified "with rights of survivorship and not as tenants in common," so that either person can dispose of the property and claim it as a survivor, thus keeping it out of probate.

Land contract—A method of purchasing real property in which title does not pass until the final payment is made, avoiding need for foreclosure in case of default. Payments are amortized as in a regular mortgage, but often the seller holds the contract; he can, however, sell it to an investor.

Legal reserve life insurance—Insurance policies that maintain level premiums while accruing a reserve of the policyholder's money.

Legatee—Beneficiary of a legacy or bequest in a will leaving personal property.

Level premium life insurance—A type of policy that maintains a constant annual premium, usually by accumulating and using a reserve fund and earnings on the fund.

Leverage—Having the use of more assets than one owns, in order to increase potential earnings; the fixed borrowing commitments increase risk as well.

Lien—A claim filed against the property of another.

Life insurance—Insurance which compensates survivors of a named individual when the individual dies.

Lifetime annuity—A contract paying a guaranteed amount per year as long as you live. Insures against the risk of living too long and running out of money.

Loading—The portion of an insurance policy cost that is not used to pay benefits, but is retained by the company as expenses, profit, or unused "reserves." More generally, the expense and profit fraction of any situation, e.g., a mutual fund.

Loan value of a life insurance policy—The amount, usually less than the reserve (of your money), that you can borrow on the policy at a stated interest rate.

Marginal benefit or utility—The added benefit from a little more, which may not be the same as the average benefit (total divided by the number or amount).

Marginal cost—The cost of one unit more.

Marginal tax rate—In the federal income tax structure, the fraction of an additional dollar of income that would be taxed away.

Mechanic's lien law—The law which allows workers in the building trades to place a lien on property on which they worked (your house) for unpaid wages, even though you may already have paid the contractor. When paid, they will sign a waiver of lien.

Mortgage commitment—A written notice from a bank or other lender stating that it will advance a specified amount to enable you to buy a particular house at some interest rate.

Mortgage discount points—A one-time charge assessed by the lender in order to supplement the interest stated in the mortgage. A way of getting around FHA limits on mortgage interest rates. Officially paid by seller, who adds it to the price.

Mortgage protection insurance—Declining term life insurance sufficient to pay off the remaining mortgage on your house.

Mortgagee—The lender in a mortgage contract.

Mortgagor—The borrower in a mortgage contract.

Mutual fund—A company that reinvests your money in a diversified portfolio of investments, usually common stocks.

Negligence—A failure to take due precautions, leading to injury to another, for which you can be sued under the law of torts.

Net reproduction rate—A measure of population growth more precise than birth rate.

No-load mutual fund—A mutual fund having no difference between buying and selling price, i.e., no agent's fee. Sold directly by the fund or, if closed-end, on the stock market for the usual stockbroker's fee.

Obsolescence—Decline in value not from use but from becoming out of date or out of style.

Open-end mutual fund or investment trust—A fund that accepts additional investments after the initial investment, reinvesting in a portfolio, usually of common stocks.

Opportunity cost—The cost of any choice, measured by the value of the next best foregone alternative.

Option—A right to choose a course of action, e.g., to renew a lease or insurance policy, or to buy something within a stated period at some price. Often purchased as insurance against a rising price or unavailability.

Ordinary life insurance—A life insurance policy that combines life insurance with a savings account. This type of insurance has level premiums, constant face value, and a declining amount of pure insurance.

Outlay—An expenditure, not to be confused with an expense.

Participating insurance policy—A policy that pays dividends at the end of each year (actually a refund of part of the premium).

Participating preferred stock—Preferred stock that can also share in extra profits.

Points—*See* Mortgage discount points.

Policy loan—A loan with your life insurance reserve as security.

Portable pension—A pension that can be taken with you if you leave the company.

Preferred stock—Ownership share in a corporation with prior claim on earnings before common stockholders get anything.

Premium—The annual charge for an insurance policy.

Present value—The value now of future sums to be paid or received.

Prescriptive easement—The right to use another's property because you have been doing so in the past without his or her objection.

Price/earnings ratio—The ratio of a current stock price to the company's last year's earnings per share.

Principal—In a loan, the amount owed, not including interest.

Probability sample—A sample, each element of which has a known probability of selection.

Probate court (or surrogate court)—The court that probates wills.

Probate of a will—A judicial procedure to determine if a document is a valid will that can be enforced to dispose of the estate according to its provisions.

Progressive tax—A tax that tends to take a larger fraction of income the higher the income, and hence is redistributive.

Put—An option to sell a specified stock at a specified price within a specified period; the opposite of a call.

Random sample—A sample in which every element in a population has the same independent probability of being selected.

Real estate, real property, realty—Land, buildings, and any other attached improvements.

Real estate investment trust (R.E.I.T.)—A trust which invests your money in a portfolio of real estate instead of stocks.

Receipts—Money received, whether income or not.

Regressive tax—Tax that tends to take a larger fraction of income from those with lower incomes.

Renewable term insurance—Pure life insurance, renewable periodically without another medical exam (at higher rates, to reflect the higher probability of dying as you get older).

Repossession—The resuming of possession by a creditor of property that was security for a debt, if the debtor defaults.

Reserve—An accumulation of excess premiums and interest in a life insurance policy that reduces the amount of pure insurance and earns further interest.

Residuary trust—A trust to hold that part of an estate outside the marital exemption and deduction, on which estate tax has been paid; used to care for the surviving spouse, but can be transferred to the children when the spouse dies, to avoid another estate tax.

Revenue (or income)—Accrual of rights to goods or services, including earnings, interest, dividends, rent, and transfers, whether received in cash or not.

Risk—A chance that some (usually bad) event will happen; the term ordinarily implies some knowledge of the probability; in contrast with uncertainty, where the probability is unknown. Risks can be insured against.

Risk-adjusted yield—A way of comparing yields of investments with different levels of risk.

Rule of 72—The approximation that, in compound interest, an amount doubles when the interest rate times the number of years reaches 72.

Sampling variance (often called sampling error)—The amount an estimate based on a sample might differ from a value based on the whole population.

Savings bank life insurance—Life insurance available at savings banks to residents in New York and Massachusetts. It has lower premiums because of the lower selling costs.

Settlement options—Alternative ways of paying death benefits of a life insurance policy.

Special assessment—A tax on property for a specific purpose of local benefit, such as new sewers or sidewalks or the first paving of a street.

Stock dividend—An issue of extra shares of stock to stockholders, often instead of money.

Stock split—Same as a stock dividend.

Straight life insurance—Ordinary life insurance, with level premiums, a constant face value, and the accumulation of a cash reserve which, with accrued interest, reduces the amount of pure insurance.

Striking price—The price at which a call or put option allows you to buy or sell the stock.

Subrogation—A substitution of creditors, as when your insurance company collects compensation for damages from another person for you, subrogating your claim. The company may even collect from you for benefits paid by them and also from another source.

Term insurance—Pure insurance for a period of time at a price, with no tied-in saving program.

Testamentary trust—A trust set up by a will.

Testate—A word used to describe a person who died having left a will.

Testator, Testatrix—A person who leaves property by a will.

Time averaging—Investing a constant amount regularly in stock regardless of its price.

Title insurance—Insurance against discovering that the title to your land is incomplete, which covers any losses involved.

Title search—A check back through the various transfers of title to your property before you got it, ideally back to a valid owner.

Title 13—A provision of the Federal Bankruptcy Act allowing the insolvent person to turn his assets and income over to a lawyer for scheduled repayments of part or all debts to creditors. It avoids formal bankruptcy, saves credit rating, and can be repeated without waiting seven years.

Tontine—An ancient alternative to an annuity, wherein the last man alive got it all.

Tort law—The law dealing with injury to another.

Transfer income—Income not currently earned, though there may have been earlier contributions, as with retirement pensions. Includes welfare and Social Security benefits.

Trustee—An individual who receives and administers the property of a trust and is personally liable for its management.

Twenty-year net cost—A method of pricing life insurance which ignores interest and thus can be misleading. It is twenty years of premiums minus dividends minus the cash value at the end.

Uncertainty—The possibility of bad or good events to which no probability can be assigned and thus for which no insurance is possible.

Variable annuity—An annuity whose accumulated funds are invested in stocks or other things calculated to hedge against inflation by rising in value or yield with the price level.

Variance—A statistical measure of dispersion equal to the summed squared deviations around the mean.

Vested interest (in a pension)—Pension rights that an individual cannot be deprived of, although he or she may have to wait until age sixty-five to start receiving them.

Waiver of lien—A statement signed by members of the building trades that they have been paid for their work on a particular house; it ensures that they will not place a lien on it later for unpaid wages.

Waiver of premium—A provision that under certain conditions an insurance policy will be kept in full force without further payment of premiums. *See* Disability waiver.

Index

Accounting, 57
   principles of, 73–77
Adverse selection, 147, 168, 241
Advertising, 223
Aging Americans Act, 224
Aid to Families with Dependent Children, 21
Amino acids, 184
Amortized loans. See Loans
Annuity, 63–71, 150, 231–32, 241
   calculation tables, 232–34
   joint or survivor, 64, 70
Assessed value, 53, 241
Assets, 80–81, 124–25, 152–53, 165
   capital costs of depreciating, 127–28, 235–36
   income tax implications of, 27–28
   insurance aspects of, 165
   and life insurance needs, 152–53
   ownership patterns of, 165
   and philanthropy, 204
Attorney's funds, 47
Attractive nuisance, 173, 241
Automobile insurance, 165–70
   avoidable accidents and costs of, 166
   collision, 168
   liability, 165–67
   "no-fault," 167
   purchase of, 169–70
   theft, 168
   unavoidable accidents and costs of, 166–67
Automobiles
   and commuting, 197–98
   depreciation of, 129–31
   insurance (see Automobile insurance)
   maintenance of, 199–201
   market value vs. use value of, 132
   rental, 201
   style obsolescence of, 133
   timing of purchase of, 133
   trading costs of, 128–30

"Bait advertising," 141
Balance sheet, 75
Balloon note loan. See Loans
Bankruptcy, 93–95, 241
   Title 13 provision of, 95

Bankruptcy Act of 1978, 94–95
Bargaining, 225–26
Bathtub theorem, 58, 82. See also Budgeting
Bequests, 63, 241. See also Estate planning
Blue Cross, 171
Bonds, 97–102, 105–6
   government, 105–6
   guaranteed redemption of, 105
   ratings of, 106
   tax implications of, 34
   yield curve of, 98, 116
Book value (of stock), 109, 241
Borrowing, 84–95. See also Credit; Debt; Loans
Budgeting, 57–61, 73–83
   accounting principles of, 73–75
   bathtub theorem and, 58
   expenditure monitoring and, 80–81
   expenditures vs. expenses and, 57
   guidelines, 72–73
   and monitoring consumption, 81–83
   receipts vs. income and, 57
   sources of income and, 77–78
   sources of savings and, 78–79

Calls, 117, 241
Capital, 8–9, 241. See also Financial capital; Human capital; Physical capital
   account, 73
   budgeting aspects of, 58–59
   defined, 8, 241
   transactions, 58
Capital gains and losses, 26, 98, 102
   of bonds, 98
   of housing, 34
   and investments, 107
   and philanthropy, 204
Capitalized value, 231–32, 241
   applied to housing costs, 49
   effects of property tax on, 54–55
   of income stream, 96
Career choice, on-the-job training and, 13–14, 16–17
Car pools, 198–99
Cars. See Automobiles

Casualty losses. *See* Losses, casualty
Charitable contributions. *See also* Philanthropy
  capital gains tax on, 121–22
Charitable trust, 179
Chattel mortgage, 93, 241
Checking accounts, 120
Chicago Board of Options Exchange, 117
Children, costs and benefits of, 21–22
Closed-end funds. *See* Mutual funds
Clothing, 194–97
Coinsurance, 171, 173, 242
Collision insurance. *See* Automobile insurance
Commodity futures, 118, 242
Common stocks. *See* Stocks
Common tenancy, 103
Condominiums, 43, 242
Constructive eviction, 46
Consumer durables. *See* Durables
Consumer information. *See* Information
Consumer information systems, 208, 221–22
Consumer Reports, 134, 135, 140, 169, 191, 219, 220, 225
Consumers Research, 219
Consumers Union, 89–90, 134, 139, 169, 218, 219
Consumption, 58–59
Contingent fee, 166, 242
Cooperatives, 42
Corporate profits tax, 27
Credit, 84–95. *See also* Borrowing; Debt; Loans
  cards, 89–91
  counselors, 95
  rating, 91–92
  unions, 88–89, 131

Debt, 84–95. *See also* Borrowing; Credit; Loans
  costs of, 91
Debt adjusters, 95
Depreciation, 107, 126–28, 129–33, 242
  of automobile, 129–33
  budget aspects of, 79–80
  declining balance, 242
  double declining balance, 107
  of durables, 126–28
  of housing, 31–32
  implications for investments of, 107–8
Diet. *See* Nutrition
Diet for a Small Planet, 184
Disability insurance, 148
  waiver of premium, 158–59, 242
Discounting, 86, 242. *See also* Present value
  on loans, 86
Dissonance reduction, 227

Dividends, 99–100, 242
  effects on stock prices, 99–100
Divorce
  economic implications of, 24
  implications for insurance needs, 154
Do-it-yourself repairs, 137–38
Drugs, 191
Dunning letters, 93
Durables, 91, 126–43
  benefits of, 135–36
  budgeting aspects of, 61–62, 142
  capital theory aspects of, 126–28
  market value vs. use value of, 126–27
  owning vs. renting of, 137
  repair aspects of, 137–39
  repair records on, 134–35
  shopping for, 135
  sources of information on, 139–40
  timing of purchases of, 91, 141–42

Easement, 44, 242
Economies of scale defined, 19–20
Economy of fear, 76
Economy of love, 76
Education, 8–13
  budgeting aspects of, 62
  costs and benefits of, 9–10
  payoffs to, 13
  rate of return on, 12–13
Efficiency, 213–14
  conditions for, 213–14
  defined, 242
Efficiency frontier curve, 242
Employee Retirement Income Security Act, 68, 70, 103
Equity, 215
  defined, 243
Estate planning, 123, 176–79. *See also* Bequests
  investment aspects of, 123
Estate tax, 29, 102–3, 177
Exercise, 185–86
Expectancy, 211
Expected value, 12–13, 145, 174, 211, 243
  applied to gambling, 174
  defined, 3, 243
  in theory of motivation, 211
Expenditures, 57, 243
Expenses, 57
  defined, 73, 243
Externalities, 215

Fair Credit Reporting Act, 92, 237–40
Family composition, economic implications of, 24
Family decision making, 213
Family planning, 21–22. *See also* Children
Family well-being, 22–25

Federal Credit Union Act, 88
Federal Deposit Insurance Corporation, 104
Federal Housing Administration, 40
Federal income tax. *See* Income tax
Federal poverty needs standard, 24
Federal Real Estate Settlement Procedures Act, 40
Federal Savings and Loan Insurance Corporation, 104
Federal Trade Commission (U.S.), 94, 160–61
Federal transfer tax, 176–77
Fee splitting, 190, 243
Financial capital. *See also* Capital
  in household balance sheet, 73
Financial planning, 57–83
  long-range goals and, 61–62
Flight insurance, 146–47
Food expenditures, 191–94
Freedom of Information Act, 224
Fringe benefits, 18
Funerals, 175–76
Future value, 231–32. *See also* Present value

G.I. insurance, 164, 243
Gambling, 174
Garnishment, 86, 93–94, 165
  defined, 93, 243
  use of, 94
Gift tax, 177
Good Housekeeping, 225
Group practice, 190, 243

Health care. *See* Medical care
Health maintenance organizations, 243
Hedge, 101, 243
Hire purchase, 243
Holder in due course doctrine, 243
Home ownership, 34. *See also* Housing
Home production, 19
Hours of work, 18
Household insurance, 33, 172–73
  coinsurance and, 173
Housework, 19
Housing, 30–56, 107, 138–39
  additions and repairs to, 138–39
  appreciation, 32
  costs of, 30–43, 55–56
  depreciation, 32
  design and style considerations of, 52
  as an investment, 107
  legal considerations of, 43–46
  neighborhood considerations, 48–50
  owning vs. renting of, 30, 31, 35–43
  property taxes on, 52–55
  tax effects of, 25–27
  transactions, 46–47

Human capital, 8–9, 75–77, 243. *See also* Capital
  in household balance sheet, 75

Imputation, 3, 5
Imputed cost, 3
Imputed income. *See* Income
Imputed interest. *See* Interest
Income, 57, 243
  defined, 73, 243
  imputed, 3, 26, 34, 77–78, 243
  as a measure of family well-being, 22–25
  nonmoney, 23
  ratio to needs, 23–24
  redistribution, 25–29
  sources of, 77–78
  total family money, defined, 23
Income account, 73
Income protection life insurance. *See* Life insurance
Income tax, 76, 102–3, 105–6
  advantages for homeowners, 35–36
  deductions, 25–27, 29
  effects on costs and benefits, 3–4
  effects on do-it-yourself activity, 19
  effects on home production, 36
  effects on housing choices, 33–34
  effects on housing closing costs, 40
  effects on investment, 121–22
  effects on market work, 17–18
  implications for casualty insurance, 168
  implications for financial investments, 102–3
  implications for philanthropy, 204
  income exempt from, 25
  loopholes, 27
  major features of, 25–26
  marginal tax rate (*See* Marginal tax rate)
  state, 28
  tax exempt government bonds and, 105–6
  treatment of capital gains and losses, 26
Individual Retirement Account, 70, 103
Inflation, 101–2, 116, 127–28, 132, 162–63, 243
  effects on durable goods, 127–28, 132
  effects on housing costs, 36
  effects on life insurance needs, 162–63
  effects on saving goals, 62
  investment strategies against, 101, 116
Information, 210–26
  from government, 223–25
  implications for efficiency of, 215–16
  insights and, 217–19
  on local services, 221–22
  and record-keeping, 222–23

Information (*continued*)
  from sellers, 223
  social good aspects of, 217
  sources of, 217–19
Information systems, 208, 221–22
Insurable interest, 146
Insurable risk, 144–46
Insurance, 88, 144–74, 182, 243. *See also* Automobile insurance; Disability insurance; Flight insurance; G.I. insurance; Household insurance; Life insurance; Medical insurance; Theft insurance; Title insurance; Worker's compensation
  availability, 147–48
  budgetary aspects of, 77
  experience rating, 172
  face value vs. real amount of, 158–59
  household behavior and, 173–74
  optimal amounts of, 146–47
  premium cost vs. real cost of, 157–58
  principles of, 144–45
Interest, 243. *See also* Interest costs; Interest rate
  imputed, 3, 243
Interest costs, 84–85, 127–28
  of durables, 127–28
  of housing, 32–33
  of housing closing charges, 39–40
  pattern of, in an amortized loan, 84–85
Interest rates, 84–86, 96, 97, 127–28, 149–51, 159–61, 243
  of bonds, 97–98
  calculation on loans, 84–86
  effects on bond prices, 97
  effects on life insurance costs, 159–60
  of financial investments, 96
  real vs. nominal (market), 3, 9–10, 32–33, 127, 235–36
  relationship with inflation rate, 9–10
  shopping for, 87
  true annual, 85–86
  use of 3 percent rule and, 231–35, 236
Internal rate of return
  defined, 11
  relationship to present value, 11
Investment, 96, 100–102, 115–17, 118–21, 243. *See also* Stocks
  in art and antiques, 121
  aspects of home ownership, 33–34
  behavior, 124–25
  in bonds (*see* Bonds)
  budgetary aspects of, 59
  calculation of net benefits of, 10–11
  characteristics of, 100–102
  in commodity futures, 118
  in debentures, 119–20
  in human capital, 8–9
  information and management costs of, 103–4
  information considerations of, 122–23
  liquidity considerations of, 101
  in money market funds, 120
  in mutual real estate investment trusts, 122
  in on-the-job training, 13
  in options market, 117–18
  in preferred stock, 119–20
  principles of, 96–97
  protection against inflation by, 101
  in real estate, 106–8
  risk considerations of, 101
  in small businesses, 118–19
  tax considerations of, 102–3
  timing of, 115–16
  in trusts, 112–14

Joint or survivor annuity. *See* Annuity
Joint tenancy, 103, 178, 243

Keogh plan, 103

Labor supply, 16–17
Land contract, 45, 244
Lawyers, 205–6
  information sources on, 205
Leverage, 109, 110
  applied to housing investment, 42
  defined, 109, 244
Licensing, 207
Lien, 44, 244. *See also* Mechanic's lien laws
Life insurance, 149–65, 244
  cash surrender value of, 155, 241
  costs of, 159–62
  decreasing term, 155–56
  disability waiver of premium for, 158–59, 242
  face value of, 155, 243
  family income, 158, 243
  family life-cycle needs and, 150
  income protection, 158
  interest-adjusted net costs of, 159–61
  mortgage protection, 158–59
  needs for, 149–51, 151–53
  nonparticipating policy, 157
  "paid up," 157
  participating policy, 157, 244
  present values and, 236
  renewable term, 155–56, 245
  return on savings in, 158
  rules of thumb, 162–63
  savings bank, 164
  term, 155–56, 245
  term vs. cash value, 155–60
  twenty-year net costs of, 159–60
  whole, 156
Liquidity, 101
"Loading," 174, 244
  on mutual fund, 112–13

Loans, 84–95, 129. *See also* Borrowing; Credit; Debt; Packing; Sum of digits method
  amortized, 84–86, 241
  balloon note, 131
  calculation of interest rate on, 85–86
  defaulting on, 86
  sources of, 88–90
Loopholes. *See* Income tax
Losses, casualty
  tax deductibility of, 168
Lotteries, 174
"Low balling," 141

M-Reit, 122
Marginal tax rate, 5–6, 26, 105–6, 244. *See also* Income tax
  defined, 5–6, 244
  effects on bond yields, 105–6
  effects on housing costs, 34
  implications for casualty insurance of, 168
  implications for philanthropy of, 25, 204
Marriage, 19–21
  career choice implications of, 20
  implications for financial planning of, 70–71
  legal aspects of, 20
Martindale-Hubbel Directory, 205
Mechanic's lien laws, 44, 244
Medicaid, 224
Medical care, 182–83, 189–90
  costs of, 190
  drugs and, 191
  fee-splitting in, 190
  group practice in, 190
  information about, 189–90
  insurance (*see* Medical insurance)
  and mental health, 188–89
  preventive, 182–83
Medical insurance, 60, 170–71
Medicare, 224
Mental health. *See* Medical care, and mental health
Money market funds, 120
Mortgage, 87
  budgetary aspects of, 80
  calculation of payment, 35–36
  commitment, 244
  costs of, 37–43
  effects of extending length of, 38–39
  income tax considerations of, 26
  payments, 31
  points (*see* Points)
  savings aspects of, 35–36
Motivation, 210–13
Mutual funds, 112–15, 244
  no-load, 133, 244
  open-end, 113, 244
  selection strategies for, 114–15

National Bureau of Standards, 219, 224
Needs standard, family, 23–25
Neighborhood, effects on house prices of, 48–50
No-fault. *See* Automobile insurance
No-load mutual funds. *See* Mutual funds
Nominal interest rate. *See* Interest rates, real vs. nominal (market)
Nonmoney income. *See* Income
Nutrition, 183–85
  cholesterol and, 184–85
  protein balance and, 185
  salt intake and, 185

On-the-job training, 13–14, 16
Open-end mutual funds. *See* Mutual funds
Opportunity, alternative, 5
Opportunity cost principle, 5
  applied to consumption choices, 181
  defined, 244
Options market, 117–18
Option value of education, 12
Owning a home. *See* Housing, owning vs. renting of

Packing, 87–88. *See also* Loans
Pensions, 61, 63–64, 67–71
Philanthropy, 26, 76, 121–22, 179, 203–5. *See also* Charitable contributions
  tax expenditures and, 204–5
Physical capital, 8. *See also* Capital
Points, 40, 244. *See also* Mortgage
  conversion to interest costs, 40
  defined, 40, 244
Poverty line. *See* Federal poverty needs standard
Prescription drugs. *See* Drugs
Prescriptive easement, 44, 245
Present value, 2–3, 10–11, 12–13, 96–97, 127–28, 149–51, 231–36, 244
  applied to on-the-job training, 16–17
  of bonds, 97
  calculation table, 232, 233, 234
  of depreciation, 127–28
  discounted, 231
  of financial investments, 96
  of foregone interest, 127–28
  of life insurance needs, 149–51
  rule of thumb, 231
Price-earnings ratio, 100, 111, 245
Probability samples, 229, 245
Property tax, 29, 33, 52–55
Puts, 117, 245

Rate of return, 96. *See also* Internal rate of return
Real estate investment trust (R.E.I.T.), 122, 245

Real interest rate. *See* Interest rates, real vs. nominal (market)
Realtor's fee, 47
Receipts, 57, 245
Recreation, 202–3
Recreational equipment, 202–3
Registrar of deeds, 46
Renting. *See* Housing, owning vs. renting of
Repair services, 206–9
Repossession, 93, 245
Retained earnings, 99–100
   effects on stock prices, 99–100
Retirement
   annuity, 236
   savings implications for, 63–72
"Riding the yield curve," 98
Risk, 101, 144–46, 245
   of investments, 101
Rule of 72, 107, 121, 245

Safety, 187
   of investments (*see* Risk, of investments)
Sales, 223
Sales tax, 29
Sampling errors, 228
Saving
   amount of, needed for retirement, 63–72
   budgeting aspects of, 60–61
   goals, 79–80
   goal setting, 62–63
   long-range, goals, 61–62
   sources of, 77–78
Savings and loan associations, 104–5
Savings bank life insurance, 245
Savings banks, 104–5
Savings bonds, 28
Securities and Exchange Commission, 114–15
Services, 205–9
Shopping, 181–82, 225–26
Small claims court, 93
Small-loan companies, 92
Social optimum, 213–16
Social Security, 26, 68–69, 71–72, 96, 146, 148, 149–50, 152, 153–54
   budget aspects of, 60, 72
   as component of family income, 22–23
   disability benefits, 148
   financing issues, 21–22
   implications of, for cost of children, 21
   implications of, for financial planning, 68–70
   implications of, for life insurance needs, 149–50, 153–54
   implications of, for savings goals, 63–68
   insurance aspects of, 77, 146, 148
   principles of, 71–72
   trust fund, 71
Stocks, 98–100, 108–12
   book value, 109
   dividends, 111, 245
   price averaging, 115–16
   prices of, 98–100
   principles of, 98–100
   splits of, 110–11, 245
   striking price of, 117, 245
Striking price. *See* Stocks
Sum of digits method, 86
Sunk costs
   applied to automobiles, 128
   defined, 4
Survey research, 227–30

Tax. *See* Estate tax; Federal transfer tax; Gift tax; Income tax; Property tax; Sales tax
Tax-free cash flow, 107
Taxpayer number, 27
Tenant's rights, 45
Term life insurance. *See* Life insurance, term
Theft insurance, 168, 173
Title insurance, 39, 47, 173, 245
Title search, 39, 245
Title 13. *See* Bankruptcy
Tort law, 165–66, 246
Transfer income, 22–23, 246
Transportation, 197–202. *See also* Automobiles
Trusts, 102, 121, 123, 177
   investment aspects of, 123
   relative to income tax, 27–28
   testamentary, 245
Truth in Lending Act, 85, 87

Uncertainty, 14, 246
   relationship with expected value of, 3
Unemployment, 16
Uniform Gift to Minors Act, 27–28
Usury laws, 93
Utility costs, 33

Vacations, 203
Veterans Administration, 40
Vitamins, 185

Well-being. *See* Family well-being
Whole life insurance, 156–59
Wills, 178
Worker's compensation, 77, 171–72

Yield curve (of a bond), 98, 116
   risk adjusted, 245

Zoning laws, 50